The Baltic Sea

Germany, Poland, the Baltic States,
Russia, Finland, Sweden and Denmark

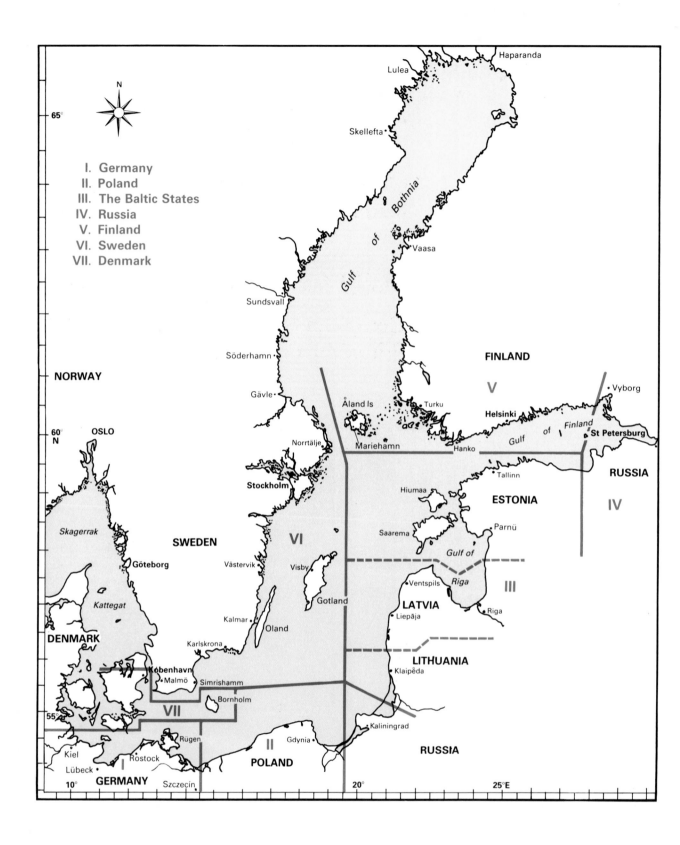

The Baltic Sea

Germany, Poland, the Baltic States, Russia, Finland, Sweden and Denmark

RCC PILOTAGE FOUNDATION

Compiled by Barry Sheffield
Edited by Oz Robinson

Imray Laurie Norie & Wilson Ltd
St Ives Cambridgeshire England

Published by
Imray, Laurie, Norie & Wilson Ltd
Wych House, St Ives, Huntingdon,
Cambridgeshire, PE17 4BT, England.
☎ (0480) 62114 *Fax* (0480) 496109

First published 1992

© Text: Royal Cruising Club Pilotage Foundation 1992
© Plans: Imray, Laurie, Norie & Wilson Ltd 1992
© Photographs: Barry Sheffield 1992

British Library Cataloguing in Publication Data
A catalogue record for this book is available from the British Library.

ISBN 0 85288 175 4

CAUTION
Every effort has been made to ensure the accuracy of this book. It contains selected information and thus is not definitive and does not include all known information on the subject in hand; this is particularly relevant to the plans, which should not be used for navigation. The Pilotage Foundation believes that its selection is a useful aid to prudent navigation, but the safety of a vessel depends ultimately on the judgement of the navigator, who should assess all information, published or unpublished, available to him.

PLANS
The plans in this guide are not to be used for navigation. They are designed to support the text and should at all times be used with navigational charts.

CORRECTIONAL SUPPLEMENTS
Imray pilot books are amended at intervals by the issue of correctional supplements. Supplements, if available, are supplied free of charge with the books when they are purchased. Further supplements are available from the publishers. The following should be quoted:

1. Name of book
2. Date of edition (above)
3. Date of last supplement (if applicable)
4. Name and address to which supplement should be sent.
5. Enclose payment of £2.00, or if paying by Visa, Access/Mastercard or American Express, the card number, expiry date and holder's name.

The last input of technical information was October 1992.

Printed in Great Britain at Tabro Litho Ltd, Ramsey Forty-Foot, Huntingdon, Cambridgeshire.

Contents

ALSO BY THE RCC PILOTAGE FOUNDATION

Published by Imray, Laurie, Norie & Wilson Ltd

Atlantic Islands
Azores, Madeira, Canary and Cape Verde Islands
Compiled by Anne Hammick and Nick Heath

Atlantic Spain & Portugal
El Ferrol to Gibraltar
Compiled by Oz Robinson and Mike Sadler

Lesser Antilles
Grenada to the Virgin Islands
Based on the pilot produced by the French Service
Hydrographique et Océanographique de la Marine
Edited by Oz Robinson

North Brittany
St-Malo to Ouessant
K. Adlard Coles. Revised by Nick Heath

North Africa
Gibraltar to Morocco, Algeria, Tunisia & Malta
Compiled by Hans van Rijn

Published by A & C Black Ltd

North Biscay Pilot
Brest to the Gironde
K. Adlard Coles and A. N. Black
Revised by Nick Heath

Atlantic Crossing Guide
Philip Allen. Revised by Anne Hammick

Foreword

The RCC Pilotage Foundation, a registered charity, is based on a very generous benefaction by an American member of the Royal Cruising Club, Dr Fred Ellis. Its objectives are to promote knowledge of the science of navigation and safety at sea and thus to encourage the aspiring sailor to cruise further afield with confidence and in safety. It does this in a number of ways, among them providing information where a need is recognised; its books cover a substantial part of the eastern North Atlantic seaboard, the African shore of the Mediterranean and the Lesser Antilles, and now touch the Baltic. This book has only been made possible by the work of Barry Sheffield, who sailed the area, but it also draws on contributions on specific points from members of the RCC, particularly Max Ekholm, of Helsinki, Tony Vasey and Martin Lawrence, who added significant information about Estonia.

The plans were drawn by the staff of Imrays and are based on official charts. The photographs were all taken by Barry Sheffield.

As in other parts of the world, details in the Baltic change, and are changing particularly quickly in the former Eastern-bloc countries. The Pilotage Foundation issues an annual update which is available from Imrays.

O. H. Robinson
Director, The RCC Pilotage Foundation
London 1992

Acknowledgements

My thanks are due to all the friendly and helpful people I met during my two circuits of the Baltic, especially Leif and Marja-Leena Strandström in Helsinki; Valodia, Larisa, Valery, Victor, Taya, both Igors, Alla, Konstantin and Ivan in St Petersburg; Tiina, Inga, Sirja, Peeter, Sven, Tomara, Mati, Helmut and Raimo in Tallinn; Peeter Volkov and Peeter Sober in Pärnu; Edward Smirnov and Janis Ramins in Rīga; Aleksandras Grinevicius in Klaipěda; Grigor and Monica Wisniewski in Szczecin; Bob Heal, Q. Smith and David Gawler at the British Kiel Yacht Club; and to Lufthansa for assistance in passages to Russia.

I am grateful to the twenty or so crew members who have been willing to sail with me during my three years in the Baltic, to Charles Hadfield for his encouragement and to Harry Causer and Leif Strandström, both with a detailed knowledge of the area, who were kind enough to take the trouble to cross-check a good many of my facts.

Finally, I would like to thank Oz Robinson of the RCC and Willie Wilson of Imrays for their encouragement and their patience.

Barry Sheffield
Oxford 1992

General information

Introduction

The overall objective of this guide is to provide a general introduction to the Baltic Sea and the Gulf of Finland, to enable yachtsmen contemplating a visit to the area to form a view of its merits as a cruising ground. It aims to give an overall impression of the countries on the shores of the Baltic, to provide basic pilotage information for the major ports of each and to indicate potentially interesting lesser ports worthy of exploration. It also deals with the practical and administrative problems likely to be encountered during a visit to the area.

A basic problem facing the authors was to evolve a presentation balanced between countries which differ widely. Finland, Sweden, Denmark and the Schleswig-Holstein region of Germany have well established yachting communities, their ports are open and their facilities are well documented (though not necessarily in English). In the Mecklenburg-Vorpommern region of Germany (the former East Germany), Poland, Lithuania, Latvia, Estonia and Russia, yachting is far less well developed, minor ports are only now being opened to foreigners and documentation is very scanty. By dint of collecting available information in the less developed areas and sailing where it was allowed there, and skimming the resources available in the better developed areas, a balance has been achieved. But the reader will recall that this book is an introduction, that there is a great deal more information available on the developed countries and a great deal more to be found out about the others; here, one of the aims of the Pilotage Foundation is to encourage such exploration.

The format of the book, following the general information section, is to describe the countries in an anticlockwise direction from Germany via Poland and the Baltic States to St Petersburg in Russia, then back again via Finland, Sweden and Denmark.

The former Eastern-bloc countries

The southern and eastern coasts of the Baltic Sea and the Gulf of Finland are low-lying and lacking in major features, sometimes with sand-dune walls connecting islands and protecting lagoons. They are geologically recent, often alluvial with glacial deposits. There are numerous inland seas in Poland and in Mecklenburg-Vorpommern, formerly in East Germany, called *Bodden*. These are a collection of lagoons, shoal, often reed-smothered, a good habitat for birds. In summer the countryside is pleasant but not spectacular. Land use is a mix of arable with livestock and, in the east, much commercial timber.

There are marked regional cultures. The countries have had complex histories since the comparatively ordered era of the Hanseatic League, when the Baltic was virtually a German sea, and they are emerging once again from decades of repression. They have deep religious backgrounds, and towns with artistic and architectural undertones still remaining despite war damage and a general lack of preservation.

Economic conditions are difficult and they become progressively more so towards the east; the shops are emptier, the food supply is more dependent on the season of the year and the life style is poorer, with fewer trimmings. But throughout the region everyone likes to meet and talk to Westerners and, as there is a strong seafaring tradition, the sea is a good starting point for an acquaintanceship.

Finland, Scandinavia and Schleswig-Holstein

The south coast of Finland and the East coast of Sweden, both with similar geological origins, are protected by a maze of islands – tens of thousands of them – forming a fascinating and sheltered cruising area with excellent facilities everywhere.

Southern Sweden, Denmark and Schleswig-Holstein are low-lying, less rocky and relatively well populated. Like Eastern Sweden and Southern Finland, they have excellent and widespread yachting facilities.

Languages

Each country has its own language which, except in the case of German, is not likely to be spoken by the usual English visitor. The most useful second language is English; it is widely spoken in the Scandinavian countries, and unless you are fluent, there is little point in attempting to converse in the local language. In Russia and the Baltic States there are usually enough English speakers amongst customs officials and yacht club administrators to deal with most problems; even the captains of Russian patrol boats can manage enough English for a straightforward interchange of information. German is fairly widely spoken throughout the area and can be useful, especially in the Baltic Republics.

Reaching the Baltic

The quickest approach to the Baltic from southern England is through the Kiel Canal, the entrance of which is a few days' sailing from Harwich. The British Kiel Yacht Club, a unit of the British Army, makes visitors welcome, and Kiel is a good place to store ship for a long cruise. Visitors from Scotland or northern England may well prefer to reach the area via the Kattegat.

For those interested in cruising in inland waterways and with ample time, it is also possible to go through Limfjord or the Eider River and Gieselau canal without unstepping masts. The Göta Canal offers an interesting but slower route to Stockholm and the Åland Islands. For those with even more time, it is also possible to cross Germany by canal and emerge into the Baltic either through the Elbe-Lübeck Canal at Travemünde or, with a draught of not more than 1.3m, through Berlin to Szczecin in Poland. Szczecin has good marina facilities, but it is best to stock up with food before leaving Berlin.

Cruise planning

The northern side of the Baltic and the Gulf of Finland can be explored very comfortably on a day-sailing basis but ports along the southeastern shores are more widely spaced and some passages may be more than 100M. If the aim is to get to Russia or Estonia, a more direct passage may be taken, calling perhaps only at Bornholm, southern Sweden or Gotland before taking a departure from Helsinki.

For the round trip, the choice is between the two obvious options. An argument for going anticlockwise is that the navigation and yachting facilities of the south and east shores of the Baltic are the lesser known quantities and best visited first so that towards the end of the cruise, when time begins to run out, the yacht is in the area with the better established yachting and communications facilities. An argument for sailing the other way round is that it gives time to become accustomed to the Baltic and, perhaps, that it is far simpler to

arrange the necessary paper work for Russia and the Baltic states in Helsinki than it is in London.

Climate

The sailing season is from June through to September, but July and August are the best months when the sea has warmed up and the almost constant daylight, together with moderate and steady winds, provides good cruising conditions. The sea temperature at the junction of the Gulfs of Finland and Bothnia rises from about 6°C in May to 15°C in August, when it reaches some 17°C off St Petersburg and as much as 24°C amongst the islands of Sweden and Finland. The middle reaches of the Baltic, south of Gotland, are warmest in September at 14–15°C.

Mean air temperatures during June, July and August are around 20°C at both ends of the Baltic but can be much higher in sheltered waters and inland. Take a swimsuit as well as oilies and sweaters.

The average annual precipitation is roughly equivalent to that of East Anglia. Poor visibility is least likely to occur in summer – possibly one day in ten when it is less than a mile in the worst areas, which are at the entrance of the Baltic, around Gotland and a patch northwest of Hiiumaa. Elsewhere the likelihood is one day in twenty or so.

Winds tend to be moderate and gales rare. The overall tendency is for winds to be from south through to west, but they are fairly evenly distributed and the weather patterns are such that winds often become established for four or five days in the same direction.

Charts and guides

British Hydrographic Office charts are excellent for sea areas, but as a major part of the attraction of the Baltic is navigating among the coastal islands and through inshore channels, detailed local charts are necessary. Most can be ordered through Imray, Laurie, Norie & Wilson Ltd, Wych House, St Ives, Huntingdon, PE17 4BT ☎ 0480 62114 *Fax* 0480 496109, and UK chart agents, but it may be easier and cheaper to buy them in Kiel or in the countries themselves. Indices for all charts are included in the appendix at page 179 together with the addresses of publishers and suppliers.

For the shores of the former Soviet bloc, the British Hydrographic Office pilots have accurate and detailed navigational information on every port but lack much of the specific information needed by the yachtsman. Edition Maritim publish two useful books in German, *Küstenhandbuch Mecklenburg-Vorpommern* and *Hafenführer Polen*.

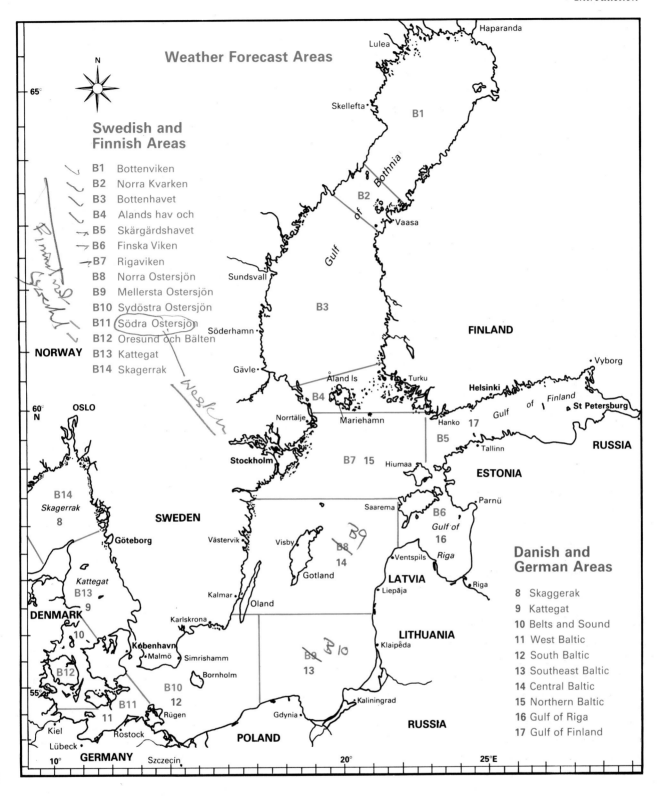

Weather Forecast Areas

Swedish and Finnish Areas

B1 Bottenviken
B2 Norra Kvarken
B3 Bottenhavet
B4 Alands hav och
B5 Skärgärdshavet
B6 Finska Viken
B7 Rigaviken
B8 Norra Ostersjön
B9 Mellersta Ostersjön
B10 Sydöstra Ostersjön
B11 Södra Ostersjön
B12 Oresund och Bälten
B13 Kattegat
B14 Skagerrak

Danish and German Areas

8 Skaggerak
9 Kattegat
10 Belts and Sound
11 West Baltic
12 South Baltic
13 Southeast Baltic
14 Central Baltic
15 Northern Baltic
16 Gulf of Riga
17 Gulf of Finland

Published lists of radio signals and lights are useful, and Reeds now publish a Baltic edition of their almanac. Russian charts, which are essential for cruising amongst the Estonian islands, can be obtained from the Estum Agency (see page 10).

A bibliography of pilot books, sailing directions and guide books for the coasts is in the appendix at page 179. Some are well illustrated with colour photographs of ports taken from the air, which can be valuable not only as an aid to navigation but also as a means of assessing the attractiveness of ports when planning the cruise.

Unless otherwise stated, references are to publications of the British Hydrographic Office.

Navigation

The geodetic base

Caution Positions of lights and other marks given in this publication have been taken from a variety of sources and will not necessarily agree exactly with positions given in other publications working to different geodetic systems or with Decca, Loran or GPS readings. Do not use for specific waypoints without referring to charts.

Buoyage

IALA System A has been adopted by all countries. In Finland and Sweden buoys may not have topmarks and cardinal buoys have to be identified by colour code which is black and white, not black and yellow.

Tides, currents and sea level

There is no appreciable tide, but prolonged winds in one direction and changes in atmospheric pressure can produce significant variations in depth. The datum of charts of the Baltic is generally mean sea level, not the lowest astronomical tide.

Because the Baltic collects more fresh water than evaporates from its surface there is a weak but steady surface outflow of low density, less saline, water through the Kattegat into the North Sea, partially balanced by a return flow of more saline water at a lower level. Within the Baltic surface currents are weak and tend to run towards Denmark, parallel to the associated coastline. Wind patterns can produce their own surface currents. Currents can flow in almost any direction, even upwind, since their direction is influenced not only by the wind but also by the shapes of the basins. Following a blow which upsets sea levels, surface and submarine currents may be markedly different.

In extreme wind conditions, which are very unlikely to occur in summer, surface currents of 4 knots and local sea level aberrations of 2m have been noted (remember chart datum may be mean sea level). Long term prediction is not possible and the best course is to consider the effect of the weather pattern of the previous days on the surface of the water – and when in doubt ask locally.

VHF coast radio stations

Germany, Finland, Sweden and Denmark operate a system of outstations controlled remotely from a centre – see diagrams at pages 5–7 which also list working channels. Except in emergency, stations answer calls on working channels and not on channel 16. Listen to check that a working channel is clear. If uncertain turn up the squelch; if there is no hiss the channel is in use and another, if available, should be used. Call an outstation with the call sign of the controlling station. The answer may be a regular tone until the operator is free to speak.

VHF stations of the former Eastern-bloc are also shown on pages 5–7.

Station	Channel	Traffic lists
Szczecin	16 24[1] 25[2] 26[3] 27[3]	Ch 26 every 4 hrs from 0000
Witowo	12 16[4] 25 26	None
Gdynia	12 16 24 26 27	Ch 26 at 0035 0435 0835 1235 1635 2035
Kaliningrad	03 16	None
Klaipěda	16 27	None
Ventspils	07 16	None
Rīga	16 27	None
Tallinn	01 16	None
St Petersburg	16	None
Vyborg	02 16	None

1. Located at Świnoujście-Szczecin passage and Szczecin lagoon.
2. Located at Świnoujście roadstead-port.
3. Located at Bay of Pomerania-Świnoujście roadstead.
4. Located at 54°11'N 15°34'E as well as at Witowo.

Weather forecasts

German coast radio stations broadcast a forecast at dictation speed in German and can be asked for a forecast in English.

Polish coast radio stations can be asked for a forecast in English on VHF Ch 12.

The Baltic States and Russia have not developed a public weather forecasting system and though a summary broadcast in English from Rīga Broadcasting Station has been advertised it has not been heard.

In Finland and Sweden forecasts are broadcast in English twice daily on VHF. See country sections for timings. Coast radio stations can also be asked for forecasts.

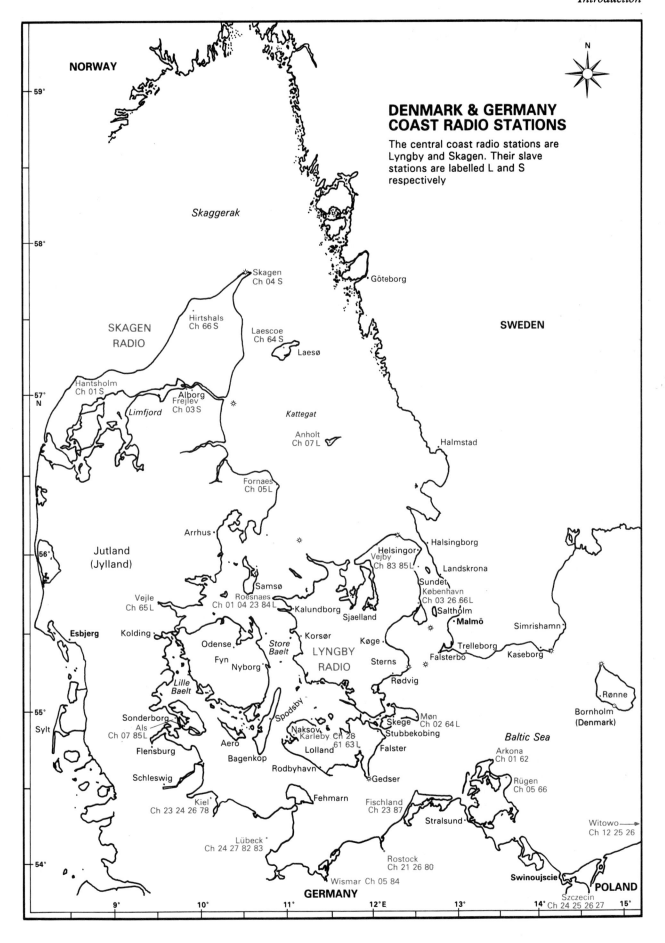

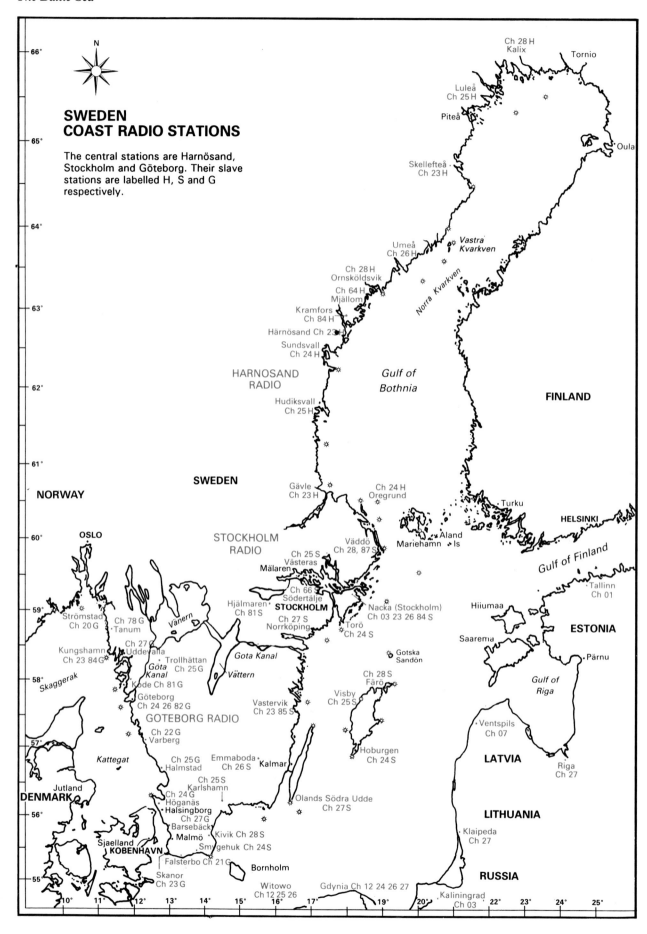

N

SWEDEN
COAST RADIO STATIONS

The central stations are Harnösand,
Stockholm and Göteborg. Their slave
stations are labelled H, S and G
respectively.

Ch 28 H
Kalix

Tornio

Luleå
Ch 25 H

Piteå

Oula

Skellefteå
Ch 23 H

Vastra
Kvarkven

Umeå
Ch 26 H

Norra Kvarkven

Ch 28 H
Ornsköldsvik

Ch 64 H
Mjällom

Kramfors
Ch 84 H

Härnösand Ch 23 H

Sundsvall
Ch 24 H

HARNOSAND
RADIO

Gulf of
Bothnia

FINLAND

Hudiksvall
Ch 25 H

SWEDEN

NORWAY

Gävle
Ch 23 H

Ch 24 H
Oregrund

Turku

HELSINKI

Gulf of Finland

OSLO

STOCKHOLM
RADIO

Väddö
Ch 28, 87 S

Aland
Mariehamn Is

Tallinn
Ch 01

Ch 25 S
Västeras

Mälaren

Ch 66 S
Södertälje

Hiiumaa

ESTONIA

Hjälmaren
Ch 81 S

STOCKHOLM

Nacka (Stockholm)
Ch 03 23 26 84 S

Strömstad
Ch 20 G

Ch 78 G
Tanum

Vänern

Ch 27 S
Norrköping

Torö
Ch 24 S

Saarema

Pärnu

Kungshamn
Ch 23 84 G

Uddevalla

Trollhättan
Ch 25 G

Gota Kanal

Gota
Kanal

Göta
Kanal

Vättern

Gotska
Sandön

Gulf of
Riga

Skaggerak

Köde Ch 81 G

Göteborg
Ch 24 26 82 G

Vastervik
Ch 23 85 S

Ch 28 S
Färö

GOTEBORG RADIO

Visby
Ch 25 S

Ventspils
Ch 07

Ch 22 G
Varberg

Kattegat

Ch 25 G
Halmstad

Emmaboda
Ch 26 S

Kalmar

Hoburgen
Ch 24 S

LATVIA

Riga
Ch 27

Ch 25 S
Karlshamn

Jutland

Ch 24 G
Höganäs

Halsingborg
Ch 27 G

Barsebäck

DENMARK

Olands Södra Udde
Ch 27 S

LITHUANIA

Malmö

Kivik Ch 28 S

Klaipeda
Ch 27

Sjaelland

KOBENHAVN

Smygehuk Ch 24 S

Falsterbo Ch 21 G

Bornholm

Skanor
Ch 23 G

Witowo
Ch 12 25 26

Gdynia Ch 12 24 26 27

Kaliningrad
Ch 03

RUSSIA

66°
65°
64°
63°
62°
61°
60°
59°
58°
57°
56°
55°

10° 11° 12° 13° 14° 15° 16° 17° 18° 19° 20° 21° 22° 23° 24° 25°

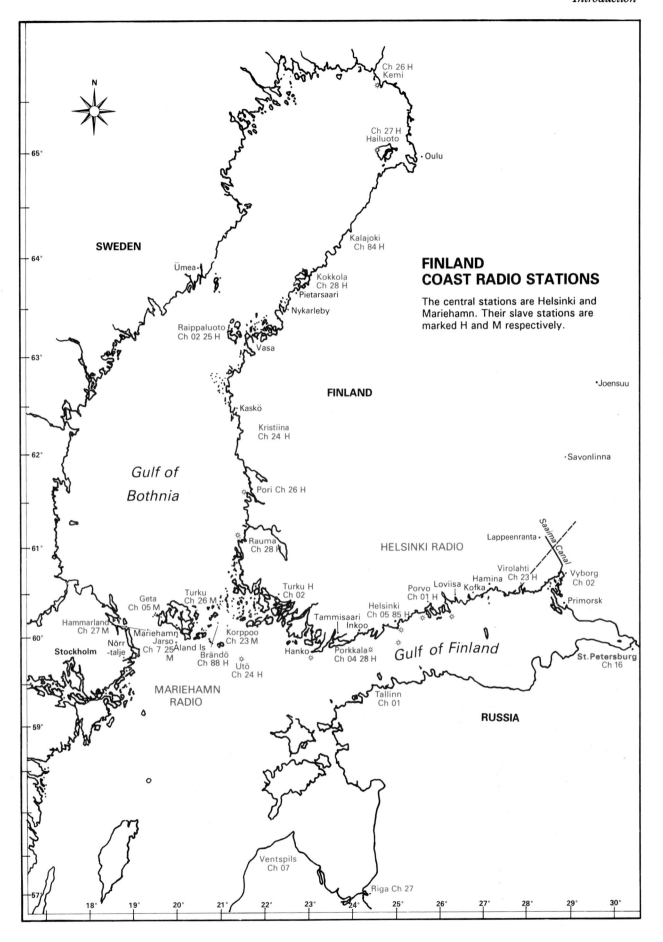

N

65°

SWEDEN

Ch 26 H
Kemi

Ch 27 H
Hailuoto

• Oulu

Kalajoki
Ch 84 H

64°

Ümea •

Kokkola
Ch 28 H
Pietarsaari

Nykarleby

**FINLAND
COAST RADIO STATIONS**

The central stations are Helsinki and
Mariehamn. Their slave stations are
marked H and M respectively.

Raippaluoto
Ch 02 25 H

Vasa

63°

FINLAND

• Joensuu

Kaskö

62°

Kristiina
Ch 24 H

• Savonlinna

*Gulf of
Bothnia*

Pori Ch 26 H

Lappeenranta •

Saimaa Canal

61°

Rauma
Ch 28 H

HELSINKI RADIO

Virolahti
Ch 23 H

Vyborg
Ch 02

Porvo
Ch 01 H

Loviisa

Hamina
Kotka

• Primorsk

Turku
Ch 26 M

Turku H
Ch 02

Helsinki
Ch 05 85 H

Geta
Ch 05 M

Tammisaari
Inkoo

Hammarland
Ch 27 M

Korppoo
Ch 23 M

Gulf of Finland

60°

Mariehamn
Jarso
Ch 7 25 Åland Is
M

Hanko

Porkkala
Ch 04 28 H

St.Petersburg
Ch 16

Stockholm

Nörr
-talje

Brändö
Ch 88 H

Utö
Ch 24 H

MARIEHAMN
RADIO

Tallinn
Ch 01

59°

RUSSIA

Ventspils
Ch 07

57°

18°   19°   20°   21°   22°   23°   24°   25°   26°   27°   28°   29°   30°

Riga Ch 27

7

In Denmark, Lyngby broadcasts a forecast in Danish but can be asked for a forecast in English. The forecast from Göteborg may be helpful.

See diagram of forecast areas on page 3.

Radio aids to navigation

See the caution in *The geodetic base* above.

Decca There are six relevant Decca chains: Danish (7B), South Baltic (0A), North Baltic (4B), Gulf of Finland (6E), South Bothnian (8C) and North Bothnian (5F). Decca is of doubtful value in the area between Åland and Turku, around Rīga and offshore from Ventspils, and is said to have poor accuracy in fog and rain.

Decca chains

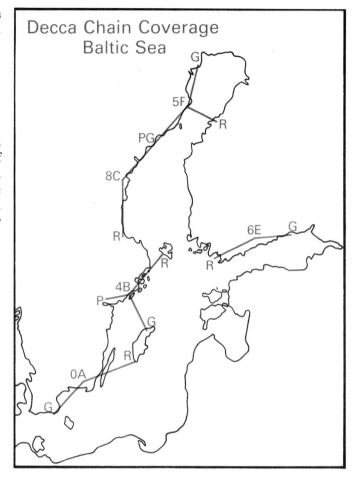

Decca Chain Coverage
Baltic Sea

Danish (7B)

Samsø	A Master	55°57'N 10°35'E	85·365
Møn	B Red Slave	54°57'N 12°28'E	113·820
Eøjer	C Green Slave	55°01'N 08°42'E	128·047
Hjorring	D Purple Slave	57°27'N 10°03'E	71·138

South Baltic (0A)

Holmsjö	A Master	56°27'N 15°40'E	84·100
Sandhammaren	B Red Slave	57°02'N 18°15'E	112·133
Burgsvik	C Green Slave	55°24'N 14°11'E	126·150

North Baltic (4B)

Nynäshamn	A Master	58°57'N 17°57'E	84·825
Åland	B Red Slave	60°07'N 19°49'E	113·100
Ar	C Green Slave	57°55'N 18°57'E	127·238
Björkvik	D Purple Slave	58°51'N 16°34'E	70·688

Gulf of Finland (6E)

Mäntsälä	A Master	60°31'N 25°11'E	85·270
Padva	B Red Slave	60°00'N 22°50'E	113·693
Sydänkylä	C Green Slave	60°31'N 27°26'E	127·905

South Bothnian (8C)

Njurunda	A Master	62°17'N 17°25'E	88·550
Skutskär	B Red Slave	60°37'N 17°27'E	114·067
Jarnas	C Green Slave	63°29'N 19°39'E	128·325

North Bothnian (5F)

Lovanger	A Master	64°21'N 21°21'E	85·095
Gamla Karleby	B Red Slave	63°52'N 23°11'E	113·460
Kallax	C Green Slave	65°32'N 22°04'E	127·6425
Jarnas	D Purple Slave	63°29'N 19°39'E	70·9125

Loran C Dependent upon the Norwegian Sea Chain; reports indicate that reliability in the Baltic is unsatisfactory.

Radar beacons (Racon) are logged when they occur with lights; there are many not mentioned in the text.

RADIOBEACONS
Denmark
Donna, Dan Oil Field Aero *DON* 355 kHz 75M
55°28'·22N 05°08'·13E
Blåvandshuk Lt *BH* 296 kHz 50M
55°33'·52N 08°05'·07E
Thyboron Lt *TN* 306 kHz 100M
56°42'·53N 08°13'·00E

Skagen W Lt *SW* 298·5 kHz 50M
57°44'·98N 10°35'·78E
Frederikshavn, NE breakwater Lt *FK* 414 kHz 10M
57°26'·02N 10°33'·43E
Hals Barre Lt *HB* 299 kHz 50M
56°57'·32N 10°25'·60E
Sjaellands Rev N Lt *SG* 310·5 kHz 50M
56°06'·08N 11°12'·17E
Nakkehoved Lt *NA* 306·5 kHz 50M
56°07'·18N 12°20'·81E
København, Svanemollevaerket Calib Stn *MU* 309 kHz 10M 55°42'·83N 12°35'·38E
Stevns Klint Lt *ST* 290 kHz 50M
55°17'·47N 12°27'·53E
Gedser Lt *GR* 303·5 kHz 50M
54°33'·88N 11°57'·89E
Rønne, Fauna Aero *FAU* 334 kHz 50M
55°01'·67N 14°54'·10E
Hammerodde Lt, Bornholm *MN* 289·5 kHz 50M
55°17'·97N 14°46'·43E

Germany (Baltic coast)
Kiel Lt *KI* 310 kHz 20M
54°30'·02N 10°16'·47E
Friedrichsort Lt Calib Stn *FB* 312·6 kHz
54°23'·48N 10°11'·68E
Fehmarnbelt Lanby *FE* 304 kHz 10M
54°36'·00N 11°09'·00E
Travemünde Lt Calib Stn *UB* 312·6 kHz
53°57'·77N 10°52'·97E
Timmendorf Calib Stn *02* 311 kHz
53°59'·55N 11°22'·73E

Warnemünde Calib Stn *LHD* 311 kHz
54°10'·72N 12°05'·92E
Sassnitz Calib Stn *SAZ* 311 kHz
54°30'·70N 13°38'·70E

Poland
Rozewie *RO* 287·3 kHz Seq 1 Cont 50M
54°49'·97N 18°20'·15E
Leba Rear Lt *LE* 287·3 kHz Seq 2 Cont 50M
54°46'·02N 17°33'·50E
Jarosławiec *JA* 287·3 kHz Seq 3 Cont 50M
54°32'·60N 16°33'·10E
Kołobrzeg Lt *KB* 287·3 kHz Seq 4 Cont 50M
54°11'·28N 15°33'·55E
Świnoujście main Lt *OD* 287·3 kHz Seq 5 Cont 50M
53°55'·05N 14°17'·17E
Świnoujście main Lt Calib Stn *S* 306·5 kHz
53°55'·05N 14°17'·17E
Kołobrzeg Lt Calib Stn *K* 296·5 kHz
54°11'·28N 15°33'·55E
Darłowo Lt Calib Stn *D* 309 kHz
54°26'·50N 16°22'·90E
Ustka Lt Calib Stn *U* 306·5 kHz
54°35'·37N 16°51'·42E
Krynica Morska Lt *KM* 310·3 kHz Seq 3, 4 Cont 50M
54°23'·23N 19°27'·18E
Hel Lt *HL* 310·3 kHz Seq 5, 6 Cont 50M
54°36'·08N 18°48'·90E
Hel Lt Calib Stn *H* 306·5 kHz
54°36'·08N 18°48'·90E
Gdynia Calib Stn *G* 296·5 kHz
54°31'·82N 18°33'·72E

Russia (Baltic coast)
Baltysk *BK* 299 kHz 80M
54°38'·25N 19°53'·90E
Akmenrags *AK* 312·5 kHz Seq 2 Cont (Latvia) 100M
56°50'·17N 21°03'·92E
Liepāja *LB* 312·5 kHz Seq 3 Cont (Latvia) 120M
56°31'·07N 20°59'·52E
Klaipēda *KA* 312·5 kHz Seq 4 Cont (Lithuania) 120M
56°31'·07N 20°59'·52E
Mys Taran *BT* 312·5 kHz Seq 5 Cont (Latvia) 120M
54°57'·60N 19°58'·87E

Latvia
Ventspils *WW* 309 kHz 100M
57°23'·74N 21°32'·40E
Ventspils Calib Stn *P* 300·5 kHz 20M
57°23'·74N 21°32'·40E
Irbenskiy Lt *YuH* 285·5 kHz 35M
57°45'·40N 21°43'·80E
Kolkasrags (grouped with Estonia Kübassaar Lt, Saaremaa)
Mãersrags Lt *MR* 291·5 kHz 15M
57°22'·00N 23°07'·35E
Rīga, Daugagrãiva Lt *DG* 286·5 kHz 30M
57°03'·58N 24°01'·43E

Estonia
Kübassaar Lt, Saaremaa *KR* 306·5 kHz Seq 1 Cont
100M 58°25'·65N 23°17'·90E
Ostrov Osmussaar *OR* 306·5 kHz Seq 2 Cont 80M
59°18'·23N 23°21'·67E
Ristna *RS* 306·5 kHz Seq 3 Cont 100M
58°56'·35N 22°03'·15E
Vilsandi *WD* 306·5 kHz Seq 4 Cont 50M
58°23'·25N 21°49'·17E
Sörve *SY* 306·5 kHz Seq 5 Cont 100M
57°54'·90N 22°03'·75E

Kolkasrags *KL* 306·5 kHz Seq 6 Cont 100M
57°44'·90N 22°35·50E
Tallinn Lt *TN* 300·5 kHz 25M
59°42'·70N 24°44'·00E
Mys Lounatrivi Lt, Ostrov Gogland *UG* 294·5 kHz 50M
60°00'·65N 27°00'·60E
Kaybolovo *KA* 294·5 kHz Seq 1 Cont 60M
59°44'·75N 28°02'·33E
Mohni Lt *MH* 294·5 kHz Seq 4 Cont 75M
59°41'·05N 25°47'·83E
Piksaäre Ots Lt, Naissaar *NG* 294·5 kHz Seq 5 Cont
75M 59°36'·25N 24°30'·83E
Pakrineem *PA* 294·5 kHz Seq 6 Cont 80M
59°23'·25N 24°02'·40E

Finland
Heka Aero *HEK* 344 kHz 25M
60°15'·35N 25°29'·70E
Porkkala pilot station *PR* 284·5 kHz 60M
59°58'·51N 24°23'·72E
Finno, Kökar Aero *FIN* 354 kHz 20M
59°55'·97N 20°54'·20E
Godby Aero *GDY* 392 kHz 25M
60°11'·20N 19°57'·47E
Mäntyluoto *MA* 297·5 kHz 60M
61°35'·58N 21°27'·90E
Laanila Aero *LAA* 350 kHz 40M
64°58'·00N 25°12'·90E

Sweden
Bjuröklubb main Lt *BB* 303 kHz 70M
64°28'·87N 21°34'·75E
Nordvalen Lt *KV* 300·5 kHz 65M
63°32'·23N 20°46'·60E
Skagsudde Lt *SE* 306 kHz 70M
63°11'·35N 19°01'·20E
Sundsvall Aero *OS* 378 kHz 25M
62°27'·67N 17°29'·33E
Söderhamn, Skallen Aero *OZ* 337 kHz 50M
61°13'·67N 17°10'·97E
Orskär Lt *OR* 291 kHz 70M
60°31'·67N 18°22'·63E
Understen Lt *UN* 299 kHz 70M
60°16'·55N 18°55'·40E
Almagrundet Lt *AL* 286·5 kHz 70M
59°09'·30N 19°07'·75E
Landsort S Lt, Oja RC *LO* 289·5 kHz 55M
58°44'·40N 17°52'·15E
Hoburg Lt *OB* 301·5 kHz 70M
56°55'·40N 18°09'·20E
Visby approach Lt *VY* 290·5 kHz 30M
57°38'·10N 18°16'·60E
Visby Aero *OV* 351 kHz 25M
57°43'·88N 18°23'·88E
Ölands Södra Grund Lt *OG* 313·5 kHz 70M
56°04'·13N 16°40'·92E
Falsterborev Lt *FV* 303 kHz 40M
55°18'·53N 12°39'·50E
Kullen high Lt *KUL* 294 kHz 70M
56°18'·10N 12°27'·35E
Hällö Lt *LL* 290·5 kHz 55M
58°20'·18N 11°13'·20E
Grebbestad Aero *GRE* 418 kHz 50M
58°41'·87N 11°14'·70E

General

Berthing

Details are contained in country sections. In many Scandinavian clubs and harbours there is a system by which each berth shows a small plate, red if boat is returning that day, green if she is not.

Formalities

Customs are considered in the country sections.

EC citizens do not need visas for Germany, Finland, Sweden and Denmark.

In Poland, Lithuania, Latvia and Estonia a bureaucracy remains which to some degree restricts freedom of movement, though now that there are more visiting yachtsmen the procedures are becoming well known and the authorities less exacting. Every visitor is supposed to be in possession of a valid visa on arrival, but in Poland and Lithuania it is possible to obtain visas at the major ports on arrival. It is easy to obtain visas for these countries in London (for further details see the country sections under *Formalities*) or through the Estum Agency in Helsinki (see below). Each member of the crew should have at least three passport photographs and three photographs of the opening pages of his passport.

The Russian bureaucracy remains obdurate but not impossible. A visa is essential but obtaining one through the Russian consulate in London is still a laborious and frustrating process. It is better to try in Helsinki.

In Helsinki, the Estum Agency specialises in handling administrative arrangements for foreigners (especially yachtsmen) wishing to visit Russia or the Baltic States. Estum keeps itself up to date with the local situation. Its address in Finnish is Vuorimiehenkatu 23A, 00140 Helsinki, and in Swedish is Bergmansgaten 23A 00140 Helsingfors; ☎ (358) 0-629 299 and *Fax* (358) 0-629 390.

Currency

In Finland, Scandinavia and Schleswig-Holstein exchange is straightforward: Eurocheques, traveller's cheques and credit cards are widely accepted. In Mecklenburg-Vorpommern the deutschmark is currency and whilst Eurocheques and traveller's cheques are becoming fairly widely accepted few places take a credit card. In Poland the złoty is not freely convertible; Eurocheques and traveller's cheques are accepted only at Orbis, the official tourist agency. US dollars are, however, more easily exchanged. In the other countries there is sharp inflation. Exchange is difficult and direct dealing in US dollars or deutschmarks is becoming widespread

(see the country section for detail). Foreign currency therefore has to be the main source of finance, so pay particular attention to security, both ashore and aboard when alongside; loss of this resource through theft would be disastrous.

Provisioning

Stock up as well as possible before arriving in the area. Housekeeping constraints apart, the point to watch is the necessity of bonding alcohol in Scandinavia and Finland.

Food

In descending order, food in Sweden, Finland, Denmark and Schleswig-Holstein is somewhere between 30% and 5% more expensive than it is in the UK and supply is extremely good.

In Mecklenburg-Vorpommern and Poland, basic foodstuffs can be bought without undue difficulty, but up to now there has been little variety. Prices are a little lower than in the UK but the rate of inflation is high.

In Russia and the Baltic States, fresh produce can be bought in the markets during the summer months, at prices almost prohibitive to the local population but cheap to visitors from the West. Otherwise, most basic foodstuffs (except milk products and bread) are rationed and almost impossible to buy. Most shops have long queues all day long.

The conclusion is that it is best to stock up with food before leaving the former West Germany, buying drinks duty-free if possible. If staying for any length of time in the old Soviet countries it would be wise to try to be self-sufficient, even to the point of including dried milk and bread-making materials.

Alcohol

In Germany and Denmark, drink can be purchased more or less as easily as in the UK and at similar prices.

In Sweden and Finland, low alcohol (2·8%) beer can be purchased in supermarkets but all stronger beverages can be bought only at special state-controlled shops where prices approach twice those of the UK.

In Poland most types of drink are available at prices lower than in the UK. The quality of certain drinks, especially beer, may be less than ideal for British tastes.

In the Baltic States and Russia, it is usually possible to buy beer, champagne, vodka, cognac and table wine locally for local currency, but supply is unpredictable. It is, however, always possible to buy foreign brands of drinks in hard-currency shops at prices more or less similar to those in England.

Water

In general, the quality of the main water supplies at the major yacht harbours described is good. In some out of the way ports of Poland and the Baltic States it would probably be prudent to boil locally obtained water before drinking it.

Health

In the former Eastern-bloc countries satisfactory medical supplies are difficult for the foreigner to find. The situation in Scandinavia and Finland is satisfactory, although familiar brands may not be found. Stock up before leaving the UK.

Mosquitos can occasionally be a nuisance and have been particularly remarked in St Petersburg. It is probably not worth netting the boat but it is certainly worthwhile taking a supply of mosquito coils.

Fuel

Petrol and diesel are widely available in Germany, Denmark and Sweden at prices roughly the same as petrol station prices in the UK. In Finland diesel costs about half as much.

The purchase of fuel in Poland, the Baltic States and Russia (apart from Tallinn, in Estonia, where there is a hard-currency fuel berth in the harbour) is generally a matter of negotiation through yacht club administrators or perhaps via local yacht captains. It is not always available, but when found it can usually be purchased at roughly the Finnish price.

Gas

Most British yachts use butane, either *Camping Gaz* or *Calor Gas*. Butane is not generally available in the Baltic, though in southern Sweden *Camping Gaz* may occasionally be found. The situation is detailed in the country sections.

A yacht intending to cruise extensively in the Baltic should either be sufficiently well stocked with its own brand of butane (*Camping Gaz* or *Calor Gas*) or be equipped to use propane. Most modern appliances will run on either fuel and one may only need a propane regulator and the appropriate connectors. For detailed advice consult Jonathan Barker, Boating Industry Liaison, Calor Gas Ltd, Appleton Park, Slough, SL3 9JG, ☎ 0753 568037.

Propane bottles can be refilled in most major ports, though the process is likely to take a couple of days or so.

Electricity

A 220-volt electricity supply is available in most yacht harbours throughout the Baltic. Continental 2-pin plugs are the norm, although it is as well to be equipped with both the sizes in common use. The new (blue) European standard connectors are also beginning to be used and it is advisable to have on board at least an adaptor for this type of connector.

Garbage

Finland and the Scandinavian countries are particularly fastidious about garbage and there is every reason to take similar care elsewhere. Garbage dumping at sea is a matter of international law. Take bin liners and when full dump in authorised places. Do not pump ship in anchorages or harbours.

Repairs

There are good facilities for most types of repair in Kiel, Scandinavia and Finland. Because a large proportion of the technical equipment used by local yachtsmen and yacht builders comes from the same sources as that used on British yachts, a wide range of compatible spares is also available. The exception may be those for a UK designed and built engine.

In Poland, technical skills are readily available and labour rates are relatively low by Western standards. However, proprietary spare parts are virtually impossible to obtain. If you can bring in your own gear, Poland is at present worth considering for major repairs or even complete refits.

In the Baltic States and Russia, many yacht clubs have quite large repair and maintenance staffs but lack modern facilities and some basic materials. Major work is impracticable though emergency repairs might be arranged. An exception is Tallinn, where there are excellent facilities, dating from the 1980 yachting Olympics, but proprietary spare parts are unobtainable.

Laying up

There is no shortage of places for winter storage in Schleswig-Holstein, Finland or Scandinavia. Enquiries at any of the larger ports will unearth a variety of facilities from which to choose.

In Finland, a foreign yacht may stay for up to 12 months without payment of duty so long as its owner remains in the country. The period can be extended to three years. There are no definite rules about laying up and leaving the boat and the situation is negotiable. Owners wishing to lay up should make their intentions known to the coastguard authorities at the earliest opportunity.

In Sweden, a foreign yacht may stay for up to a year without payment of import dues so long as its owner remains in the country. If the owner wishes to leave the boat, duty or a bond, which may be 25% of the value of the boat, may be required unless repairs, modifications or additions are being made.

On the eastern shore there are two proven locations, one in Poland, one in Estonia: Marina Marco at Szczecin and the Kalev Yacht Club at Tallinn. Both have been used successfully by British yachtsmen and both have satisfactory security, good facilities and reasonable prices. In both countries the rules are flexible. If it is intended to leave a yacht for any length of time, inform customs on entry and negotiate.

At St Petersburg, both the River Yacht Club and the Baltic Shipping Company Yacht Club are developing their facilities to attract visitors and may be able to offer secure conditions for winter storage in the future. There are no specific rules governing the temporary import of yachts.

Telecommunications

Telecommunications are dealt with on a country basis but the following general points about conditions in the former Eastern-bloc countries are worth making here.

International calls can be made only from certain private telephones (including those in tourist hotels and service bureaux) or through the operator-controlled call offices in major post offices, which are almost impossible to use without good knowledge of the local language. Facsimile is becoming common. Telex is available at many hotels and commercial establishments, and may be both quicker to use and more reliable than telephone or facsimile. Inside Russia, however, and to a lesser extent in the Baltic States, telex machines generally have Cyrillic keyboards.

Travel

AIR

Airports handling traffic from Britain, either direct or, in the case of the Baltic States, via København, Warsaw or St Petersburg:

Germany	Hamburg, Berlin
Poland	Gdańsk
Lithuania	Vilnius
Estonia	Tallinn
Latvia	Rīga
Russia	St Petersburg
Finland	Helsinki, Turku, Mariehamn
Sweden	Stockholm, Göteborg
Denmark	København

Other airports conveniently situated but served only by internal flights are:

Denmark	Ålborg, Århus, Rønne (Bornholm)
Germany	Kiel
Russia	Kaliningrad
Lithuania	Palanga (for Klaipěda)
Sweden	Nyköping, Norrköping, Visby (Gotland), Oskarshamn, Kalmar, Ronneby (for Karlskrona), Kristianstad

RAIL

Trans-European rail services are good – about 24 hours to København and 36 hours to Stockholm or Poland, whilst the interesting train/ferry journey from London to Helsinki takes 2½ days as does St Petersburg via Berlin and Warsaw. Few of the major ports in this guide are not on national rail networks and those which are not can be reached by coach or ferry. The Thomas Cook *European Rail Timetable*, published monthly, is an invaluable guide for planning rail and ferry travel in Europe and Scandinavia.

COACH

There are good and very cheap coach/ferry services from London to all three Scandinavian capitals and to Germany.

FERRY

The following ship and ferry routes are potentially useful to yachtsmen and their crews travelling to and from the Baltic:

Gedser – Rostock
Gedser – Travemünde
Grisslehamn – Eckerö
Harwich – Esbjerg
Harwich – Hamburg
Harwich – Hoek van Holland
Helsinki – Tallinn

Hull – Helsinki
København – Malmö
København – Rønne
Malmö – Ystad – Świnoujście
Newcastle – Esbjerg
Newcastle – Göteborg
Nynäshamn – Visby
Oskarshamn – Visby
Oxelösund – Gdańsk
Puttgarden – Rødby
Rønne – Sassnitz
Stockholm – Mariehamn – Turku – Helsinki
Stockholm – Rīga
Stockholm – St Petersburg
Stockholm – Tallinn
Travemünde – Helsinki
Travemünde – Trelleborg
Ystad – Gdańsk
Ystad – Rønne

The Thomas Cook *European Rail Timetable* gives details of ferry sailings.

Pets

Animals may be moved from the UK to and between countries of continental Europe except Sweden where permission from the National Board of Agriculture is required. There are very strict rules governing the import (and re-import) of animals into the United Kingdom without prior permission – which is unlikely to be given without a six month quarantine period. Attempted illegal importation may lead not only to a heavy fine but probably also to the demise of the pet.

Photography

Nowadays there are few restrictions on photography, even in Russia, but it is prudent to avoid taking photographs of military installations in any country.

I. Germany

The provinces *(Länder)* of the Federal Republic of Germany have well marked individual characteristics and strong local governments. The cultural differences between the pair considered in this guide are overlaid by the economic success of the West German economy contrasted with the acknowledged failure of the old East German system.

The country

Germany's Baltic coastline falls naturally into two parts: the former West German province of Schleswig-Holstein and the former East German province of Mecklenburg-Vorpommern.

Neither part of the coast has any dramatic physical feature but each has considerable interest in other respects. The western segment, from Kiel to Travemünde, has excellent yachting centres at Kiel, Heiligenhafen and Travemünde. It is an agricultural country with scattered farms, hillocks, small valleys, lakes and estuaries leading to important ports such as the historic and beautiful city of Lübeck.

The eastern part offers that slightly mysterious fascination of what was until recently forbidden territory, securely guarded. Today's visitor frequently encounters reminders of life as it was under communist rule but can also enjoy a countryside where wildlife has been left undisturbed. The coast has spits, bars and islands enclosing irregular inland seas known as *Bodden*, often backed by sand dunes planted with Norway spruce. There are a number of historically significant cities, each with its own character.

History

Schleswig-Holstein has been for centuries a no-man's-land between Denmark and greater Germany, and both parties have used force to establish their claims. It became a province of Prussia in the last part of the 19th century. Following a plebiscite after the First World War the border was changed and the northern part was given to Denmark. The arrangement left significant minorities on the wrong side of the border; nevertheless, Schleswig-Holstein remained a political unit, and, while it was part of the British zone of occupation after the Second World War, its status was changed to that of an autonomous German *Land*.

In Mecklenburg-Vorpommern there is a marked contrast between the development of the trading towns and that of the countryside. In the middle of the 13th century, the volume of trade and the dangers attending it led Wismar to join Rostock and Lübeck in a union designed to protect it from piracy on the lawless Baltic. From this the Hanseatic League emerged and developed into one of the world's most powerful trading cartels. But neither the wealth nor the ideas behind the social development in the Hanseatic cities filtered outwards to the countryside, and up to 1918, Mecklenburg was the most backward part of Germany, with large estates whose owners forcibly repressed agricultural workers. Even after that date there was serious trouble between labourers and landowners, leading to the area becoming a centre of reaction and later a stronghold for Hitler's National Socialists. The large estates were eventually broken up in 1945 through legislation introduced when Mecklenburg was part of the USSR's zone of occupation, but under East German rule there was little economic advance.

The economy

Schleswig-Holstein depends largely on agriculture and the service industries, which include the maintenance of a considerable volume of shipping in transit.

The mainstays of Mecklenburg-Vorpommern are agriculture, the shipping industry at Rostock and Wismar, fishing and tourism. There is very little manufacturing industry apart from that associated with shipping. The tourist industry has been established since the end of the 19th century when the immense beaches of the province became popular; a 20th-century development is that many of the sun-worshippers now take the logical step of wearing no clothes.

An immediate effect of reunification has been the closure of much old and inefficient industry, with a corresponding steep rise in unemployment. This, coupled to the problems of bringing prices into line with Western levels and to feelings that the relatively poor members of the local population are being exploited by their wealthier kinsmen, has caused tension. This should be short-lived, but meanwhile it is prudent for visiting yachtsmen not to align themselves too closely with either side.

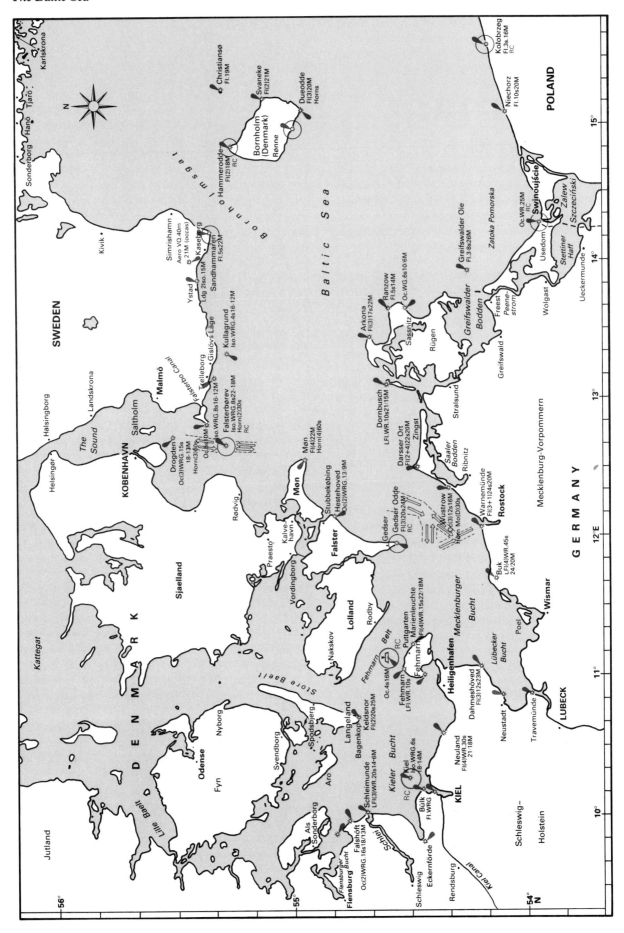

Although English is widely used throughout the rest of Germany, especially among the business community, in Mecklenburg, as a result of its isolation, relatively little English is spoken.

Money

The currency throughout is the deutschmark. In Schleswig-Holstein the usual credit facilities and cash dispensers which take Eurocheque cards (with PIN numbers) are commonplace. In Mecklenburg-Vorpommern credit facilities are rare but becoming more common.

Yacht services and chandlery

Moorings are considerably cheaper than they are in the UK: in ports with few facilities there may well be no charges at all for overnight mooring.

In Schleswig-Holstein yachts are well provided for. Fuel and gas (but not butane) are both easily available.

In Mecklenburg-Vorpommern facilities are scarce and less well developed. Obtaining fuel and gas can be a problem. When available, both are slightly more expensive than they are in Britain. But basic facilities can be found in most places – and there is an attraction in visiting ports where yachtsmen are welcomed as travellers from distant lands rather than simply as sources of revenue.

Formalities

EC citizens do not need visas, but passports must be held and the yacht should carry the Small Ship's or the Department of Trade and Industry's *Certificate of Registration*. It is sensible for the skipper to have a *Certificate of Competence,* although it would be unusual for this to be inspected. Appropriate radio licences should also be carried, but it is unlikely that they will be asked for.

Yachts can obtain customs clearance on the Baltic coast at Laboe (in Kiel fjord), Travemünde, Wismar, Warnemünde, Barhöft (on the west side of the northern arm of the Strelasund) and Stralsund.

Yachts can be kept in Germany for up to a year without paying import duty, provided that they are used solely for pleasure.

The flag is three horizontal stripes of black, red and gold.

Representation

Kiel British Consulate United Baltic Corporation GmbH, Schleuse, PO Box 8080, 2300 Kiel 17 ☎ (49) 431 30632 *Fax* (49) 431 35895 *Telex* 299829.

German Embassy in London 23 Belgrave Square, London SW1X 8BJ ☎ 071-235 5033.

Navigation

Admiralty charts are excellent for all sea areas, but if it is intended to spend any length of time exploring the newly opened cruising area along the Mecklenburg coast, it is worth considering purchasing, at Kiel or Travemünde, a set of German charts such as the *Sportschiffahrtskarten,* published by Nautische Veröffentlichung. The appropriate title is *Serie 4 Rund um Rügen – Stettin Bornholm,* comprising a set of one 1:240,000 sheet, one 1:80,000, one 1:30,000 and seven 1:60,000 sheets, all contained in a large plastic envelope for cockpit use.

The *Baltic Pilot Volumes I* and *II (NP 18* and *19)* are useful for reference, but they are not ideally suited to the needs of the yachtsman. Brian Navin's *Cruising Guide to Germany and Denmark,* published by Imray, is recommended. There are several pilot books available in German covering the Mecklenburg coast, for instance *Küstenhandbuch Mecklenburg-Vorpommern* by M. Brandenburg, published by DK Edition Maritim, and *Der Grosse NV Hafen Lotse Volume 4,* published by Nautische Veröffentlichung.

Note that there is a traffic separation scheme in Mecklenburger Bucht.

Communications

Facsimile and telex are easily available in Schleswig-Holstein and practically all telephone kiosks can be used for international calls. In Mecklenburg-Vorpommern, these facilities are hard to find but the telephone system is being modernised. The code for the UK is 00 44.

Letters take between four and five days to reach England.

Coast radio stations at Kiel, Lübeck, Rostock and Rügen handle public correspondence traffic, with English-speaking operators, and provide weather bulletins at dictation speed in German.

Travel

The major airports serving the Baltic coast area are at Hamburg and Berlin.

There are good train services throughout Germany, complemented by local bus services, good in Schleswig-Holstein but not yet so good in Mecklenburg-Vorpommern. There are excellent express coach services from London to Hamburg and Travemünde.

Ferry services operate on the following routes:

Kiel – Trelleborg
Kiel – Bagenkop
Puttgarden – Rødby
Travemünde – Gedser

Travemünde – Helsinki
Travemünde – København
Travemünde – Świnoujście
Warnemünde – Gedser
Sassnitz – Trelleborg

Time

Germany is one hour ahead of UT in winter and two hours ahead from the last Sunday in March until the Saturday before the last Sunday in September.

Cruising areas

The major ports to the west of the now defunct dividing line between East and West are Kiel and Travemünde, and it is from one or other of these two ports that yachts coming from western Europe are most likely to emerge into the Baltic.

The coast heading east from Kiel is low-lying and well populated. Yachts aiming for the Mecklenburg coast will sail past the mammoth new Heiligenhafen yacht harbour before passing under the impressive Fehmarnsund bridge (clearance 23m, but winds from north or east can raise sea level by up to 1·5m) connecting Fehmarn Island to the mainland. Those heading for southern Sweden will skirt the northern side of Fehmarn.

Sailing east from Kiel, whether passing under the Fehmarnsund bridge or skirting the north of Fehmarn island, there is little shore interest, but Travemünde and Lübeck are both extremely enjoyable places to visit.

East of Wismar the coast has hills and woods as far as Heiligendamm, some 6 miles away, but then flattens out. There are no more ports until Warnemünde.

Continuing eastwards, the coastline is wooded between Warnemünde and the corner at Darsser Ort. Inland lies the Mecklenburg lake district, densely wooded and boasting more than a thousand lakes. It is an unspoilt region ideal for walking, cycling or indeed exploring by boat – via a system of shallow canals linking major lakes. The coastline, however, is low lying and seemingly featureless from seaward.

But appearances are deceptive: immediately behind the tree-lined spits and sandbars forming much of this coast lie the *Bodden* – large unspoilt lagoons, often bordered by immense expanses of reeds, and remarkable for their birds, isolation, shoal waters and small fishing ports. As yet little explored by yachtsmen, they have a special ambience derived from their isolation and the simple lives of the people who dwell in the villages and farms around their shores.

For navigation in the *Bodden* German charts (and perhaps one of the German pilot books) are necessary. Details of appropriate charts are given in the appendix.

The more important centres are Schwerin, the capital of Mecklenburg, and the ports of Wismar, Rostock (which has the oldest university in northern Europe) and Stralsund.

Behind the coasts of Darss and Zingst lie three *Bodden* which may be entered from the eastern end: Barther, Bodstedter and Saaler. Dredged, buoyed channels 19m to 25m wide are maintained with depths of 3·2m up to Barth and 2·4m beyond (the offshoot to Prerow is 2·1m, that to Wustrow 1·5m and that to Ribnitz 1·6m). Depending on the winds, sea levels may change by as much as +2m to −1m.

The coastal islands of Rügen, Usedom and Hiddensee, with their long, wide, sandy beaches alternating with steep cliffs, are fast becoming a popular but far from overcrowded holiday area: secluded fishing villages and breeding grounds for swans, geese and other wild birds are still to be found.

Behind the western and northern coasts of Rügen Island is another area of *Bodden* which can be entered from the north or the south, with depths of 3m in the dredged channels, but very shoal and sometimes stony outside them.

Amongst the dunes and woods along the Zingst coast, not far short of Kloster, lies the entrance to the Strelasund, the buoyed channel which separates the island of Rügen from the mainland. Just inside the entrance is a major breeding ground for wild geese and swans, of which many thousands are frequently to be seen.

The clearly marked channel winds past Barhöft, a convenient place for customs clearance if entering Germany, to the charming, if poorly maintained, city of Stralsund. The double lifting bridge, the Ziegelgrabenbrücke, leads through to the Strelasund South, which meanders through marshes and meadows to Stahlbrode and Palmer Ort, where the comparatively deep (8m) Greifswalder Bodden begins.

The small islands of Ruden and Greifswalder Oie lie off the eastern entrance of the Greifswalder Bodden, the shores of which hide perhaps a dozen small harbours tucked into inlets.

To the south the Peenestrom, a well buoyed, landlocked channel, leads through green countryside past Peenemünde (of wartime V1 and V2 fame – and currently with many laid-up military vessels in evidence) and behind the island of Usedom to cross the border into Poland. There are two opening bridges, at Wolgast and Zecherin, to negotiate on the way. The times of opening for these bridges can be obtained from the harbour office at Stralsund or the harbourmasters of most of the smaller ports in the area. Dredged depths are 6m as far as Wolgast and 2·5m afterwards. This is an interesting route to Szczecin in Poland.

South of Wolgast, on the east side of the Peenestrom, the Achterwasser is an extensive area of water with an attractive small harbour at Zinnowitz.

The seaward side of Usedom Island, from Peenemünde to Świnoujście approaches, is generally low – less than 60m – and featureless; the best marks are the churches of Zinnowitz, Heringsdorf and Ahlbeck (the border lies about 1·5M southeast of Ahlbeck Church). There are no harbours.

Yachts continuing into Poland through the Peenestrom must show their papers to the Polish patrol boat permanently stationed where the channel passes through the chain of yellow buoys marking the border across the Stettiner Haff (or Zalew Szczeciński in Polish) which, like the Greifswalder Bodden, has a number of interesting small harbours hidden away in inlets.

Kiel
54°21'N 10°10'E

Distances
Travemünde 65M, Gislövs Läge 130M, København 145M, Stubbekøbing 85M.

Charts and guides
Admiralty charts *33* and *696*
German charts *32*, *33* and *34*
Baltic Pilot Volume I (NP 18)
Cruising guide to Germany and Denmark Brian Navin, Imray
Cruising Association Handbook
NV Nord-Ostseekanal

Lights
1. **Kiel light** 54°30'N 10°16'·5E Iso.WRG.6s29m18-14M Horn Mo(KI)30s White round tower, red gallery and base, floodlit, 33m 071°-R-088°-W-091·3°-G-148·5°-W-220°-R-246·5°-W-295°-R-358°-W-025·5°-G-056°
See diagram on chart.

The British Kiel Yacht Club at Stickenhorn, Kiel.

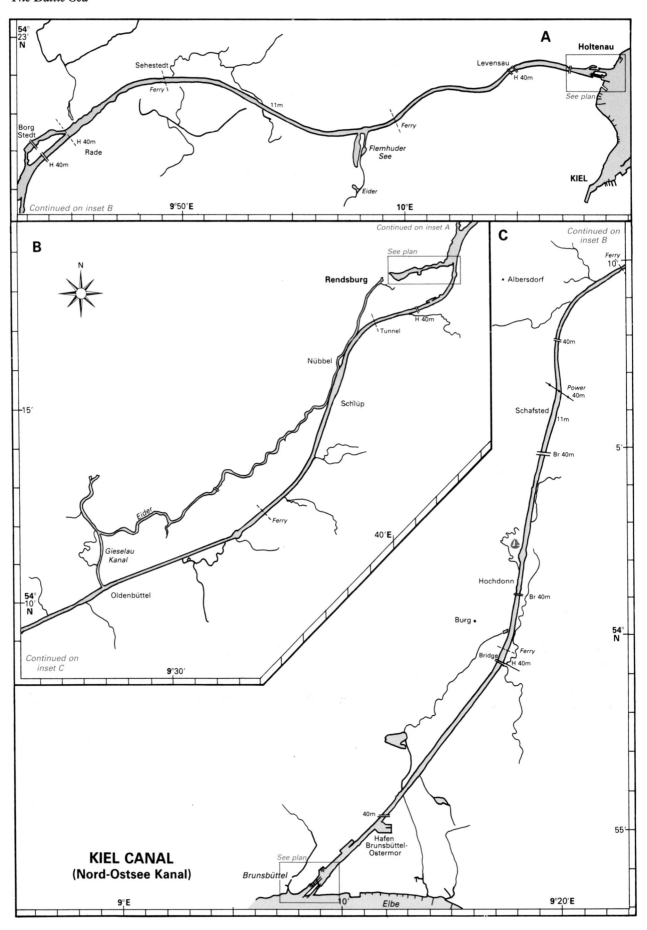

A

Holtenau

Levensau
H 40m

See plan

KIEL

Sehestedt

Ferry

11m

Ferry

*Flemhuder
See*

Borg
Stedt

H 40m
Rade
H 40m

Eider

Continued on inset B 9°50′E 10°E

B

N

Continued on inset A

See plan

Rendsburg

• Albersdorf

C

*Continued on
inset B*

Ferry
10′

H 40m

Tunnel

Nübbel

Schlüp

Schafsted

40m

Power
40m

11m

Br 40m

15′

5′

Eider

Ferry

40′E

Gieselau
Kanal

54°
10′
N
Oldenbüttel

Hochdonn

Br 40m

Burg •

54°
N

Bridge

Ferry
H 40m

*Continued on
inset C* 9°30′

KIEL CANAL
(Nord-Ostsee Kanal)

40m

Hafen
Brunsbüttel-
Ostermor

55′

See plan

Brunsbüttel

9°E 10′ *Elbe* 9°20′E

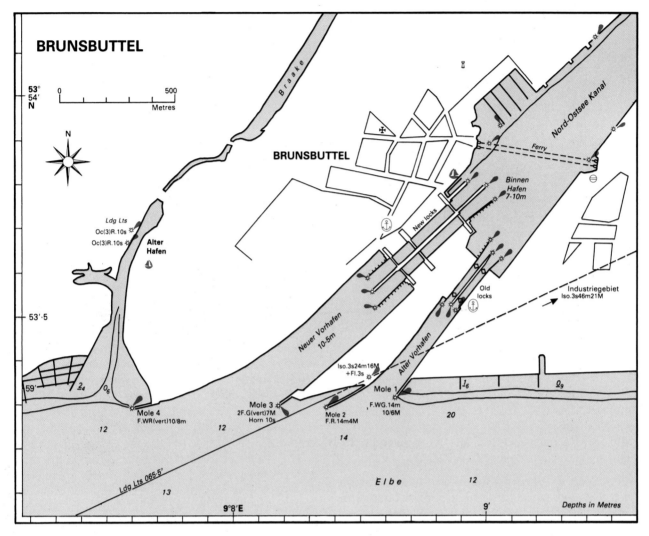

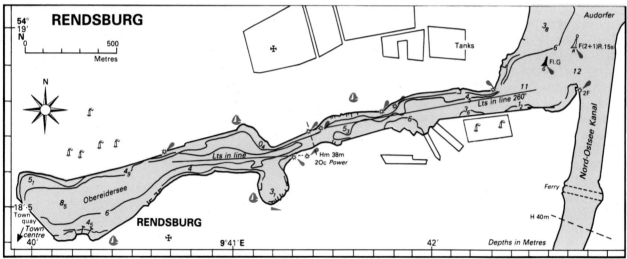

2. **Friedrichsort** 54°23'·5N 10°11'·7E F.WG.32m18/6M
Horn Mo(F)30s White round tower, green bands on
gallery and base, floodlit, 32m 202°-W-209° 224°-W-
280°-G-300°-W-032°-G-090°
  a. Fl(2)WR.9s17/14M 209°-W-214°-R-224°
  b. Fl(3)WG.12s17M/13M 171·5°-G-188°-W-195°
  c. Oc.6s18M 195°-vis-202° Also shows when fog
    signal working.
See diagram on chart.

General

Kiel is a major naval base, a commercial port and
easily the largest yachting centre in the Baltic; at one
end of the Kiel Canal, it is always busy. Kiel fjord on
a Sunday in summer can be compared to the Solent
– only with a constant stream of shipping entering
and leaving the canal.

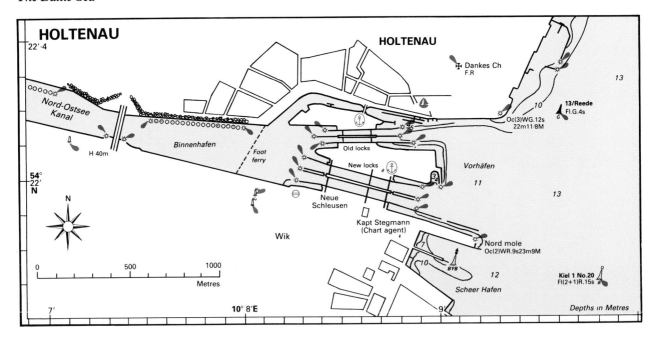

The town has a superb shopping centre, modern, busy and with great variety. For yachts entering the Baltic it is an excellent place to store ship for the whole Baltic cruise or to have repairs carried out. With first class travel facilities, it is an ideal place for crew changes.

For British yachtsmen it is also an opportunity to enjoy the pleasures of the British Kiel Yacht Club.

The Kiel Canal

The Nord-Ostsee Kanal, or Kiel Canal, is a fascinating piece of engineering. Built so that the fleet moving between the Baltic and the North Sea did not have to move through the Kattegat, it was opened in 1895. It is 54M long. Near Rendsburg, roughly halfway along the canal, is one of the few remaining transporter bridges in the world. Its moving section passes across the canal at a height of 12m. All other bridges have a clearance of 40m.

There are two pairs of locks at each end: at Brünsbuttel, at the entrance from the Elbe, and at Holtenau (a suburb of Kiel) where the canal enters Kiel fjord. At Brünsbuttel yachts are usually directed to the southern lock, and at Holtenau to the northern lock, except in winter. Yachts should make it clear that they wish to enter the canal simply by hovering in full view of the control tower, in the area in front of the lock gates, but take good care to keep well clear of commercial shipping. There is a confusing array of flashing lights for the benefit of the large ships, but these should all be ignored until a flashing white is seen, indicating that the lock-keepers are ready to accept yachts – usually after one or more larger vessels have entered. It is usually best not to try to communicate with the lock-keepers, either by radio or by going ashore.

Mooring in the locks is to floating wooden staging only a couple of inches above water level – so fenders need to be touching the water. The rise and fall is very small at both ends and there is no turbulence; it is normally not even possible to distinguish whether the lock is being filled or emptied.

The canal can comfortably be traversed in one day at a speed of 5 knots; if a more leisurely passage is preferred it is permitted to moor for the night at Rendsburg or in the Gieselau Canal on staging 0·5M into the canal – but nowhere else. There is a yacht harbour with good facilities at Rendsburg, about 1·5M inside the entrance to the River Eider.

It is important during the transit to keep well clear of commercial shipping, but this is not difficult as the canal is very wide and dredged to 11m. There can be a great deal of wash.

Canal dues, modest, are payable at the small brick-built newspaper kiosk on the north side of the locks at the Holtenau end. The procedure is to pay at the kiosk, then to take the ticket up to the control tower to get it stamped by the lock-keepers. The kiosk also sells charts.

Approach

If arriving from the Baltic, either north or south of Fehmarn Island, it should be noted that there is a military firing range extending 3M from the coast immediately east of the entrance to Kiel fjord. If it should be in use, yachts are intercepted by a patrol-boat with instructions (on VHF Ch 13).

Major landmarks at the entrance to Kiel fjord are the Kiel light tower[1] and (in daylight) the impressive German navy war memorial just north of Laboe, the customs clearance point for yachts. The fjord is very

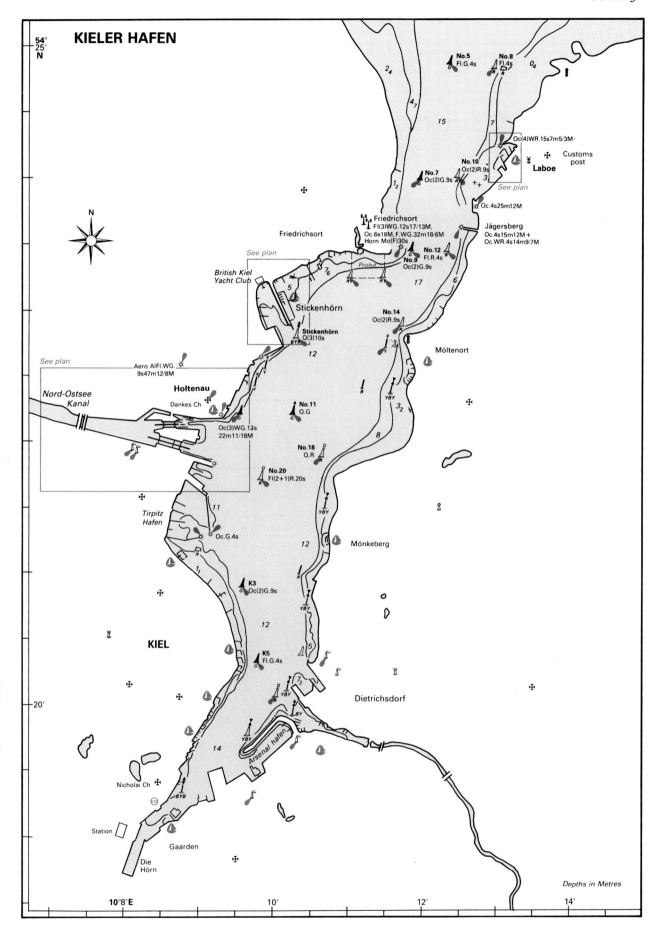

KIELER HAFEN

54° 25' N

No.5 Fl.G.4s
No.8 Fl.4s
No.7 Oc(2)G.9s
No.10 Oc(2)R.9s
Oc(4)WR.15s7m5/3M
Customs post
Laboe
See plan
Oc.4s25m12M
Jägersberg Oc.4s15m12M + Oc.WR.4s14m9/7M
Friedrichsort Fl(3)WG.12s17/13M, Oc.6s18M, F.WG.32m18/6M Horn Mo(F)30s
Friedrichsort
No.12 Fl.R.4s
No.9 Oc(2)G.9s
Prohd
See plan
British Kiel Yacht Club
Stickenhörn
Stickenhörn Q(3)10s
No.14 Oc(2)R.9s
Möltenort
Aero AlFl.WG. 9s47m12/8M
Holtenau
Dankes Ch
No.11 Q.G
Oc(3)WG.12s 22m11/18M
Nord-Ostsee Kanal
See plan
No.18 Q.R
No.20 Fl(2+1)R.20s
Tirpitz Hafen
Oc.G.4s
KIEL
K3 Oc(2)G.9s
Mönkeberg
K5 Fl.G.4s
Dietrichsdorf
Arsenal hafen
Nicholai Ch
Station
Gaarden
Die Hörn

Depths in Metres

10°8'E   10'   12'   14'

well buoyed throughout, but there is a large area of shoal water extending from the shore near the naval war memorial. Friedrichsort light[2] is a prominent landmark when approaching the British Kiel Yacht Club at Stickenhorn. The entrance to the canal is about 1M further south.

Anchorage

There are no restrictions on anchoring in Kiel fjord, but because of the heavy volume of commercial traffic it is strongly recommended that yachts should seek berths at one of the many yacht harbours.

Although there are many yacht harbours to choose from, most British yachts are likely to berth at the British Kiel Yacht Club at Stickenhorn (54°23'N 10°10'E), or the small yacht harbour immediately outside the Holtenau entrance to the canal, on the north bank.

If intending to stay at BKYC it is best to call Sailtrain on VHF Ch 67 well before arrival to ask for instructions. Berthing is stern-to with bow lines to posts. Most cruising yachts are unlikely to carry out their berthing manoeuvres under sail as do the smartly handled training yachts which are based here.

If it is more convenient to stay near the canal entrance in the yacht harbour just outside the Holtenau lock, mooring is mostly rafted alongside staging. There are few facilities, except the nearby fuelling barge and two small chandleries ashore.

Formalities

Yachts arriving from the North Sea should clear customs at Cuxhaven. From Scandinavia or the Baltic, clearance for yachts is at Laboe. The customs office is near the root of the solid jetty to starboard about 50m inside the harbour. Beware the frequent ferry traffic from the inner side of the outer mole; it is best not to round the mole head too closely.

For yachts leaving Germany, outward clearance is also at Laboe, where the correct documentation relating to any duty-free goods purchased in Germany must be produced.

General facilities

BKYC is a British army establishment, situated within a German naval base. Entry by land is through either of two gates, both guarded by sentries day and night. Passes must be obtained from the British personnel in the charter office in the clubhouse.

There are water and electricity on the jetty and there are excellent showers and toilets in the clubhouse. There are also two bars, a cafeteria and a part-time shop selling sailing clothes.

A supermarket and other shops for everyday supplies are to be found in Friedrichsort, about 15 minutes' walk away. There are also banks,

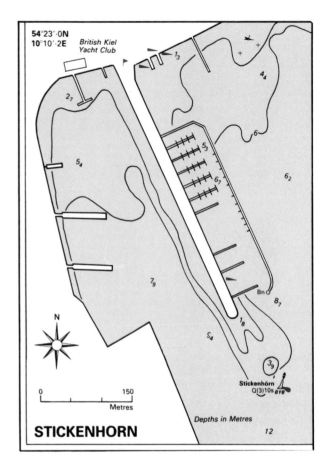

STICKENHORN

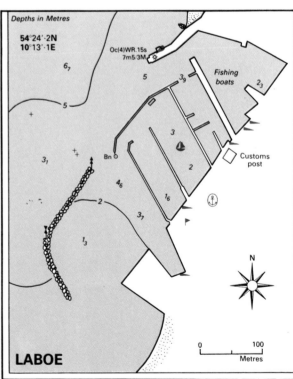

LABOE

restaurants and pubs. Duty-free drink, certain foodstuffs and some clothing can be bought at Willi Ludwig, just outside the camp gates, and purchases will be delivered to the boat immediately before sailing.

There are a couple of interesting restaurants near the quay and yacht harbour in Holtenau, outside the lock gates, and the airport restaurant is also good value.

The nearest launderette is in Wik, immediately to the south of the Holtenau lock, and this can be reached either by a short bus ride or via the charming little foot ferry which operates to and fro across the canal about half a mile west of the locks.

The excellent shopping centre in Kiel itself is about 15 minutes on the bus from outside the camp gates.

Yachting services

The best place to buy fuel is at the bunker boat moored near the yacht harbour outside the Holtenau locks. *Camping Gaz* can be purchased from certain petrol stations in the vicinity of BKYC. There is a very large and well stocked chandlery in Kiel town centre, and two smaller ones on the quayside at Holtenau, immediately outside the locks.

The chart agent, Kapitän Stegmann, is to be found on the south side of the Holtenau locks in a small trading estate together with Elna, a marine electronics company. Stegmann also has a shop between the two new locks.

There is a well equipped boatyard adjacent to BKYC.

Weather forecasts are posted daily on the BKYC notice board.

Communications

International calls can be made without difficulty from all telephone kiosks, including the one at BKYC. Link calls can be made through Kiel Radio. Kiel Radio also transmits at prearranged times short messages for vessels carrying only a receiver; this service might be used, for instance, to cause someone to telephone.

Travel

Hamburg is the nearest international airport. Kiel has good train and coach services to all parts of Europe.

Travemünde
53°57'N 10°47'E

Distances
Kiel 65M, Wismar 25M.

Charts and guides
Admiralty chart *2364*
German charts *35, 51* and *52*
Cruising guide to Germany and Denmark Brian Navin, Imray
Küstenhandbuch Mecklenburg-Vorpommern M. Brandenburg, DK Edition Maritim

Lights
Approach
1. **Travemünde** 53°57'·8N 10°53'E Fl.WR.4s114m19/15M Building 113m 165°-R-214°-W-234°-R-245°
Entrance
2. **Priwall** Ldg Lts 215·9° *Front* 53°57'·5N 10°53'·2E Oc(2)9s14m17M
   Red ▲ on white mast, red bands, 13m
   Rear 365m from front 53°57'·3N 10°53'E Oc(2)9s24m 17M Red ▼ on white framework tower, 21m
3. **N mole head** 53°57'·8N 10°53'·4E Oc.RG.4s10m 6/5M Horn Mo(TD)30s White tower, black bands, floodlit 123°-R-201°-G-066°

General
Travemünde is the outer port for Lübeck. It is a holiday resort and a busy ferry and commercial port with two major yacht harbours (depths up to 7m). Its shopping centre is adequate, but not extensive.

Approach
The most prominent landmark is a 37-floor tower block (with Travemünde light[1] on top) immediately north of the harbour entrance, visible from a considerable distance out to sea.

The fairway leading into the harbour is well buoyed, with powerful leading lights on a bearing of 216°. The frequent arrivals and departures of ferries also serve to indicate the harbour entrance.

Anchorage
It is possible to anchor close inshore along the coasts both to the east and to the west of Travemünde, but it is not practicable to anchor inside the harbour or in the river.

Berthing
There are two major yacht harbours, the Passathafen, immediately to port on entry, behind the permanently moored square-rigger *Passat*, and the Marina Baltica, about half a mile further in on the starboard hand. It is also possible to berth in the fishing harbour, to starboard just before reaching the

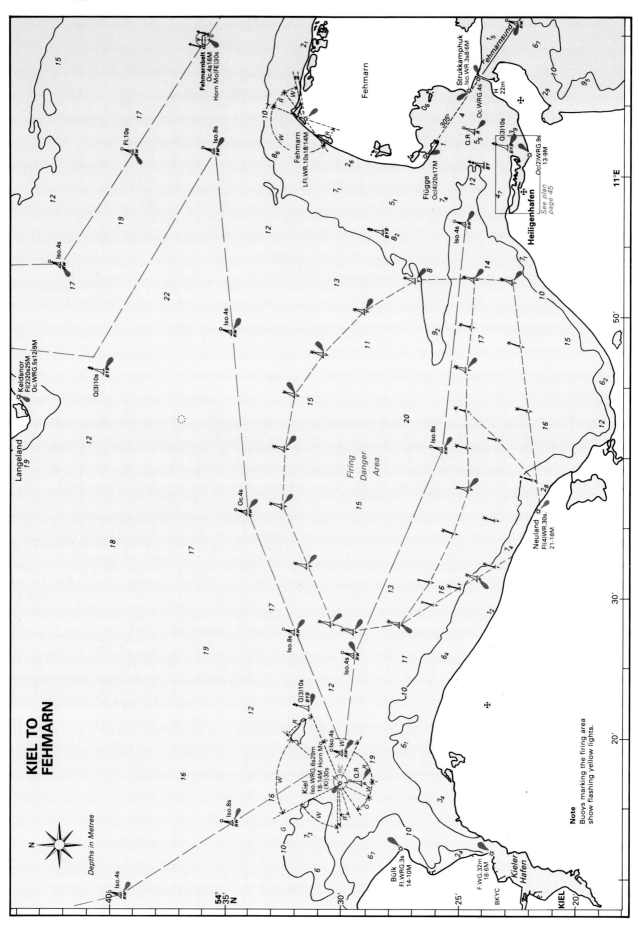

KIEL TO
FEHMARN

N

Depths in Metres

Iso.4s
RW

Bülk
Fl.WRG.3s
14·10M

F.WG.32m
18·6M

BKYC

*Kieler
Hafen*

KIEL

54°
35'
N

40'

30'

25'

20'

Kiel Iso.WRG.6s29m
18-14M Horn Mo
(KI)30s

Q(3)10s
BYB

Iso.8s
RW

Iso.4s
RW

Iso.8s
RW

Oc.4s
RW

Iso.4s
RW

Iso.4s
RW

*Firing
Danger
Area*

Iso.8s
RW

Iso.8s
RW

Q(3)10s
BYB

Keldsnor
Fl(2)20s25M
Oc.WRG.5s12/9M

Langeland

Fl.10s
RW

Fehmarnbelt Oc.4s16M
Horn Mo(FE)30s

Fehmarn

Fehmarn
LFl.WR.10s18·14M

Flügge
Oc(4)20s17M

Q.R

Oc.WRG.4s

Strukkamphuk
Iso.WR.3s8·6M

Fehmarnsund

Q(3)10s
BYB

Oc(2)WRG.9s
13·9M

Heiligenhafen

*See plan
page 45*

Neuland
Fl(4)WR.30s.
21·18M

11°E

50'

30'

Note
Buoys marking the firing area
show flashing yellow lights.

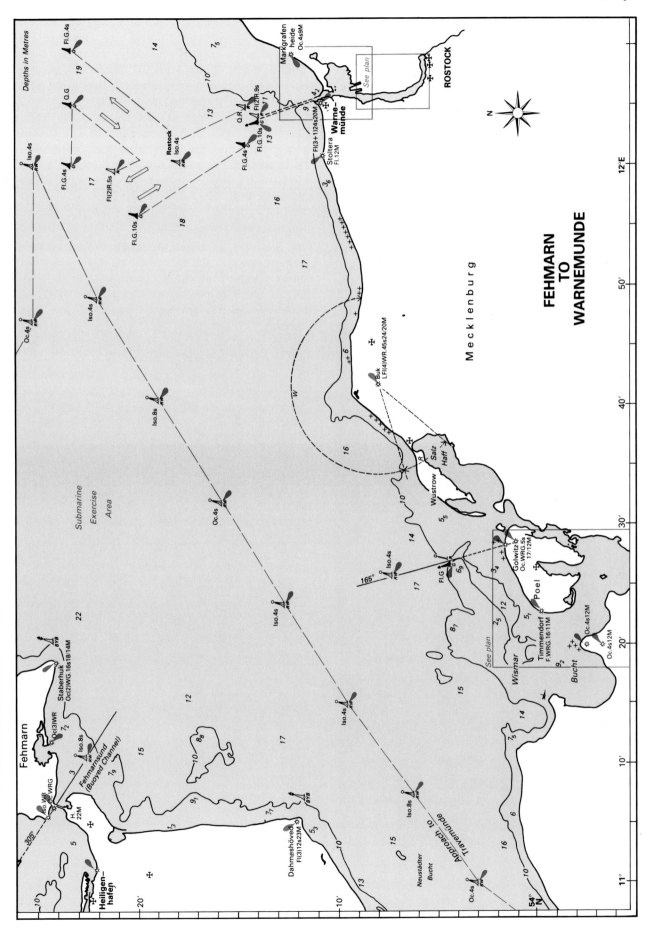

**FEHMARN
TO
WARNEMÜNDE**

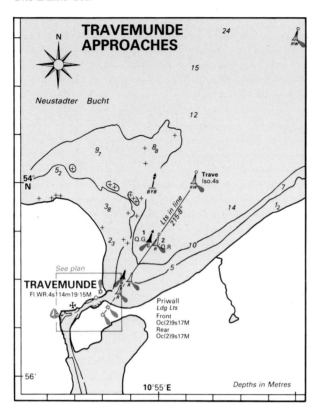

Marina Baltica, where there is a more traditional ambience, but there are fewer facilities.

Formalities

If entering or leaving Germany at this point, customs clearance can be obtained. Call on VHF Ch 16 or contact customs through either of the two yacht harbours.

General facilities

Both yacht harbours have excellent facilities. The Passathafen is perhaps slightly more attractive visually, but both are efficient. There is a crane at the Passathafen if it is required to step masts after emerging from the Elbe-Lübeck Canal.

The shopping centre is on the north bank, about 10 minutes' walk from Marina Baltica and a short ferry ride across the river from the Passathafen. There are banks, restaurants, hotels and a tourist information office in the centre of the town. There is no launderette.

Yachting services

Fuel can be obtained at either of two bunker stations, one on each side of the river. *Camping Gaz* can be bought from the hardware store in the town centre. There is no full-scale chandlery shop, but there are several boatyards equipped for most repairs.

Weather forecasts can be obtained from both yacht harbours or Lübeck Radio.

Communications

There are good rail services to Lübeck and Hamburg, where there is an international airport.

Tourism

The Hanseatic city of Lübeck, 11M up the River Trave from Travemünde, should not be missed. It has a population of 200,000 and it is full of historic buildings which have been painstakingly restored

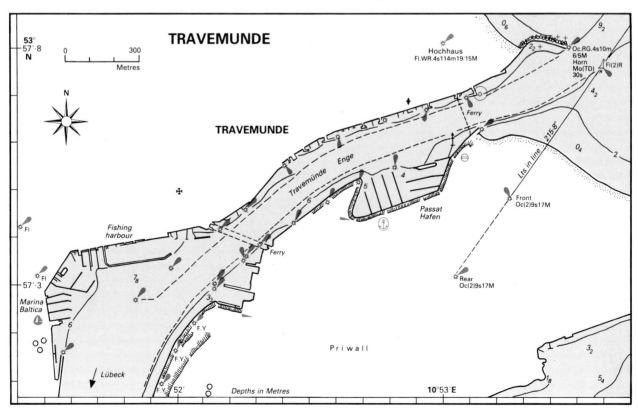

Fehmarnsund bridge at sunrise.

The Passathafen, in the busy port of Travemünde.

Nansen's polar expedition vessel *Fridthjof* and others in the historic ship harbour at Lübeck.

Yachts in the Alten Hafen at Wismar.

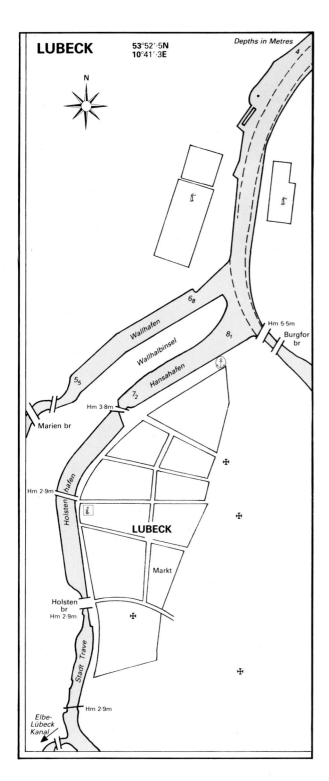

and maintained following the bomb damage of the Second World War. There is also an interesting historic ship harbour, the Hansahafen, where a number of carefully preserved old ships lie, including the *Fridthjof*, one of Nansen's polar expedition vessels, now beautifully restored by Horst and Ilsa Greiser.

It is a pleasant trip by boat, and it is possible to moor quite close to the centre of the city, although there are no facilities. There is also a convenient train service from Travemünde.

Wismar

53°54'N 11°26'E

Distances

Travemünde 25M, Warnemünde 35M.

Charts and guides

Admiralty chart *2364*
German chart *1641*. Essential for entry at night.
Cruising guide to Germany and Denmark Brian Navin, Imray
Baltic Pilot Volume I (NP 18)
Küstenhandbuch Mecklenburg-Vorpommern M. Brandenburg, DK Edition Maritim
Der Grosse NV Hafen Lotse Volume 4 Nautische Veröffentlichung

Lights
Approach

1. **Insel Poel** 53°59'·6N 11°22'·6E F.WRG.21m16-11M Horn 30s White round tower, red top, white lantern, red cupola on building, 21m 049°-R-060°-W-069·5°-G-125·5°-W-136·5°-R-196°-G-202·5°-W-211·5°-R-229°
2. **Wismar** Ldg Lts 150° *Front* 53°54'N 11°27'·1E Oc.3s 27m10M
   Black ▲ on metal frame tower with 2 galleries, 24m
   Rear 700m from front 53°53'·7N 11°27'·4E Oc.3s46m 10M Black metal framework tower
3. **W side. Dolphin 39** 53°54'·5N 11°26'·6E Q.G.5m5M Black pedestal on dolphin
4. **E side. Dolphin 2** 53°54'·3N 11°27'·1E Q.R.5m3M Red pedestal on dolphin
5. **W side. Dolphin 41** 53°54'·3N 11°26'·8E Fl.G.4s5m 6M Black pedestal on dolphin

General

Wismar, a historic town of some 60,000 inhabitants, is principally engaged in shipbuilding and repairs. The old town has remarkable baroque and Gothic architecture and the Alte Markt is a reminder of the greatness of the Hanseatic League. It is one of the largest squares in Germany, with many gabled houses including the 'Alte Schwede', built in 1380 though taking its name from the pub opened there in the late 19th century, a reminder that Wismar belonged to Sweden in the 17th and 18th centuries. The old town has a preservation order and much restoration has been carried out, though of the medieval fortifications only the Wassertor and bits of the town wall remain. The church of St Nicholas and the museum in the Schabbel-haus are worth visiting.

Approach

The fairway is entered off the island of Poel, and is clearly marked by buoys and leading lights. Note

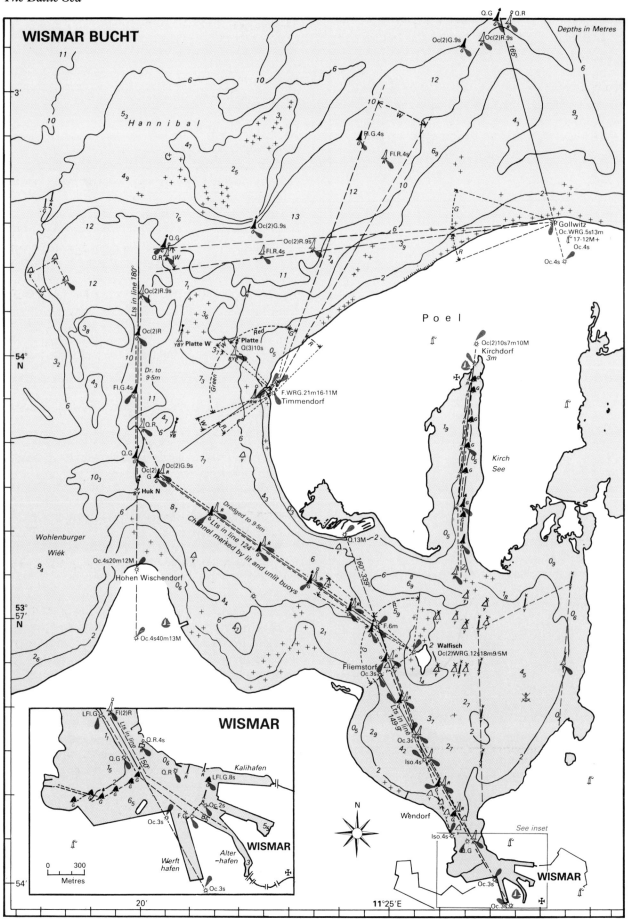

WISMAR BUCHT

Depths in Metres

Q.G Q.R

Oc(2)G.9s Oc(2)R.9s

165

11

H a n n i b a l

6 10 6 12 9₃ 6

5₃ 10 10 W

10 3₁ 4₁ 4₇ Fl.G.4s Fl.R.4s 6₉ 4₃

4₉ 2₅ 12 10 2

7₆ 13 Oc(2)G.9s 6 G Gollwitz
Oc.WRG.5s13m

12 Q.G Oc(2)R.9s Fl.R.4s 3₉ 17-12M+
Q.R W 7₄ Oc.4s

Lts in line 180° Oc(2)R.9s 7₁ 11 2 R Oc.4s

12 3₆ *P o e l*

3₈ Oc(2)R Red Oc(2)10s7m10M
Y BV Platte W Platte 3₇ G Kirchdorf
54° Q(3)10s O₅ R 3m
N 3₂ BV Green G
4₃ 10 7₃ F.WRG.21m16-11M 1₉
Fl.G.4s 11 R W Timmendorf
6 Q.R W R Kirch
4₁ 6 See
Q.G Y8 7₇
10₃ Oc(2) Oc(2)G.9s 0₅
G G
Huk N 8₇ 4₃ 0₃
6 Dredged to 9·5m Q.13M 2
Wohlenburger 6 Lts in line 124° R 0₅
Wiék Channel marked by lit and unlit buoys 6 0₉
9₄ 160° 339° 8 1₈
Oc.4s20m12M R 6₉ 0₆
Hohen Wischendorf 0₆ R 5₉ 1₈
4₄ F.6m 2 Walfisch
Oc.4s40m13M 4₇ 2₁ G Oc(2)WRG.12s18m9/5M
6 **Fliemstorf** 1₄ 4₅
2₆ Oc.3s 0₁
0₅ 2₉ 3₇ 2₇
Oc.3s
4₂ 2₇
Iso.4s

N

Wendorf *See inset*
Iso.4s
0.G
WISMAR
Oc.3s
Oc.3s

53°
57'
N

WISMAR

LFl.G Fl(2)R
1₁ Lts in line 150°
Q.R.4s
Q.G 0₆
1₅ Q.R LFl.G.8s
6₅ R
Oc.2s
F.G 8₅
Oc.3s 5₅

0 300 *Kalihafen*
WISMAR

Werft *Alter*
hafen *–hafen* 3
Metres Oc.3s

that a number of buoys are unlit, but in conditions of good visibility the ambient light is sufficient to enable them to be seen at night.

Anchorage

Anchor outside the shipping channel with appropriate warning signals. There is considerable professional shipping in Wismarbucht, and it is preferable to berth in Alten Hafen.

Berthing

Visiting yachts normally moor alongside on the east side of the picturesque Alten Hafen, just past the harbourmaster's office on the quayside, and ten minutes' walk from the town centre. The harbourmaster can be contacted on VHF Ch 14 and 16.

At popular times yachts moor two or three abreast. Avoid mooring outside one of the tripper vessels which also use this part of the quay.

In 1990 an overnight mooring fee of about £7 was charged for a yacht 12 metres in length.

There is some weed in the water in both the Alten Hafen and the main fairway through Wismarbucht; check water intake strainers.

Formalities

Foreign yachts may be visited by immigration officials, but usually the formalities comprise only a courteous examination of passports.

General facilities

Water, electricity and toilet facilities (but not showers) are available at the quayside. There is a launderette in the town. Bread, green groceries, fast food and leather goods can be bought from stalls near the quay. Groceries, gas and most other supplies can be bought in the town centre.

There is a tourist information office in the town, and banks, restaurants and hotels abound.

Yachting services

Fuel can be obtained only from service stations ashore or by arrangement through the harbourmaster. In 1991, *Camping Gaz* could not be bought, but it is likely that this deficiency will soon be rectified as facilities are brought nearer to West German standards.

There are no specialist facilities for yacht repairs, although the ship repair yard could no doubt be approached in connection with serious problems. There is no yacht chandlery or sailmaker.

Weather forecasts are available on request from the harbourmaster's office.

Communications

There are many telephone kiosks within easy reach of the harbour, but these may not yet be usable for international calls.

Link calls can be made via Lübeck Radio, although reception is sometimes poor in Wismar.

Travel

There are good train services to Hamburg, Berlin and Rostock.

Tourism

From Wismar, ships of the 'White Fleet' (*Weisse Flotte*) take an hour to run to the island of Poel, which is popular for its beaches. Poel also has a museum illustrating the island.

Schwerin, on the edge of the Mecklenburg Lake District, is some 30km by rail from Wismar. Its castle, inspired by Château Chambord, was the seat of the Dukes of Mecklenburg until they were thrown out in 1918; it is both amazingly grand and unsatisfactorily dull. Its gardens and orangery are pleasant enough. The museum of Schwerin has a collection of Dutch and French paintings. Outside the city, Schweriner See is the largest (65km²) of many lakes which contribute to a pretty countryside.

Warnemünde

54°13'·9N 12°04'E

Distances

Wismar 35M, Rostock 12M, Stralsund 54M.

Charts and guides

Admiralty charts *2365* and *2370*

German charts *1671* and *1672*

Cruising guide to Germany and Denmark Brian Navin, Imray

Baltic Pilot Volume I (NP 18)

Küstenhandbuch Mecklenburg-Vorpommern M. Brandenburg, DK Edition Maritim

Der Grosse NV Hafen Lotse Volume 4 Nautische Veröffentlichung

Lights

1. **Warnemünde** W side of entrance 54°10'·9N 12°05'·2E Fl(3+1)24s34m20M White round tower, black bands, copper cupola, 31m
2. **Warnemünde Hafen** Ldg Lts 175·8° *Front* middle mole head 54°11'·1N 12°05'·3E Oc.5s10m13M Yellow ▲ on red mast, white bands, 8m
   Rear Alte Strom. E side. 360m from front 54°10'·9N 12°05'·3E Oc.5s20m13M, Yellow ▼ on yellow framework tower, 19m
3. **Wustrow** 54°20'·2N 12°22'·6E Oc(3)12s12m16M Horn Mo(D)30s Square red tower, 2 white galleries on building, 10m
4. **Darsser Ort** 54°28'·4N 12°30'·2E Fl(2+4)22s33m 20M Round red tower, brown cupola, building, 35m

Fishing boats in the Alter Strom, Warnemünde.

Entrance

5. **W mole head** 54°11'·3N 12°05'·3E Iso.G.4s14m5M Horn Mo(WN)30s Green conical tower, white band and lantern, two galleries, floodlit, 13m
6. **Middle mole** 54°11'·1N 12°05'·3E Iso.4s15m8M Yellow hexagonal tower with platform, floodlit, 11m

General

Warnemünde, a holiday resort and ferry terminal, still maintains an inshore fishing fleet which ties up with yachts in the Alten Strom alongside gabled houses. It lies at the entrance to the huge commercial port of Rostock, whose docks and shipyards stretch inland for 15 miles along the River Warnow, due south from Warnemünde.

In the summer most of the fishing vessels find it more profitable to operate as tripper boats.

Approach

The harbour mouth is very obvious both by day and by night, and is equipped with powerful leading lights. There are no dangerous hazards outside the harbour, and there is a well buoyed fairway extending about two miles out to sea for the benefit of shipping.

The harbour mouth is divided into two, the eastern side being the deep-water channel to the commercial port and to Rostock, whilst the western

side leads to the yacht harbour and the fishing port. Immediately inside the western entrance, there are again two channels, the left-hand one leading past the entrance to the yacht harbour before rejoining the deep-water channel, and the right-hand one being the Alter Strom, from which the fishing boats and tripper vessels scurry back and forth. At night, beware several unlit dolphins at the seaward end of the dividing wall between the yacht harbour and the Alter Strom.

Anchorage

Do not anchor in this busy waterway.

Berthing

It is pleasant to lie alongside the rough staging in the Alter Strom, but yachts should moor only on the eastern side. Mooring on the western side can be hazardous, as many of the skippers of the commercial craft which also use this side seem to object to yachts invading what they regard as their territory. It is also possible to enter the yacht harbour and berth bows-to in 2 metres of water.

Formalities

There is a customs control point on the jetty at the left-hand side of the entrance to the Alter Strom, where it is very easy to moor alongside for clearance,

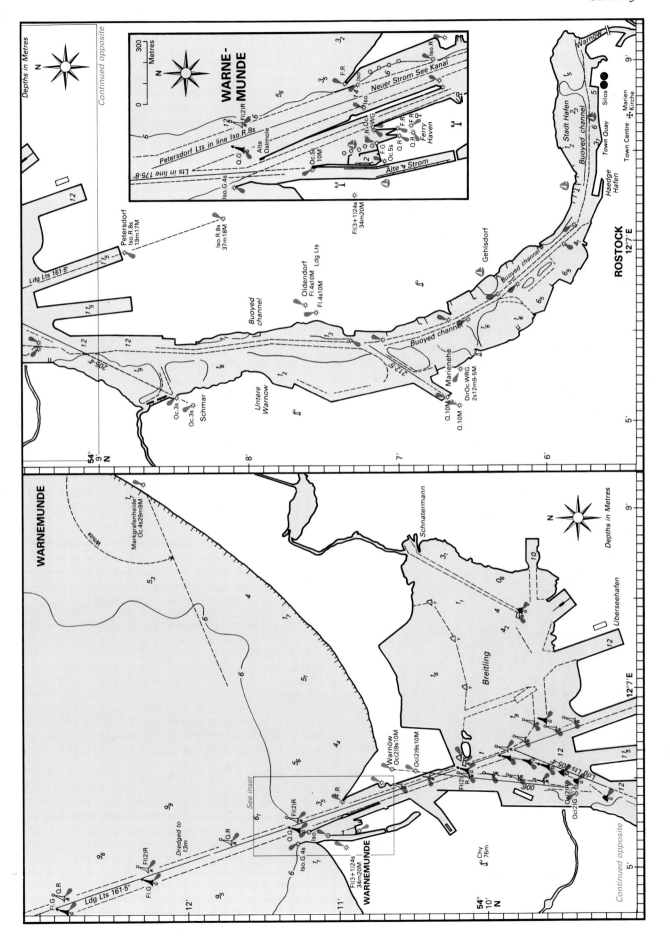

Depths in Metres

N

Continued opposite

WARNE-MUNDE

300
Metres
0

N

F.R

Iso.R

5·6

3·2

3·5

Neuer Strom See Kanal

Iso.R

Fl(2)R

Petersdorf Lts in line Iso.R.8s

Lts in line 175·8

Alte Ostmole

Q.G

7·2

6

F.R Oc.I

F.WG

F.G

Oc.5s

Q.R

F.R
F.R
Ferry Haven

Alte Strom

Oc.5s
10M

Iso.G.4s

Fl(3+1)24s
34m20M

Warnow

1·5

5

Stadt Hafen
2·3

Buoyed channel

5

Silos

Town Quay

Town Centre Marien
Kirche

Haedge
Hafen

ROSTOCK
12°7′E

Petersdorf
Iso.R.8s
19m17M

Iso.R.8s
37m18M

Ldg Lts 161·5

11·5

11·5

Buoyed
channel

Oldendorf
Fl.4s10M   Ldg Lts
Fl.4s10M

7·3

6

Buoyed channel

Gehlsdorf

6·5

6·5

6

6

5·6

5·6

Buoyed channel

Marienehe

21·5

Q.10M

DirOc.WRG
2s12m9·5M

Q.10M

1·2

12

12

6

205·4

1·9

11

Oc.3s

Oc.3s

Schmar

Untere
Warnow

12

54°9′
N

9′

8′

7′

6′

5′

12°7′E

WARNEMUNDE

White

Markgrafenheide
Oc.4s29m9M

5·3

4

6

5·1

4·4

5·6

Dredged to
13m

9·9

6·1

3·5

F.R

See inset

Q.G

Fl(2)R

Iso.

Iso.G.4s

Fl(3+1)24s
34m20M

WARNEMUNDE

Q.R

Fl(2)R

Fl.G

Ldg Lts 161·5

9·6

9·5

12

11′

Fl.G Q.R

54°
10′
N

Chy
76m

1·7

Schnatermann

3·1

10

0·6

Überseehafen

12

Breitling

4

4·2

1·1

1·6

Warnow
Oc(2)9s10M

Oci(2)9s10M

Fl(2)R

900

Oc(2)G

Oc(2)R

Ldg Lts 205·4

12

1·5

12

N

Depths in Metres

9′

12°7′E

5′

Continued opposite

should it be required, at any time of the day or night. If the customs point is not manned, customs officials can usually be contacted at the nearby ferry terminal.

General facilities

Water, electricity, toilets and showers are available in the yacht harbour but not in the Alter Strom.

Provisions are available from nearby shops, and there are stalls selling pancakes, hot dogs and other forms of fast food. Since this is a holiday resort, there is a very wide range of restaurants, hotels and banks to choose from. There is also a tourist information office in the town.

Yachting services

Petrol and diesel can be obtained at the yacht harbour.

There is a crane capable of lifting 2·5 tonnes at the yacht harbour, and a larger one capable of handling 8 tonnes is at the nearby boatyard.

Communications

International calls cannot be made from the old East German telephone kiosks, but the main post office in the marketplace provides an operator-controlled international call service.

VHF correspondence services can be obtained through Rostock Radio or (if Rostock is not operating) via Lübeck Radio.

Travel

It is a ten-minute ride on the S-bahn railway to the centre of Rostock.

There is a regular ferry sailing to Gedser in Denmark.

Rostock

54°05'N 12°07'E

Distances

Warnemünde 12M.

Charts and guides

Admiralty chart *2370*
German charts *1671* and *1672*
Cruising guide to Germany and Denmark Brian Navin, Imray
Baltic Pilot Volume I (NP 18)
Küstenhandbuch Mecklenburg-Vorpommern M. Brandenburg, DK Edition Maritim
Der Grosse NV Hafen Lotse Volume 4 Nautische Veröffentlichung

General

Rostock is the largest city in the area, with about 200,000 inhabitants. It was founded at the first bridge over the Warnow and was a most important member of the Hanseatic League. Today, together with Uberseehafen, 2 miles up from Warnemünde, it has extensive cargo handling and shipbuilding facilities as well as a specially built deep-sea fishing harbour. For the visitor its chief attractions are its buildings, many of which survive despite heavy bombing during the Second World War. The Steintor and the surviving houses of the merchants are good evidence of the Hanseatic commercial influence, but the centrepiece is the Marienkirche, an immense Gothic edifice built over a period of 400 years, which houses a late 15th-century astronomical clock and a famous baroque organ. The Maritime Museum (Schiffahrtsmuseum) has over 100 models of sailing ships, including some of the Hanseatic period. More recent shipping is recorded in the Schiffbaumuseum.

There are now wide, elegant streets and a smart pedestrian-only shopping centre with a sparkling fountain, waterfalls, and bright umbrellas at pavement cafés.

Approach

From Warnemünde take the well marked main channel past the shipyards and docks for 12 miles to the town quay (Stadthafen) on the starboard hand. Pilotage is straightforward if the German chart is used, and at night the numerous unlit buoys are reasonably well seen because of the high ambient light level.

A number of low wooden jetties project deceptively far out from the north bank shortly before the town is reached. At night these are very difficult to see.

Anchorage

Do not anchor in this waterway.

Berthing

There is a small yacht harbour at Gehlsdorf on the north side of the waterway before Rostock itself, but it is not well situated for exploring the town. Visiting yachts will find it more convenient to berth alongside at the free but somewhat uncomfortable town quay (Stadthafen), opposite No. 56 red buoy and a five-minute walk from the shopping centre.

General facilities

The town quay is without facilities for yachts, except electricity, which can be obtained from one of the extension boxes fed from the supply points for commercial vessels. There are rubbish skips across the nearby road, outside a block of flats.

The town quay at Rostock.

All normal shopping facilities, hotels, banks and restaurants are available in the town centre.

Yachting services

It is not possible to buy fuel, gas or chandlery conveniently, and yacht repair facilities are non-existent.

Weather forecasts in German are broadcast on VHF by Rostock Radio and Lübeck Radio.

Communications

There are many telephone kiosks, but these may not yet have been upgraded to enable international calls to be made.

The Bundespost main post office provides operator-controlled international calls, together with all normal communications facilities.

Travel

Rostock has good rail connections with Berlin and Hamburg.

Tourism

Outside Rostock is the open air Klockenhagen Museum illustrating a regional farmhouse and farming. It is possible to take the train further afield, from Warnemünde to Rostock and on to Bad Doberan, which has the Doberaner Münster, a great brick church built by the Cistercians between 1294 and 1368. The Molli, a steam railway which has a gauge of only 90cm and is a great tourist attraction, runs from Bad Doberan through Heiligendamm to Kühlungsborn, on the coast 25km west of Warnemünde. Heiligendamm was established in 1793 as a spa; it is known as 'The White Town by the Sea' because of its white-painted, period buildings. Kühlungsborn is the largest seaside resort in Mecklenburg.

Stralsund

54°19'N 13°06'E

Distances

Warnemünde 51M, Świnoujście 50M, Szczecin 85M.

Charts and guides

Admiralty chart *2365* (unsuitable for safe navigation of the inshore passages).
German charts *1579 1511* and *1622*
Cruising guide to Germany and Denmark Brian Navin, Imray
Baltic Pilot Volume I (NP 18)
Küstenhandbuch Mecklenburg-Vorpommern, M. Brandenburg, DK Edition Maritim
Der Grosse NV Hafen Lotse Volume 4, Nautische Veröffentlichung

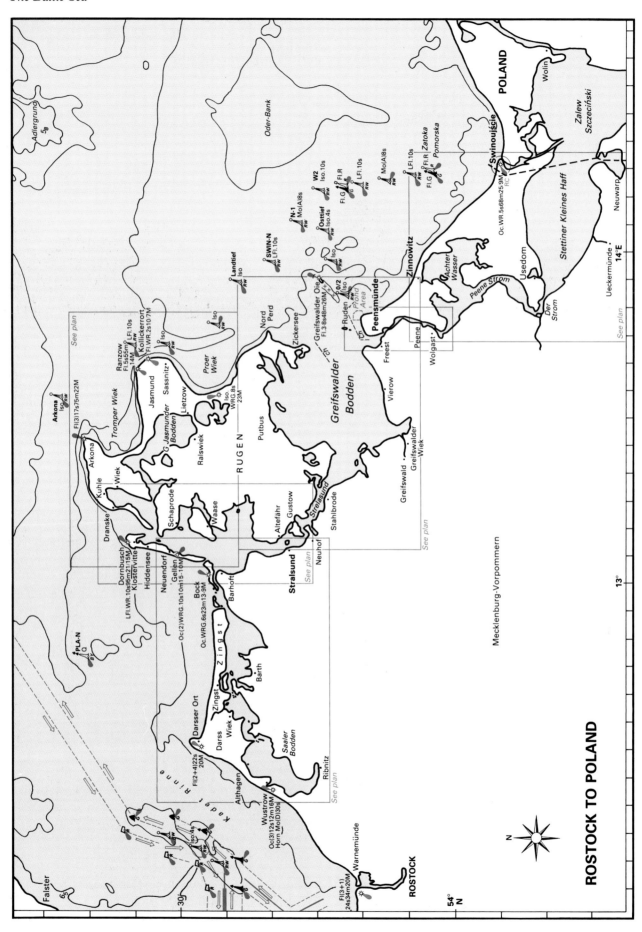

ROSTOCK TO POLAND

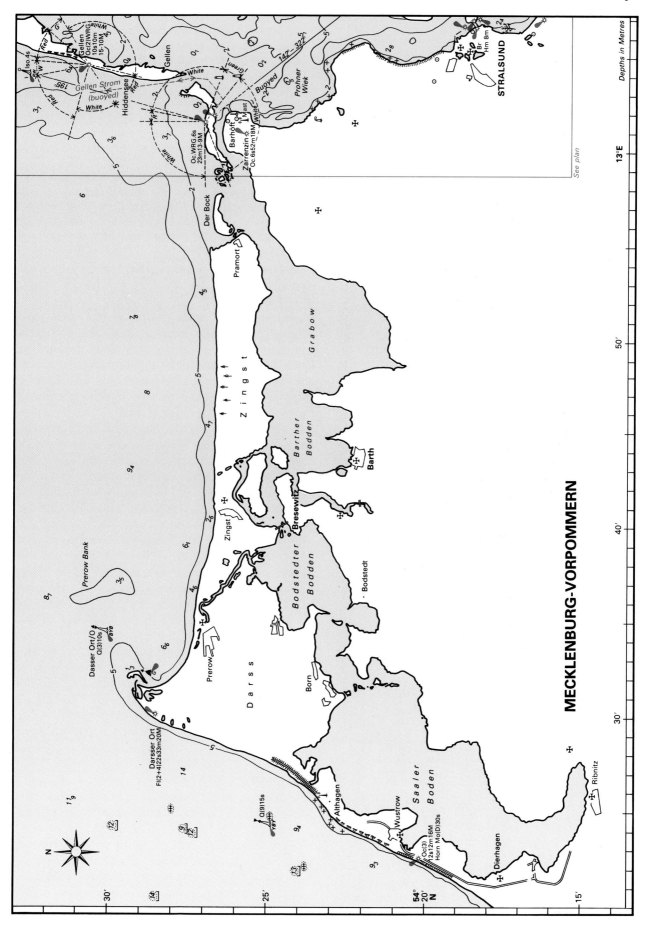

MECKLENBURG-VORPOMMERN

STRALSUND

Gellen
Oc(2)WRG
10s10m
15-10M

Iso.4s
W

195

Gellen Strom
(buoyed)

Hiddensee

White

Red

White

Green

Green

142 – 322.5

Prohrer
Wiek

Buoyed

White

Oc.WRG.6s
23m13.9M

Barhöft

Zarrenzin
Oc.6s52m118M

Mast

White

Der Bock

Pramort

Grabow

Zingst

Barther
Bodden

Barth

Bresewitz

Zingst

Bodstedter
Bodden

Bodstedt

Prerow Bank

Darss

Dasser Ort/O
Q(3)10s

BYB

Prerow

Born

Darsser Ort
Fl(2+4)22s33m20M

Saaler
Boden

Althagen

Q(9)15s
VQ(9)

Wustrow

Oc(3)
12s12m16M
Horn Mo(D)30s

Dierhagen

Ribnitz

N

54°
20'
N

25'

30'

15'

30'

40'

50'

13°E

54°20'N

See plan

Depths in Metres

39

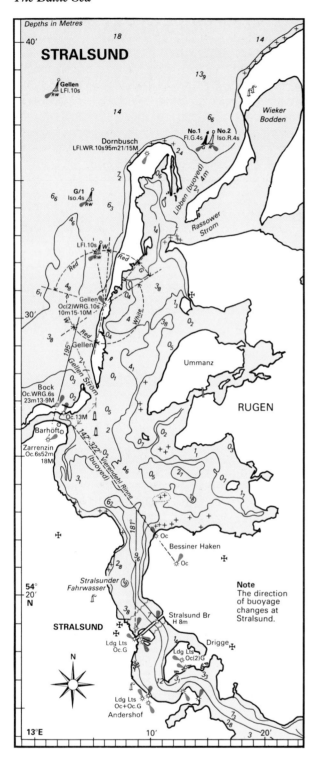

Lights

Approach

1. **Darsser Ort** 54°28'·4N 12°30'·2E Fl(2+4)22s33m 20M Round red tower, brown cupola, building, 35m
2. **Bock** Ldg Lts 195·1° *Front* 54°26'·9N 13°01'·6E Oc.WRG.6s23m13-9M White framework tower, red lantern and gallery 195° with white roof, grey stone base, white stripe, 23m 089°-W-180°-R-191°-W-290°-G-308°-W-069°

Rear (Zarrenzin) 1·3M from front 54°25'·6N 13°01'E Oc.6s52m18M White metal framework tower, red bands and lantern, white cupola, 23m

3. **Kap Arkona** 54°40'·9N 13°26'·1E Fl(3)17·1s75m22M Red lantern on yellow round tower with two galleries, 35m

Channel

4. **Bock** Ldg Lts 322·1° *Front* 54°26'·6N 13°02'E Oc.6s 12m13M White framework tower, red lantern and gallery with white roof, grey stone base, white stripe, 12m 302°-vis-342°

Rear 54°26'·9N 13°01'·6E Oc.WRG.6s23m13-9M White framework tower, red lantern and gallery with white roof, grey stone base, white stripe, 23m 089°-W-180°-R-191°-W-290°-G-308°-W-069°. Back bearing on 322·1° can be used when moving south to Stralsund.

Light 2 front and 4 rear are the same.

General

Stralsund is the main town of this area, and although once a very prosperous trading port, it is now somewhat run down after four decades of inefficient government. It is still, however, a very attractive port and holiday resort, full of old-world charm and with many historic buildings, cobbled streets and a lively open-air market.

It was founded in 1209 and joined the Hanseatic League in 1293. Like Wismar, it was under Swedish control in the 17th and 18th centuries and came under Prussian control in 1815. It was very badly damaged in British and US air raids during the Second World War, a memory which lies not far below the surface. The fine Town Hall survived and over its windows on the market side are the arms of Hamburg, Lübeck, Wismar, Rostock, Stralsund and Greifswald. The three parish churches of St Mary, St James (Jacobikirche) and St Nicholas demonstrate the prosperity of the city – especially the last, which was started in the 13th century and largely rebuilt after a fire in 1662. The eclectic maritime museum is concerned with the biology and geology of the coast. It also has a considerable tropical aquarium, a section devoted to coral, the 15m skeleton of a fin whale and the 17m fishing boat *Adolf Reichwein* which is said to have been the doyenne of the former Democratic Republic's high-seas fleet.

Approach

The port lies on the west bank of the Strelasund, the narrow channel between the island of Rügen and the mainland.

Whether coming from the north or the south it is necessary to navigate through the Strelasund, which is tortuous but very clearly marked. There is sometimes a small current in the Strelasund, with a direction and strength dependent on wind

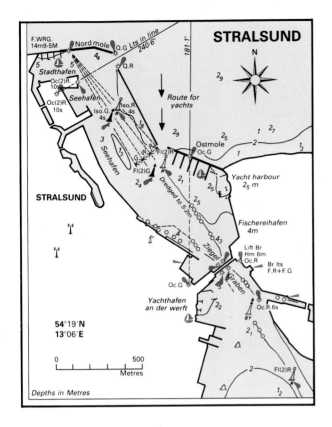

conditions over the southern Baltic. Navigation at night in the Strelasund is possible, but not recommended.

Approaching from the north, via Gellen Strom, it should be noted that the channel buoyage now starts at buoy No. 27, even though on some charts higher numbers may be shown extending further to seaward.

On the approach from the south, after the southern arm of the Strelasund from the Greifswalder Bodden has been passed through, twin lifting bridges will be encountered at the southern end of the town. These bridges open at 0230, 0800, 1245, 1800 and 2200 local time for 20 minutes. Timings may be changed; enquire at Stralsund harbourmaster's office. If it is necessary to wait it is usually possible to find a temporary mooring at the Yachthafen an der Werft, just before the bridge on the western side of the Strelasund. At the bridges the direction of buoyage changes.

There is a certain amount of weed in the channel; check inlet water strainers after navigating in this area.

Anchorage

There are numerous anchorages outside the fairway, but appropriate signals must be displayed.

Berthing

Visiting yachts normally moor in the town harbour (Stadthafen), alongside the northern mole immediately to starboard on entry via the northern entrance. It may be necessary to moor outside other yachts at busy times. The pontoons further along the mole are for shallow-draught yachts only. It is also permitted to moor alongside the commercial quays midway between the north and south entrances, provided that no larger vessels are expected.

The Yachthafen an der Werft, the yacht harbour immediately south of the twin lifting bridges, has few guest berths and it is usually difficult to find a place, especially for yachts over 2.5 metres in beam. It does, however, have toilets and showers and, although it is not as close to the city centre as the Stadthafen and has a railway line close by, in many ways it is a more pleasant harbour.

Formalities

There is a customs office (should it be needed) overlooking the Fährkanal, opposite the harbour-master's office.

General facilities

The only facilities conveniently available at the Stadthafen are public toilets (near the start of the north mole) and rubbish bins. Water may be available by negotiation at the quay used by tripper boats.

The Yachthafen an der Werft has showers and toilets. A water supply is also available.

There is a small general store opposite the harbourmaster's office at the Stadthafen, but otherwise all shops, banks and restaurants are in the city centre, about 1km from the Stadthafen and about 2km from the Yachtclub an der Werft.

Yachting facilities

There are two chandlers, but no repair facilities and no fuel supplies (except possibly by negotiation with the harbourmaster or one of the tripper boat skippers).

Weather forecasts in German – but at slow speed – are broadcast by Rügen Radio at 0930 and 2130 local time on VHF Ch 1 for north and west and on Ch 5 for south and east.

Communications

The main post office provides the normal PTT facilities, including operator-controlled international telephone calls.

Telephone kiosks are not equipped for international calls, but Rügen Radio can handle public correspondence calls.

Travel

There are good train services to Berlin and Rostock, but it should be noted that there are two railway stations – which can be very confusing.

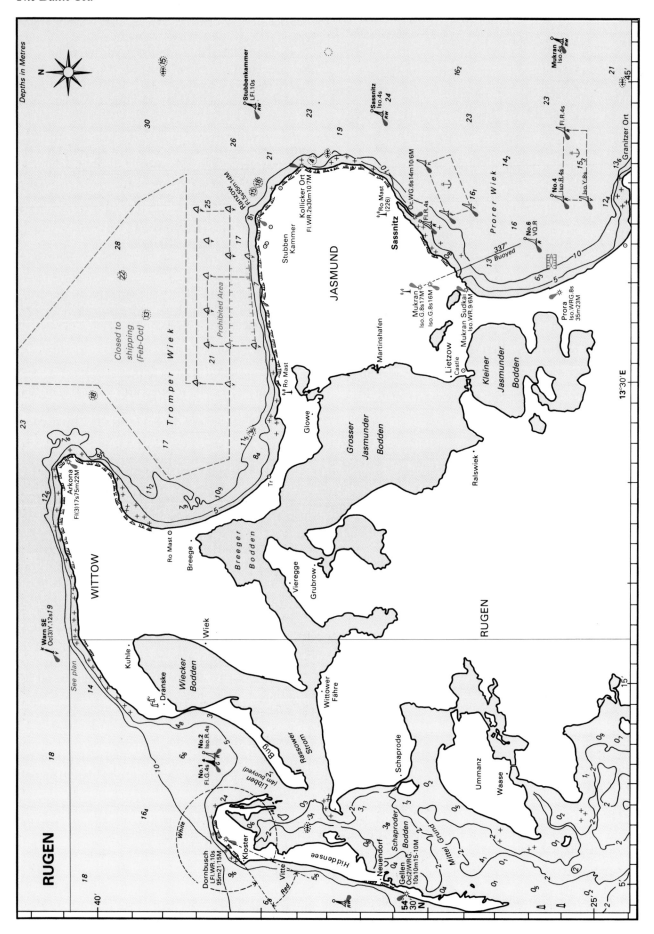

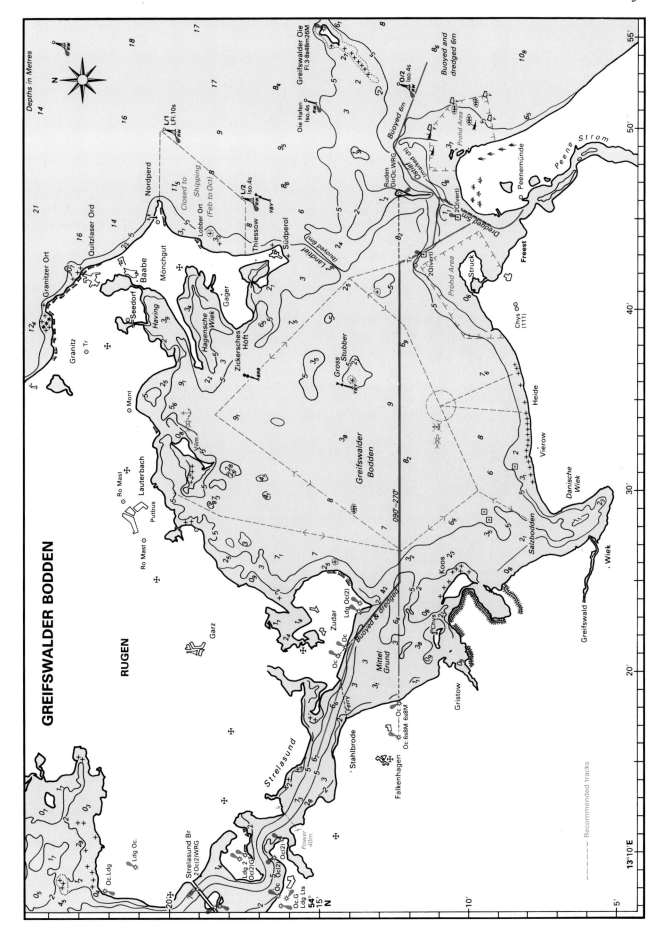

GREIFSWALDER BODDEN

RUGEN

Depths in Metres

Greifswalder Oie
Fl.3·8s48m26M

Greifswalder Oie
Fl.3·8s48m26M

Oie Hafen
Iso.4s

Ruden
DirOc.WRG

Peenemünde

Peene Strom

Freest

Struck

Buoyed 6m

Buoyed and
dredged 6m

Prohd Area

Prohd Area

Dredged 5m

2O(vert)

2O(vert)

OI/2
RW

Chys
(111)

Heide

Vierow

Danische
Wiek

Salzbodden

. Wiek

Greifswald

Gristow

Koos

Chys

Mittel
Grund

Zudar

Ldg Oc(2)

Oc.

Oc.

Stahlbrode

Falkenhagen
Oc. 6s8M

Oc. 6s8M

Ferry

Strelasund

Power
40m

Strelasund Br
2Oc(2)WRG

Ldg Oc.

Oc.Ldg

Ldg 2
Oc(2)G

Oc. Oc(2)G

Oc. G
Ldg Lts

Garz

Ro Mast

Lauterbach
Putbus

Ro Mast

Vilm

Granitz

Granitzer Ort

Seedorf
Having

Baabe

Mönchgut

Gager

Hagensche
Wiek

Zickersches
Höft

Gross
Stubber

Greifswalder
Bodden

Quitzlaser Ord

Nordperd

Lobber Ort

Thiessow

Südperol

U/1
LFl.10s
RW

U/2
Iso.4s
RW

Landtief
(buoyed 6m)

Closed to
Shipping
(Feb to Oct)

090°–270°

Recommended tracks

13°10'E

54°
15'
N

Mont

Tr

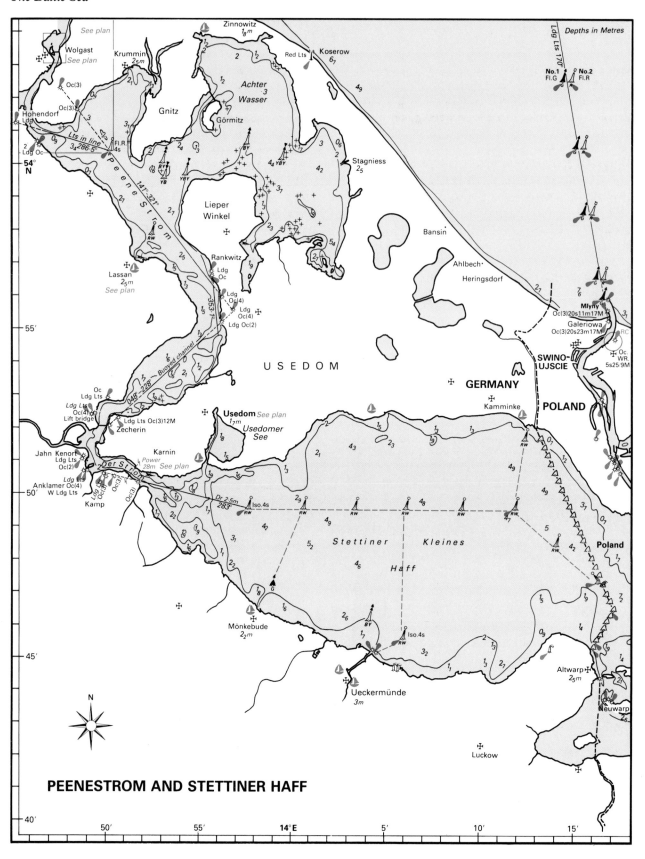

PEENESTROM AND STETTINER HAFF

Other ports

Laboe 54°24'N 10°13'E
A small fishing port and yacht harbour on the eastern side of Kiel fjord. It is the official customs clearance point for yachts entering or leaving Germany via Kiel.

Heiligenhafen 54°21'N 11°00'E (See plan)
A major yachting centre with every facility, Heiligenhafen also has a pleasant fishing harbour. Entry is through a dredged channel; the harbour has depths between 2·2–4·3m.

Burgetiefe 54°24'N 11°11'E
A yacht harbour which can take craft of up to 15m with 3m draught; it is near Burg on Fehmarn, off the Burge See, which is entered 3M east of the Fehmarnsund Bridge.

Niendorf 54°00'N 10°48'E
A fishing harbour used by yachts drawing less than 3m.

Timmendorf 53°59'N 11°22'E
On the island of Poel. Used by pilots, it has 3·5m in the approach, 1.6–2·7m in the yacht area. It is well protected by moles.

Kirchdorf 53°59'N 11°26'E
A fishing harbour at the head of a narrow fjord. It has 2·3–3·1m in the buoyed approach through banks and 3–4m inside.

Darsser Ort 54°28'N 12°31'E
Until recently a DDR patrol boat base, but now a popular yacht harbour. Dredged to a depth of 4·7m. Minimal facilities.

Zingst 54°25'N 12°41'E
Also on Barther Bodden, east of Meiningenbrücke, Zingst has a swing bridge with a clearance of 3m. In the summer of 1990 this was open only on Mondays between 1900 and 2000 and on Fridays between 1315 and 1415.

Prerow 54°26'N 12°35'E
Small harbour on Bodstedter Bodden. Depth 2·1m.

Althagen 54°22'N 12°25'E
On Saaler Bodden. Depth 2m.

Wustrow 54°20'N 12°23'E
Also on Saaler Bodden. Depth 2m.

Dierhagen 54°17'N 12°21'E
On the narrow part of the spit between Saaler Bodden and the sea. Depth 2·7m.

Ribnitz 54°14'N 12°26'E
At the extreme southeast end of Saaler Bodden. Depth only 1·6m.

Bodstedt 54°22'N 12°37'E
On the south side of Bodstedter Bodden. Depth 1·7m.

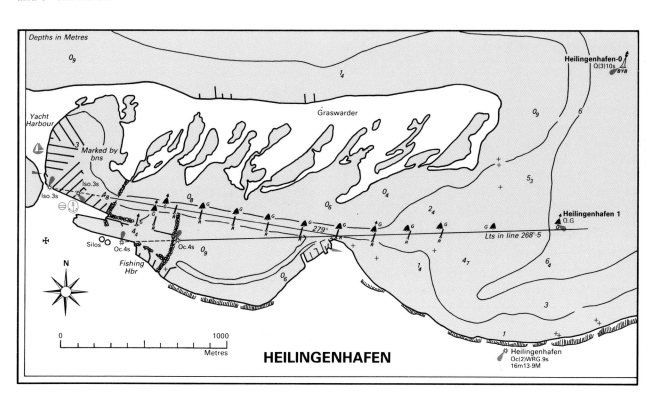

HEILINGENHAFEN

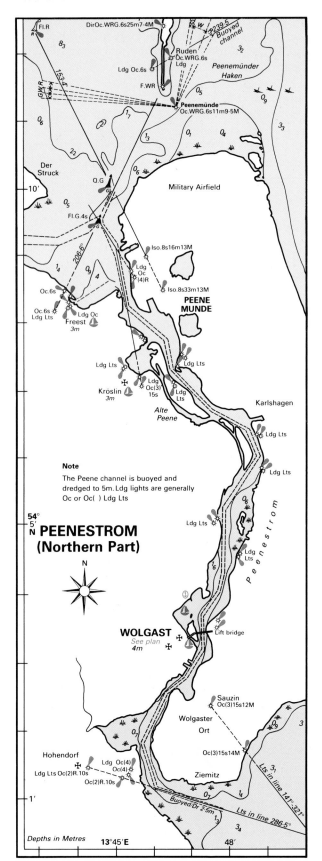

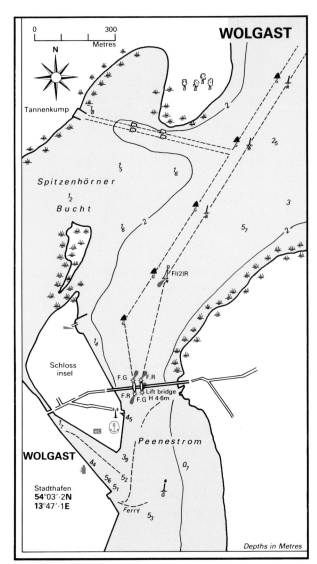

Wolgast yacht moorings, conveniently close to the town centre.

Barth 54°22'N 12°43'E
Small town on Barther Bodden with unspoilt yacht harbour. Depths 1·2–3m.

Kloster 54°35'N 13°07'E
On the seaward side of Hiddensee Island. Depth 2·7m.

Neuendorf 54°31'N 13°05'E
Fishing community straddling Hiddensee Island. There is a small harbour with a depth of 2·5m on the east side of the island, on Schaproder Bodden.

Vitte 54°34'N 13°06'E
On east side of Hiddensee with T-shaped jetty for yachts and small ferry landing. Depth 2·3m.

Kuhle 54°38'N 13°17'E
Small harbour popular with local yachtsmen. Depth 2·5m.

Wiek/Rügen 54°37'N 13°17'E
Old fishing village on Wiecker Bodden. Depth 0·5m but may be more.

Breege 54°36'N 13°21'E
Fishing harbour and ferry landing at the north end of Grosser Jasmunder Bodden. Depth 3·2m.

Martinshafen 54°31'N 13°30'E
Isolated, small commercial harbour on the east side of Grosser Jasmunder Bodden. Depth 2·5m.

Ralswiek 54°28'N 13°27'E
A must. Old castle and delightful surroundings. Depth 2·1m.

Schaprode 54°30'N 13°10'E
Village with small commercial harbour. Depth 2·5m.

Waase 54°27'N 13°10'E
Depth 2·3m.

Barhöft 54°26'N 13°02'E
On the west side of Strelasund North, just inside the entrance. Depth 3·7m. Used by pilot vessels and yachts. Customs clearance can also be obtained here.

Neuhof 54°16'N 11°11'E
Depth 4·4m.

Stahlbrode 54°14'N 13°17'E
Ferry and fishing port on the south side of Strelasund South near the entrance to Greifswalder Bodden. Depth 2·7m in the fishing harbour.

Puddemin 54°16'N 13°20'E
On the north side of Strelasund South, opposite Stahlbrode. Depth 2·3m.

Lauterbach 54°24'N 13°30'E
On the south coast of Rügen, with a depth of 2·4m in the inner harbour. Short walk (2km) to Putbus, dating from 1325. Narrow-gauge steam railway.

Seedorf 54°21'N 13°39'E
Beautiful natural harbour on Rügen, at the north end of Greifswalder Bodden. Depth 4m.

Sassnitz 54°30'N 13°38'E
On the seaward side of Rügen. A major fishing, commercial and ferry port with connections to Trelleborg in Sweden.

Vilm 54°19'N 13°32'E
Tiny island on the north side of Greifswalder Bodden. Formerly a government reserve. Depths of 3m.

Wiek 54°06'N 13°27'E (See plan)
Charming yacht harbour, with depths of about 4m, on the south side of Greifswalder Bodden at the mouth of the River Ryck. Wooden drawbridge at west end of harbour.

Greifswald 54°06'N 13°23'E
University town and small port a short distance up the River Ryck.

Freest 54°08'N 13°44'E (See plan)
Fishing port and well equipped yacht harbour at the north entrance of the Peenestrom. Depths 2·4m.

Peenemünde 54°08'N 13°46'E (See plan)
Site of wartime rocket development. Military harbour, entry prohibited.

Karlshagen 54°06'N 13°48'E
Unattractive fishing harbour with processing plant, but a convenient overnight mooring place. Depth 2·4m.

Wolgast 54°03'N 13°47'E (See plan)
Attractive town with bascule bridge over Peenestrom. Good quay near centre of town for shopping. Depth 3·4m.

Zinnowitz 54°04'N 13°55'E
Small yacht harbour, with depths of 2·5m, tucked away on north side of Achterwasser.

Stagniess 54°00'N 14°03'E
Tiny harbour on east side of Achterwasser. Depth 2·4m.

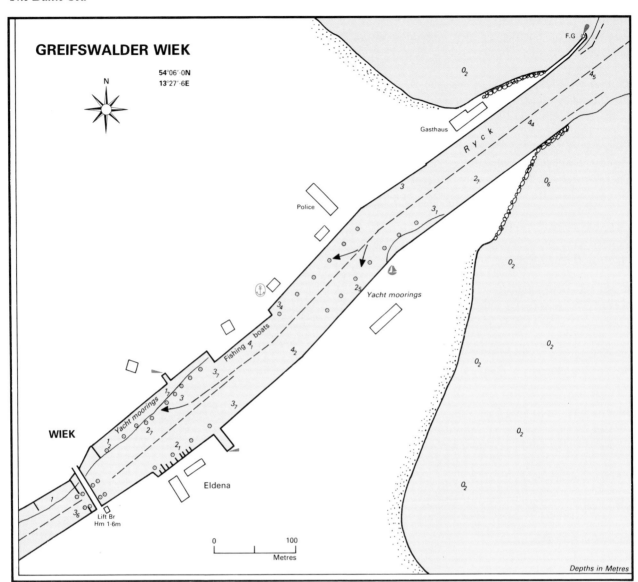

GREIFSWALDER WIEK

54°06'·0N
13°27'·6E

N

Ryck

F.G

Gasthaus

Police

Yacht moorings

Fishing boats

Yacht moorings

WIEK

Eldena

Lift Br
Hm 1·6m

0   100
Metres

Depths in Metres

Rural scene on the Peenestrom.

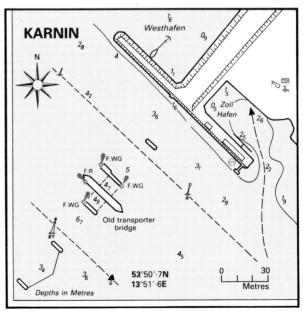

KARNIN

N

Westhafen

Zoll
Hafen

F.WG

F.R

F.WG

F.WG

5

Old transporter
bridge

BY

53°50'·7N
13°51'·6E

0   30
Metres

Depths in Metres

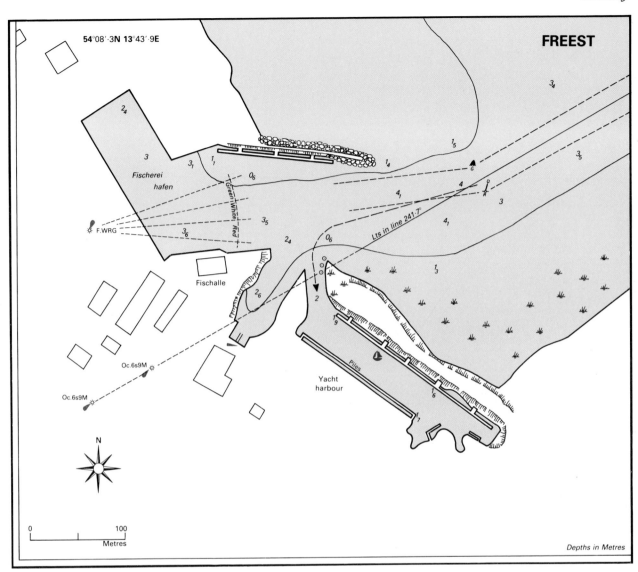

54°08'·3N 13°43'·9E

FREEST

Fischerei hafen

Green White Red

F.WRG

Fischalle

Oc.6s9M

Oc.6s9M

Yacht harbour

Piles

Lts in line 241·7

0 100
Metres

Depths in Metres

Zecherin 53°52'N 13°50'E
Bascule bridge with opening times coordinated with those of the Wolgast bridge.

Karnin 53°51'N 13°52'E (See plan)
At entrance to Kleines Haff. Shallow harbour (1·5m). Channel passes through girder structure of disused railway lift bridge, put out of action in the Second World War.

Usedom 53°52'N 13°56'E (See plan)
On south side of Usedom island. Enter through Usedomer See. Fishing harbour 2m deep.

Mönkebude 53°46'N 13°58'E
Beautiful yacht harbour on south side of Kleines Haff. Depth 2m.

Ueckermünde 53°45'N 14°04'E
Tree-lined entrance to River Uecker, leading in 1M to Stadthafen in town centre. Depth 3m.

Altwarp 53°44'N 14°16'E
Small fishing village on border with Poland. Depth 2m.

Wolgast, approaching the bascule bridge from the north.

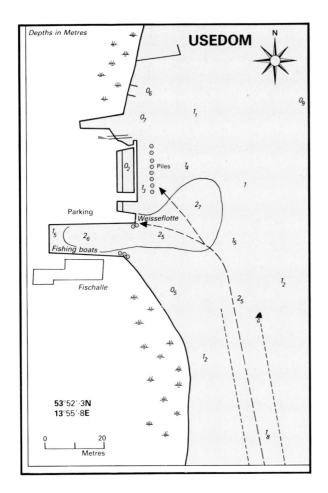

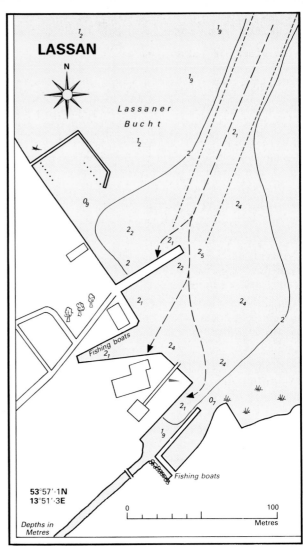

The bascule bridge at Zecherin on the Peenestrom.

A Second World War relic: the derelict transporter bridge at Karnin on the Peenestrom.

II. Poland

Poland's coastline is mostly undramatic with steep clayish cliffs often less than 100m high and low-lying beaches. It is about 250M from one end to the other, if both sides of the Hel spit are taken into account. Szczecin (pronounced Shchetsin) and Gdynia have good yacht harbours and there are a number of smaller fishing ports which can be visited. Several navigable inland seas, and extensive inland waterways, including two major routes to Berlin, give further scope for exploration, and boats drawing less than 1m can get to the border of Russia (Kaliningrad), which may by now be open.

The country

The underlying geology of the country is complicated, but the landscaping forces in the northern part were more straightforward; the surface has been influenced mainly by the last glaciation. Much clay, sand and small debris was dumped and along the coast a rolling countryside has evolved, with low hills and lakes. Outside the towns in the coastal area the land is mainly arable or pasture, though there is timber which is carefully maintained, especially in the national parks. The principle of the collective farm has generally been abandoned. Cereals (particularly wheat and rye), potatoes and sugar beet are common. Livestock is on the increase. Roads are rough.

History

In its own way, the history of Poland is as complicated as its geology, but it is much less pleasant to contemplate. The Poles are very conscious that their country was first established as a kingdom in the 11th century; that they developed into a highly cultured nation in the late middle ages; but that they have been continually threatened, invaded, carved up and even completely suppressed by a succession of predators whose number included the Teutonic Knights, the Tartars, the Swedes, the Prussians, the Austrians and the Russians amongst others. At the end of the 19th century there was no recognisable Polish state. Prussian influence and the German language dominated along the Baltic coast, Russian authority in the centre and east, and Austrian in the southwest. In the confusion at the end of the First World War, the movement to re-establish a Polish nation, supported by the USA and, interestingly, by the newly established soldiers' and workers' councils of bolshevik Russia, was successful, though it did not end the confusion. In 1920 the Poles were at war with Russia to recover territory in the Ukraine they considered Polish. The border in Silesia between Poland and Germany was unsatisfactorily and only temporarily settled by a plebiscite held in 1921. Germany retained large territories along the Baltic known as East Prussia; Poland was given access to the Baltic near Danzig (Gdańsk), cutting off East Prussia from the rest of Germany; Danzig itself was not given to Poland but established as a free state within the Polish Customs Union. During the growing tensions of the interwar years, Poland was unable to solve her political and economic difficulties, and in 1939 she was overwhelmed by Germany and the USSR acting in concert. In the ensuing Second World War, Poland lost about a quarter of her Catholic population and virtually all of her Jewish population, which had for centuries been given refuge there, as well as an enormous amount of agricultural and industrial stock. At the end of that war she again came under the influence of Russia (this time in the guise of the USSR) but with significant geographical differences. Both her eastern and western boundaries were moved west so that a part of the formerly German Silesia came to Poland and East Prussia vanished, giving Poland her present coastline. This change was accompanied by an apparent shift in the ethnography of the western area, from 85% of the population said to be German to 93% said to be Polish; however, Świnoujście and Szczecin still have a German overtone, whilst Gdańsk and other places retain echoes of the Teutonic knights, the Hanseatic League and other relicts of history.

A footnote

In Polish, the prefix 'z' before a word means 'out of'. The 'z' became 's' and objects coming from Prussia were labelled as Spruce; in 16th-century England, the area was called Sprucia or Spruce-land. The word spruce by itself is labelled by lexographers as elliptical in that it needs another word to complete its meaning, as in spruce-board, spruce-canvas and even spruce-fir. Spruce-fir might be one of a number of varieties – black spruce, Koyama's spruce, Norway spruce, red spruce, Sitka spruce, tiger tail spruce etc. The spruce found in Prussia is *Picea*

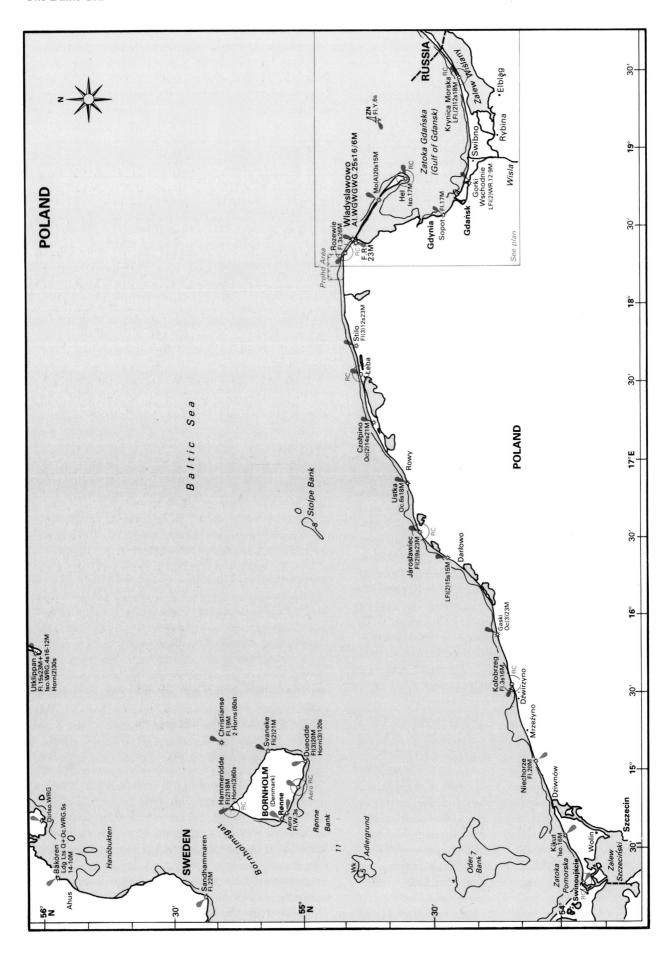

POLAND

N

RUSSIA

Krynica Morska RC
LFl.(2)12s18M

Wisłany
Zalew
Swibno • Elbląg
Wschodnie Rybina

Wisla

ZN
Fl.Y.6s

Zatoka Gdańska
(Gulf of Gdansk)

Gorki LFl.(2)WR.12.9M
Gdańsk

Wladysławowo
Al.WGWG.25s16/6M

Hel
Iso.17M
Sopot •Fl.17M

Gdynia

MolA)20s15M
RC

Rozewie
Fl.3s26M
RC

F R
23M RC

See plan

Prohd Area

Stilo
Fl(3)12s23M

Łeba
RC

Czołpino
Oc(2)14s21M

Baltic Sea

Rowy

POLAND

Stolpe Bank

Ustka
Oc.6s18M

Jarosławiec
Fl(2)9s23M RC

Darłowo

LFl(2)15s15M

Gaski
Oc(3)23M

Utklippan
Fl.1s23M+
Iso.WRG.4s16-12M
Horn(2)30s

Kołobrzeg
Fl.3s16M RC

Dźwirzyno

Christiansø
Fl.19M
2 Horns(60s)

Hammerödde
Fl(2)18M
Horn(3)60s

Svaneke
Fl(3)21M

Dueodde
Fl(3)20M
Horn(3)120s

Mrzeżyno

Niechorze
Fl.20M

BORNHOLM
(Denmark)

Rønne

Aero RC

Ørriso.WRG

Bäkören
Ldg Lts Q+Oc.WRG.5s
14-10M

Åhus

Hanöbukten

Aero
Fl.W.3s

Rønne
Bank

Adlergrund

Dziwnów

Oder
Bank

Kikut
Iso.16M

Wolin

SWEDEN

Sandhammaren
Fl.22M

Bornholmsgat

11

WK
5

8

Zatoka
Pomorska

Świnoujście
RC

Zalew
Szczeciński

Szczecin

56° N

30'

55° N

30'

30'

30'

54°

30'

15°

30'

16°

30'

17°E

30'

18°

30'

19°

30'

abies, the Norway spruce, which grows in Europe between the Alps, Norway, Russia and the Balkans.

The people and the church

One reason why throughout the centuries the Poles managed to retain a sense of national identity and a recognisable culture was the cohesion provided by the Roman Catholic Church. Some 93% of the estimated present population of 39 million are Roman Catholic and the church's demonstration of its ability to provide leadership during the recent 'communist' rule is only the latest of a series of parallel episodes. There is also a Polish Orthodox Church, with a following of some 600,000, which has from time to time been part of the Russian Orthodox Church, and which renewed its self-governing (autocephalic) position in 1948 with the consent of the Moscow patriarch.

The Polish people may seem at first reserved, or perhaps even indifferent to foreigners, but once common ground has been established they are most hospitable and friendly. Language is a problem; alternative languages to Polish are Russian and German. Few Poles speak English.

The economy

Poland was the first member of the bloc to strike away from the USSR. The industrial and agricultural policies of the last forty years have resulted in very low efficiencies and serious pollution, even of the land itself, and the government has now embarked on a wide-ranging programme of restructuring and privatising state-run industries. There are signs that a market economy is developing, but high unemployment and high inflation will continue to make life difficult. With considerable natural resources and a labour force which will for some time remain cheaper than that of the developed economies of the West, the economy of Poland is beginning to revive, but performance in both production and distribution is uneven.

Most industrial activity lies away from the coastal area. It includes the production of cement, copper, coke, chemicals (fertilisers, sulphuric acid), salt, steel and zinc, and a vehicle production capability. Along the coast there are a significant fishing fleet, food processing and shipbuilding.

The standard of living is better than in most countries of the former bloc. There are more goods available in the shops, though the quality and variety of products available remain limited. Food prices are higher than those in Russia but significantly lower than those in the UK.

State tourist office

The closest approximation to a Polish state tourist office is Polorbis, which has a London office at 82 Mortimer Street W1N 7DE (☎ 071-636 2217). Within Poland it is called Orbis and runs hotels and travel offices.

Money

The Polish złoty is convertible but, at an exchange rate of around 20,000 złotys to the pound, the amounts to be handled tend to be confusing. It is also difficult to develop a feeling for the value of goods in the shops.

Currency can be exchanged at the National Bank of Poland or at a bureau de change (*kantor* in Polish). Traveller's cheques and Eurocheques are accepted for the purchase of złotys in Orbis exchange bureaux and hotels, and for the payment of bills and purchase of goods at the Baltona and Pewex hard-currency shops, but not at normal high-street shops.

Credit cards are uncommon and are only likely to be accepted at hard-currency establishments and a small number of other shops and restaurants.

Shopping

In 1991 food prices were around a third of those in England, but inflation is high and it is difficult to guess what will happen. Most normal foodstuffs can be bought without too many problems, though sometimes queues are generated. There are designated shops (e.g. Baltona and Pewex), trading in hard currency only, where foreign products with familiar brand names may be found.

Vodka costs about £2–3 a half-litre bottle; most other alcoholic drinks are sold at UK prices. Polish beer, normally only moderately acceptable to British tastes, can be bought easily and cheaply.

Hotels and restaurants

The big towns have a range of hotels. The restaurants tend to be adequate rather than good and most finish business by 2100 hours – the exception is often the restaurants in the expensive hotels run by Orbis.

Yacht services and chandlery

An increasing number of services and commodities are being made available only in exchange for hard currency, usually deutschmarks, at prices comparable to UK prices. Diesel, for example, was sold for złotys in 1990 at a price equivalent to 14p per litre, but in 1991 it had to be paid for in deutschmarks at a price equivalent to 35p a litre.

Very little chandlery is available. Propane cylinders can usually be recharged by local arrangement but the process may take several days.

Communications

An intense effort is being made to modernise the antiquated system, but telephoning in Poland remains difficult and time-consuming. Ordinary street kiosks cannot be used for international calls. It is best to go to an Orbis hotel, some of which have direct dialling facilities. The dialling code for Britain is 00 – dial tone – 44; otherwise call the international operator on 901, 902, 903 or 904.

Facsimile and telex machines are hard to find. Again, it is best to go to an Orbis hotel or travel bureau.

Ordinary letters take 10–14 days to or from the United Kingdom.

The coast radio stations at Szczecin (VHF Ch 24, 25 and 26) and Gdynia (Ch 26) handle public correspondence.

Travel

Rail and air services to western Europe are good. Internal rail services are efficient and cheap – but understanding the timetables and booking arrangements can be something of a challenge. If travelling by rail, travel express and book through an Orbis office. The Polish national airline, LOT, flies from Warsaw to Gdańsk and to Szczecin.

Taxis are easily obtainable and very cheap. Because of the language difficulty it is best to order them through a yacht club or hotel.

Time

Polish time is one hour ahead of UT in winter and two hours ahead from the last Sunday in March until the Saturday before the last Sunday in September.

Weather forecasts are broadcast in English at 0933, 1533 and 2133 local time by Szczecin (VHF Ch 24, 25 and 26) and Gdynia (Ch 26).

Formalities

Visas are not necessary for UK citizens. The flag is horizontally white over red.

UK representation

British Embassy Consular section, Wawelska 14, 02-061 Warsaw, ☎ (48) 22-580315 *Fax* (48) 22-50328 *Telex* 816 113.

Navigation

There are no particular difficulties in navigating off the coast of Poland. The approaches are well covered by Admiralty charts. The *Baltic Pilot Volume II (NP 19)*, the only pilot book for this area in English, is an excellent guide but is written with the big ship in mind, not a yacht with its comparatively shoal draught.

Cruising areas

Poland has two regions of interest to the cruising yachtsman: the Szczecin/Świnoujście area and the Gdańsk/Gdynia area.

To explore places away from the main fairway in the Zalew Szczeciński and the other inland seas around Świnoujście and Szczecin, use the detailed German charts and the chart set *Die Boddengewässer Rügen – Stettin – Bornholm* and associated pilot *Der Grosse NV Hafen Lotse Volume 4* from Nautische Veröffentlichung (see *Appendix I. Bibliography*), or purchase the Polish *Zalew Szczeciński, Mapa żeglarsko-turystyczna* (nautical and tourist map of Zalew Szczeciński, 1:75,000) for the equivalent of a few pence from the customs officials on entry. This map provides a guide to the maze of unlit fishing stakes – difficult to avoid even in good visibility.

The inland seas between and around Szczecin and Świnoujście provide interesting sheltered sailing. The countryside is low-lying, and there are a number of unspoilt fishing harbours and several yacht harbours. As noted above, it is possible to cross the border in the western part of the Zalew Szczeciński into Germany through the Peenestrom.

Although Gdynia is a very large port and has a well equipped yacht harbour, the town is of no great interest. Most visitors leave their boats at Gdynia and travel to Gdańsk by train or taxi. It is possible to berth near the centre of Gdańsk, but there are no facilities and there may be some risk of petty larceny.

There are some interesting possibilities in the inland waterways for boats with masts that can easily be stepped. The river Odra (Oder) and the Oder-Havel and Oder-Spree canals provide links to Berlin and Frankfurt-an-der-Oder, and with a draught of less than 1m it is possible to use the Warta, Notec, Wisła and Nogat rivers to reach the Zalew Wislany inland sea and the border with Russia. The Zalew Wislany is also connected by inland waterway to Gdańsk and to the Mazurian lake district.

Świnoujście

53°55'N 14°16'E

Distances

Stralsund 50M, Rønne 72M, Szczecin 28M, Gdynia 190M.

Charts and guides

Admiralty charts *185* and *2150*
Baltic Pilot Volume II (NP 19)
Zalew Szczeciński, Mapa żeglarsko-turystyczna (nautical and tourist map of Zalew Szczeciński, 1:75,000)
Hafenführer Polen Müller

Lights

1. **Świnoujście** 53°55'N 14°17'·2E Oc.WR.5s68m25/9M Yellow round brick tower, red bands, on square building, 65m. 029°-R-057°-W-280° RC 287·3kHz *OD* (– – –/–··) 50M
2. **Kikut** 53°59'N 14°34'·9E Iso.10s91m16M Grey round stone tower with white lantern, 18m 063°-vis-241°
3. **Outer Ldg Lts** 170·1° *Front* Młyny W mole head 53°55'·7N 14°16'·8E Oc(3)20s11m17M White tower, 11m
   Rear Galeriowa 512m from front 53°55'·4N 14°16'·9E Oc(3)20s23m17M White triangle on white round tower with 3 galleries, 24m

Entrance

4. **East mole** 53°56'N 14°16'·8E F.R.13m11M Horn(3) 60s Red octagonal tower, 11m

General

Świnoujście (Swinemünde in German) is the outer port of Szczecin. It is at the mouth of the river Odra (Oder), just inside the Polish/German border at the southeastern end of Uznam (Usedom) island, and has a population of about 30,000. The Odra continues towards Szczecin and carries a large volume of traffic. As well as a commercial port, Świnoujście is a fishing harbour, a naval base and a holiday resort, popular with Germans and Swedes. It is drab and lacks facilities, but the shops have most everyday items and there is an open-air market.

Approach

The big-ship route is buoyed on the line of the leading lights from a RW pillar buoy N2, Iso.10s, Racon, 54°14'·5N 14°11'E, almost 20M from the entrance; this route goes through two big-ship anchorages centred roughly 3 and 7 miles off the entrance. There are miles of sea-room on both sides of these hazards to small craft.

The entrance itself is obvious, well marked and free from obstructions, with Świnoujście lighthouse conspicuous on the east side.

Anchorage

It is forbidden to anchor in the fairway.

Berthing

The small yacht harbour immediately to starboard after the customs and immigration clearance point is suitable only for small yachts. Visiting yachts normally use the town quay in the main harbour to starboard about half a mile beyond customs and immigration, just beyond the ferry embarkation point.

Formalities

All yachts must report to the customs and immigration authorities at a rough concrete quay immediately to port on entry to the river.

If the nationality of the visitor requires that he should have a visa but he arrives without one, he may be allowed after reporting to go to the passenger terminal (about one mile up the river on the east bank), purchase the appropriate documentation and then return to customs and immigration for clearance.

General facilities

Services at the quayside are non-existent, except for rubbish skips. There are satisfactory toilets and showers at Art Zeglarski, the small chandlery across the road from the town quay, at a charge of about 15p for a day's unlimited use.

Most basic foodstuffs can be bought in the shopping centre. Alternatively, fresh produce can be bought at the open-air market.

There are few restaurants; they include the Jantor, the Restaurant Baltyk and the Hotel Miersk. The food, if available, is decidedly plain.

Exchange bureaux and banks in the town.

Yachting services

There are no facilities for repairs, refuelling or replenishing gas bottles. Chandlery can be bought very cheaply at Art Zeglarski but the range is limited.

Communications

International telephone calls are impossible to make on normal telephones, but the public correspondence services on Szczecin Radio are very good. Reception is good throughout this area.

Bus and train services to Szczecin and onwards to Poznan and Berlin.

Polferries operate regular ferry services from Świnoujście to Ystad in Sweden and to København.

Tourism

Some 30km inland, beyond Wolin, the main road between Świnoujście and Szczecin passes through

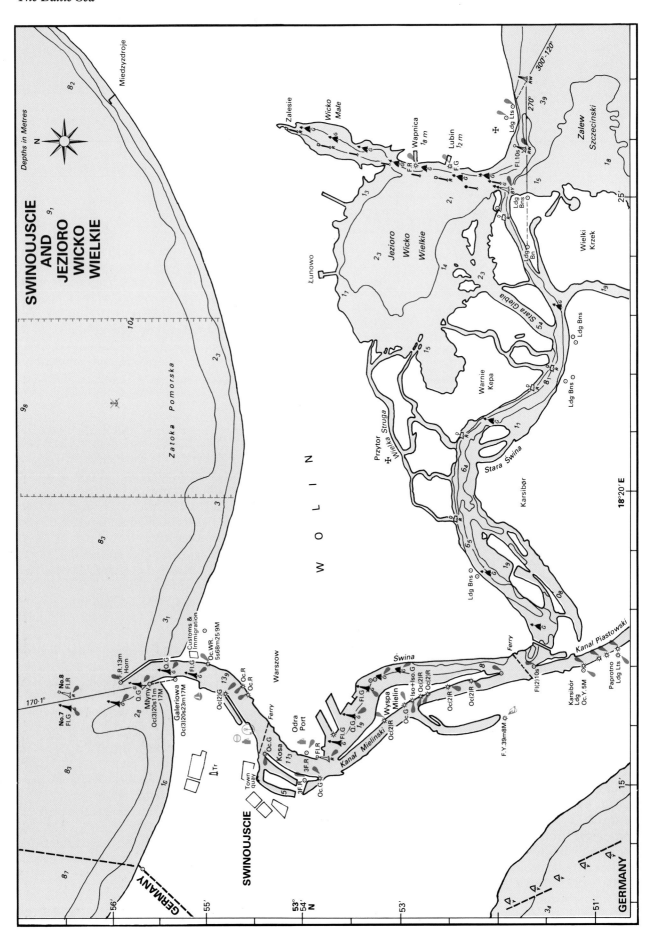

SWINOUJSCIE
AND
JEZIORO
WICKO
WIELKIE

Depths in Metres

N

Zatoka Pomorska

Miedzyzdroje

W O L I N

SWINOUJSCIE

GERMANY

Zalew
Szczecinski

Jezioro
Wicko
Wielkie

Wicko
Male

Zalesie

Wapnica

Lubin

Łunowo

Warnie
Kepa

Stara Swina

Karsibór

Przytor

Wielka Struga

Wielki
Krzek

Stara Głębia

Kanal Piastowski

Karsibór

Paprotno

Swina

Warszow

Odra
Port

Kosa

Town
quay

Kanal Mielinski

Wyspa
Mielin

Ferry

Ferry

Customs &
Immigration

ZALEW SZCZECINSKI

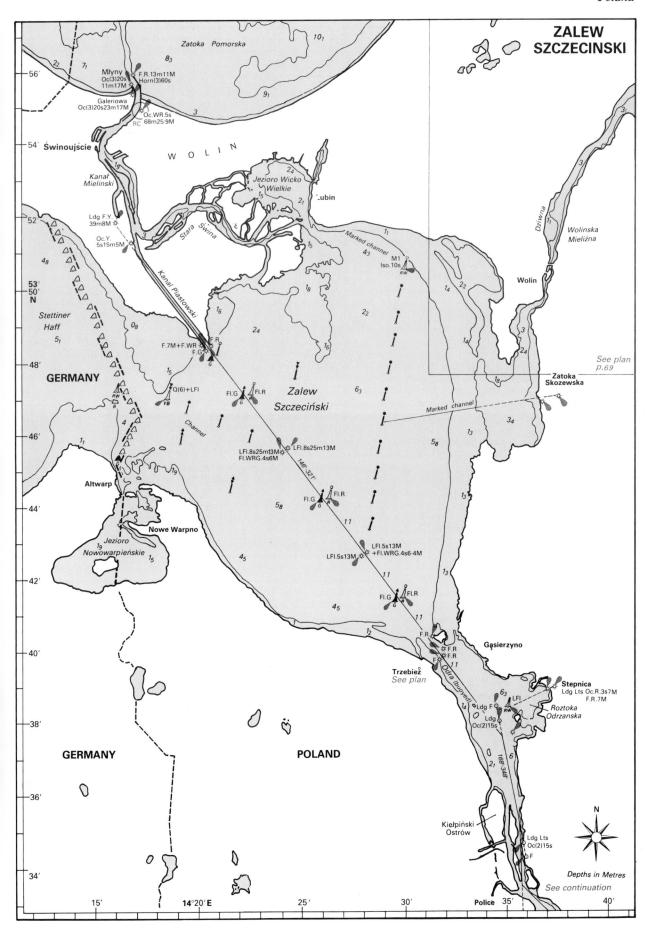

Zatoka Pomorska

10_1

2_2 7_1

8_3

Młyny
Oc(3)20s
11m17M

F.R.13m11M
Horn(3)60s

9_1

3_1

Galeriowa
Oc(3)20s23m17M

Oc.WR.5s
68m25·9M
RC

3

W O L I N

Świnoujście

1_5

Kanał
Mielinski

Jezioro Wicko
Wielkie

2_4

1_5

2_1

Lubin

Dziwna 1_1

Wolinska
Mieliźna

3_1

3

Marked channel

1_1

Wolin

3

2_4

Ldg F.Y.
39m8M

Oc.Y.
5s15m5M

3

Stara Świna

1_5

4_3

M1
Iso.10s
RW

1_4 2_2

3

Kanał Piastowski

1_6

1_8

1_6

2_2

1_4

2_4

1_8

See plan
p.69

Stettiner
Haff

5_1

0_8

2_4

6_3

3_4

Zatoka
Skozewska

F.7M+F.WR
F.R
F.G
6

F.R
6

1_5

Zalew
Szczeciński

Marked channel

5_8

1_3

GERMANY

4_8

Q(6)+LFl
YB

Fl.G
G

Fl.R

6_3

Channel

1_1

4

RW
R

1_9

LFl.8s25m13M
Fl.WRG.4s6M

LFl.8s25m13M

$146°·321°$

1_3

Altwarp

Fl.G
G

Fl.R
R

5_8

11

Nowe Warpno

Jezioro
Nowowarpieńskie
1_5

1_9

4_5

LFl.5s13M

LFl.5s13M
+Fl.WRG.4s6-4M

11

1_3

Fl.G
G

Fl.R

4_5

11

GERMANY

POLAND

1_2

F.R

F.R
F.R

11

Gąsierzyno

Trzebież
See plan

Odra (buoyed)

1_4

6_3

LFl
RW

Stepnica
Ldg Lts Oc.R.3s7M
F.R.7M

Ldg F

Ldg
Oc(2)15s

Roztoka
Odrzanska

2_1

6

$168°·348°$

Kiełpiński
Ostrów

Ldg Lts
Oc(2)15s

F

N

Depths in Metres
See continuation

Police

15'   **14°20′E**   25'   30'   35'   40'

Stakes marking fishing nets in Zalew Szczeciński.

Interster yacht harbour at Goław, near Szczecin.

the Wolinski National Park, a large and attractive oak and beech forest which has a small bison reserve. The main bison herds are in the Carpathians, which take a long time to reach from this area, but Wolinski can be visited by bus from Świnoujście or Szczecin.

The Orbis office is at ulica (street) Armii Czerwonej 2, open 1000 to 1600 Monday through Saturday.

Szczecin

53°25'N 14°33'E

Distances

Świnoujście 28M, Stralsund via the Peenestrom 85M, Mescherin 00M.

Charts and guides

Admiralty charts *185* and *2150*
Baltic Pilot Volume II (NP 19)
Hafenführer Polen Müller
Der Grosse NV Hafen Lotse Volume 4, Nautische Veröffentlichung
Boddengewässer Rügen – Stettin – Bornholm Nautische Veröffentlichung (set of charts)
Zalew Szczeciński, Mapa żeglarsko-turystyczna (nautical and tourist map of Zalew Szczeciński, 1:75,000)

It is possible, after arrival and with considerable persistence, to obtain Polish charts for navigation in the diverse waterways around Szczecin. Try the Pomerania tourist office at aleja (avenue) Jednosci Narodowej 50.

General

The city, with a population of about 400,000, is situated on the river Odra (Oder). It has a complex network of waterways which, although large enough for big ships, are often bordered by trees and green fields with a wide variety of wildlife.

Szczecin was properly Polish until the first part of the 12th century, when it passed to a succession of Polish-Pomeranian dukes. In the middle of the 17th century it was annexed by Sweden, and from 1720 onwards it belonged to Prussia and became the main entrepôt for Berlin, now ninety minutes' drive away. At the end of the Second World War it became Polish again. It is one of the major ports of Poland, handling the trade of the Oder basin, and an attempt has been made to divert the Czechoslovakian trade away from the Elbe-Hamburg route by establishing a free port here. It is an important shipbuilding and ship repair centre.

Approach

The main approach is from Świnoujście, through the Zalew Szczeciński (Stettiner Haff), which has

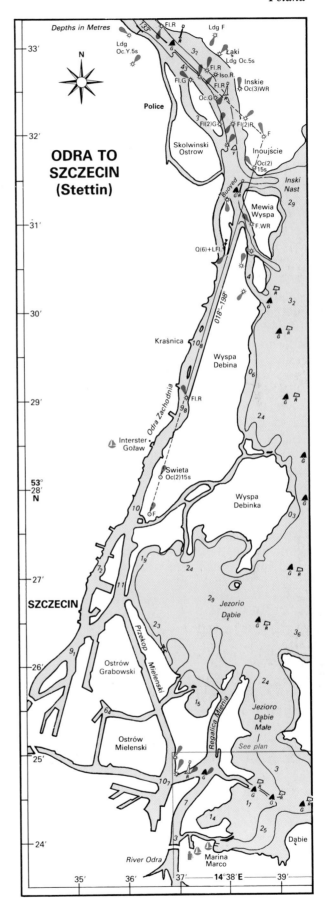

4–6m depths in most places but shoals towards the northeastern shore. The big-ship channel is buoyed all along the way. There is, however, a severe constriction on this route at Trzebież; though the gap between the west bank and the island of Chełminek is ¾M, the western shore is shoal and the width with 2m or more narrows to some 500–600m. South of this the route continues for 5M through the smaller inland water of Roztoka Odrzanska before entering the narrow waterway at Krepa, 10M north of Szczecin.

An alternative approach from Stralsund is through the Peenestrom, the Greifswalder Bodden (see page 56) and the western part of the Zalew Szczeciński to Trzebież, which is the customs post for this route.

A third route, for boats which can unstep their masts, is from the south via the river Odra, which is connected to the German canal system.

Jezioro Dąbie, which has depths of 3–3·5m, can either be entered from the south to either side of Mewia island or from the north through the river Regalica. To reach the northern entrance, continue up the Odra, passing Interster yacht harbour at Goław (see below), and at Okretowa Island take the eastern channel, Przekop Mieleński. At the junction with Canal Grabowski, large vessels signal their intentions. Continue to port up the Przekop Mieleński. 1·3M further on the Duńczyca crosses Przekop Mieleński and then, 0·8M beyond that, the larger Parnica, which 0·4M eastwards enters the Regalica. Northwards the Regalica goes into Jezioro Dąbie and southwards it leads to Dąbska Struga, which is the canal serving Marina Marco (see below). The entrance to the canal is distinctively marked by the bridge superstructure of a large ship, set up on dry land, on the starboard side of the entrance. Beware the long spit which extends 20 metres into the river at the northern side of the entrance to the canal.

Formalities

If assistance is required on arrival in Szczecin, go to the harbourmaster's office on the west bank immediately opposite Grodzka Island, which has a one-way system round it going anticlockwise. The office (☎ (48) 91-308557) is a modern two-storey building, clearly labelled 'Harbourmaster's Office' in English. Some of the harbourmaster's staff speak good English and are keen to help their relatively rare visitors from Britain.

Anchorage

Anchoring is prohibited in the fairways, but the many creeks and harbours of the area offer countless attractive anchorages.

Berthing

There are two good yacht harbours.

One of the Brama towers marking the channel into Szczecin.

Approaching Szczecin, the scenery is a mixture of industrial and rural scenes.

MARINA MARCO (54°24'N 14°37'·2E)

Formerly the yacht club of the STAL shipbuilding group, Marina Marco is about 1½ miles east of the city centre in a picturesque corner at the south end of Jezioro Dąbie. It has good access to the city centre by bus and tram. It was purchased in 1991 by a partly British joint venture company and has been energetically modernised; it has facilities comparable with those of many Western yacht harbours. It has been used by British yachts for winter storage. ☎ (48) 91-614350, *Fax* (48) 91-613693 *Telex* 422 790. The extremely hospitable manager will give advice on tourist matters and also make restaurant reservations, order taxis, etc.

Rural scene along the main shipping channel not far from the centre of Szczecin.

Szczecin is a major shipbuilding and ship repair centre.

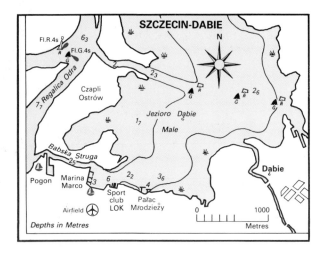

Approach

As for the north end of Jezioro Dąbie, but turn north in the Regalica and then east into Dąbska Struga. On emerging from that canal into the lake, Marina Marco is immediately to starboard. Moor either alongside the jetty or bows-to and stern to a buoy. There is about 4m of water outside the jetties and about 2.5m on the inside.

Facilities

Water and electricity on the jetties, and good showers, toilets, a snack bar and a seven-room hotel in the marina building. Laundry can be arranged. There is a night watchman. A sauna, swimming pool and gymnasium are planned.

Interster

A pleasant yacht harbour situated at Goław, on the west bank of the main channel, about two miles north of the city centre and 20 minutes away by bus or tram. Moor bows to the quayside and stern to a buoy in about 4m. Overnight charges are roughly similar to those of Marina Marco. Water and electricity on the jetties, and toilets, showers and a restaurant ashore.

Yachting services

Both yacht harbours provide fuel in cans. Marina Marco is planning to install a fuel berth in the near future. Chandlery and *Camping Gaz* are virtually impossible to obtain, but it is possible to arrange for propane bottles to be refilled, given two or three days' notice.

Marina Marco has a crane for stepping masts, which is much used by German yachtsmen from Berlin, and extensive boatyard facilities where repairs and refits can be carried out at very reasonable prices, although chandlery and proprietary equipment should be provided from a Western source. There is a Volvo agent on site, who will also deal with other makes of engine.

Communications

The central post office has a large telephone call office for operator-controlled long-distance and international calls, but as the Polish telephones are not 'user-friendly' it is better to use the telephone at Marina Marco or the excellent correspondence service through Szczecin on VHF Ch 24, 25 and 26. The operators speak English. Marina Marco has facsimile and telex (see above).

Travel

The airport for Szczecin at Goleniow, 45km north, has some international services but mainly handles internal services. If travelling by air, the best options may be to fly to Gdańsk or Berlin and complete the journey by train, or to fly to Warsaw and continue by LOT, the Polish airline. There are good train services to all parts of Poland, and through Berlin to the rest of Europe.

General facilities

Orbis is at pl Zwycięstwa 1. The city has a number of banks, several Baltona and Pewex hard-currency shops and a reasonable selection of restaurants and hotels.

For city maps try Pomerania at aleja Jednosci Narodowej 50, which may also have charts of the lakes and canals.

Tourism

The city was badly damaged in the Second World War and after four decades is still pretty drab. But despite the magnitude of the task of modernisation, there is a strong feeling of optimism about the place.

The main places of interest are north and east of the main railway station. The old cathedral was destroyed and the present building dates from 1945. The castle, which houses a museum, and the town hall have a similar history. Some buildings, such as the baroque harbour gate and the 14th-century church of Peter and Paul, survived. There is a national museum in two sections, one concentrating on the art and the other on the maritime history of the area.

Gdynia

54°32'N 18°33'E

Distances

Świnoujście 195M, Klaipěda 115M.

Charts and guides

Admiralty charts *2369* and *2377*
Baltic Pilot Volume II (NP 19)
Hafenführer Polen Müller

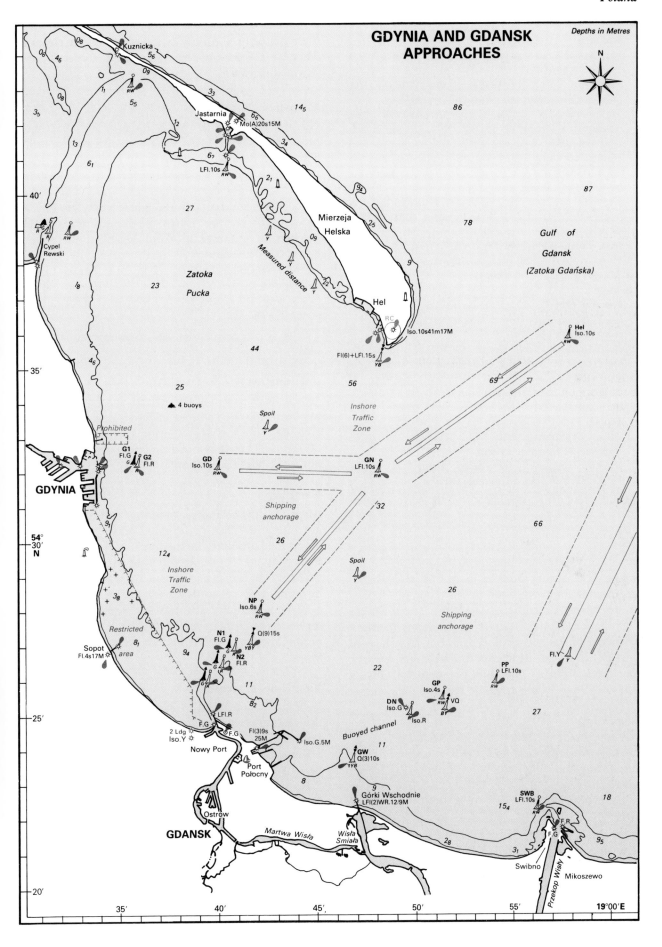

GDYNIA AND GDANSK
APPROACHES

Depths in Metres

N

Kuznicka

Jastarnia
Mo(A)20s15M

LFl.10s

Mierzeja
Helska

Measured distance

Gulf   of

Gdansk

(Zatoka Gdańska)

Hel
Iso.10s

Zatoka

Pucka

Hel

RC Iso.10s41m17M

Fl(6)+LFl.15s
YB

4 buoys

Spoil
Y

Inshore
Traffic
Zone

Cypel
Rewski

Prohibited

G1
Fl.G

G2
Fl.R

GD
Iso.10s

GN
LFl.10s

GDYNIA

Shipping
anchorage

Inshore
Traffic
Zone

Spoil
Y

Shipping
anchorage

Restricted
area

Sopot
Fl.4s17M

NP
Iso.6s

N1
Fl.G

Q(9)15s
YBY

Fl.Y
Y

N2
Fl.R

PP
LFl.10s

GP
Iso.4s

DN
Iso.G

VQ
BY

Iso.R

LFl.R

F.G

2 Ldg
Iso.Y

F.G

Fl(3)9s
25M

Iso.G.5M

Buoyed channel

GW
Q(3)10s
YB

Nowy Port

Port
Połocny

SWB
LFl.10s

Górki Wschodnie
LFl(2)WR.12/9M

Ostrow

GDANSK

Martwa Wisła

Wisła
Smiała

F.R
F.G

Swibno   Mikoszewo

Przekop Wisły

19°00'E

Lights

1. **Rozewie** 54°49'·8N 18°20'·4E Fl.3s83m26M Red round tower, red top, two galleries RC 287·3kHz *RO* (·−·/−−−) 50M
2. **Jastarnia** 54°42'·1N 18°41'·1E Oc(2)20s22m15M White round tower, red bands and cupola, 13m
3. **Hel** 54°36'·1N 18°48'9E Iso.10s41m17M Red octagonal tower 130°-vis-080° RC 310·3kHz *HL* (····/·−··) 50M
4. **Port Północny** 54°24'·1N 18°41'·9E Fl(3)9s56m 25M (Gdańsk) Grey square tower with gallery on port captain's building
5. **Krynica Morska** 54°23'·3N 19°27'·2E LFL(2)12s 53m18M Red round tower, white lantern RC 310·3kHz *KM* (−··/−−) 50M
6. **Mys Taran** 54°57'·6N 19°58'·9E Oc(3)15s55m21M Horn Mo(A)15s Red octagonal tower on building RC 312·5kHz *BT* (−···/−) 120M

Entrance

7. **Gdynia** Ldg Lts 271·5° *Front* 54°32'·3N 18°33'·1E Iso.Y.4s15m17M Front White metal framework tower, red stripe, 15m
Rear 0·57M from front 54°32'·3N 18°32'·1E Oc.Y.6s27m17M White metal framework tower, red stripe, 24m
8. **S detached breakwater S end** 54°31'·1N 18°33'·9E Oc.G.10s12m9M Detached concrete tower, glass cupola, 12m
9. **Basen Zeglarski E mole head** 54°31'·1N 18°33'·4E F.G.5m2M Concrete column
10. **Basen Zeglarski W mole head** 54°31'·1N 18°33'·4E F.R.5m2M Concrete column

Note Lights for the main (middle) and the north entrance are not described.

General

Gdynia is a large shipbuilding centre and one of the largest and most modern ports in the Baltic, accommodating vessels of up to 100,000 tonnes besides having a secure yacht harbour. The town has a population of about 200,000. It is largely modern, with wide streets laid out in a grid, but, like those of most Polish towns, its streets and buildings are in a poor state of repair. The point of coming to Gdynia is to visit Gdańsk, which has no facilities for yachts.

Caution
The area inside the Hel Peninsula (Mierzeja Helska) has been a prohibited area, with a heavy fine for trespassing, and it may still be so. Enquire at Gdynia before entering.

Approach

From the northwest, Mierzeja Helska, the 18 mile peninsula trending southeast and ending at Hel, is a line of wooded dunes not higher than 30m, quite steep-to. It is marked by Rozewie[1], Jastarnia[2] and Hel[3]. Coming from the northeast at night, Krynica Morska[5] may be visible and Port Północny[4] should be. There are two traffic separation zones, the inshore lane of one passing within 2M of Hel and the other centred 8M off; see diagram. Once clear of Mierzeja Helska and the traffic lanes, the approach is straightforward.

Entrance

Gdynia is protected by a north-south detached breakwater about 1¾M long with three entrances. The main, middle, entrance is about a mile north of the southern entrance and is covered by the leading lights. Make for the southern entrance. The yacht harbour is not part of the main complex but a separate basin, the Basen Zeglarski, whose well marked, lit entrance is 400m WSW of the south entrance – see lights[9-10].

Entry is easy at any time and under most conditions.

Anchorage

Yachts are recommended not to anchor outside the port.

Formalities

All yachts must call at the arrivals berth immediately to port inside the entrance of Basen Zeglarski. There is a 24 hour service. Customs and immigration officials will be summoned though they may possibly not come in the silent hours.

Berthing

After customs clearance, moorings can be chosen at any one of the four yacht clubs whose headquarters are in the harbour. The moorings of the Yacht Club Polski, at the opposite corner to the entrance, are probably the most convenient. Mo bows-to with bow lines to posts at the stern.

Water, electricity and rubbish skips are available on the quayside, but the best water is at the arrivals berth. There are toilets and showers at Yacht Club Polski.

Yachting services

Fuel can be obtained in cans by arrangement with the yacht club staff or one of the professional yacht skippers.

Butane is not available, but propane cylinders can be refilled by arrangement (slowly).

Boatyard facilities are provided by the Yacht Club Polski, and most repairs can be tackled, but there is considerable yachting activity locally and heavy demand on the workshops may result in some delay.

Yacht Club Polski employs a night watchman.

Weather forecasts in English for all areas of the Baltic are broadcast by Gdynia Radio on VHF at 0933, 1533 and 2133 local time.

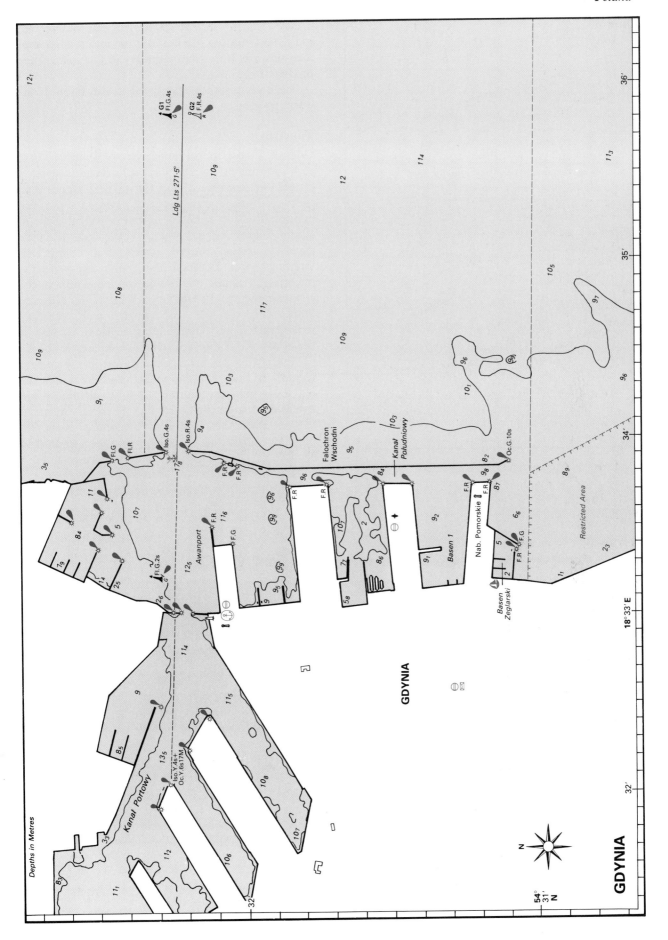

Depths in Metres

12₁

G1
Fl.G.4s
G

G2
Fl.R.4s
R

Ldg Lts 271·5°

10₉

11₄

12

11₃

36'

35'

10₅

10₈

11₇

9₇

9₁

10₉

10₃

9₆

10₉

9₃

9₆

9₆

9₉

Fl.G
Fl.R
Iso.G.4s
Iso.R.4s

9₄

10₁

10₃

Falochron
Wschodni

9₅

Kanał Południowy

35

F.R
F.R

9₆

9₆

8₄

8₂

Oc.G.10s

8₉

34'

Restricted Area

11

F.R

9₆

9₉

9₅

10₇

2

8₆

9₂

Basen 1

9₈

8₇

F.R

F.R

6₆

2₃

Awanport
11₆
F.R

8₄

5

7₉

F.G

Nab. Pomorskie

5

F.R
F.G

Fl.G.2s
G

12₅

9₉

9₅

7₇

8₆

9₁

2

Basen
Żeglarski

1₄

2₅

2₆

9

5₈

11₄

GDYNIA

9

GDYNIA

8₅

11₅

Iso.Y.4s
Oc.Y.6s17M

13₅

10₈

10₇

N

33

Kanał Portowy

11₂

10₆

32

8₃

11₁

54°
31'
N

18°33'E

32'

67

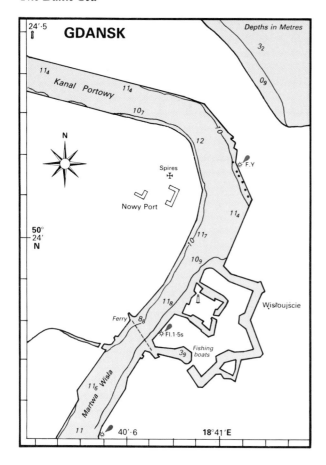

There are produce stalls near the harbour but for most food supplies it is better to go into town, a ten-minute walk. It may be necessary to queue for some products.

The hard-currency restaurant in the Orbis Hotel offers good value for money.

Tourism

Gdańsk. Under its previous name of Danzig, it was early dominated by the Teutonic Knights, later a formidable member of the Hanseatic League, then part of Prussia, then again a pawn in European politics; the city suffered miserably in the Second World War. The old town, which had defensive canals, narrow crooked streets and tall gabled buildings, was bombed flat. After the war the majority Germanic population was expelled and the city adopted the Polish form of its name, Gdańsk. Stare Miasto, the old town, was carefully reconstructed and shipbuilding revived; Gdańsk is the home of the shipyards which were the seat of the Solidarity Movement, a prime mover in the current turmoil. In Stare Miasto the Teutonic great mill, the old town hall, the churches and some of the old streets are extremely interesting. There is a museum in Stare Przedmieście with an exceptional collection of the works of Flemish painters (including Memling's *Last Judgement*) and, at a baser level, a collection of hotels and reasonable restaurants – though they can become crowded in summer.

Other ports

Clockwise round Zalew Szczeciński.

Wapnica (Kalkofen) 53°53'N 14°26'E
Tiny canal-like harbour at the northern extremity of Zalew Szczeciński.

Lubin 53°52'N 14°26'E
Small town at entrance to Jezioro Wicko Male, close to Wapnica.

Wolin (Wollin) 53°51'N 14°37'E (See plan)
Small town and minor port on river Dziwna in the northeast part of Zalew Szczeciński. Passage to interesting Zalew Kamienski but two opening bridges to negotiate and 2m draught (see also Dziwnów and Kamién Pomorski below).

Trzebież (Ziegenort) 53°40'N 14°31'E (See plan)
Attractive small yacht and fishing harbour in the south part of Zalew Szczeciński. It is also the customs clearance point for vessels entering the area from the Peenestrom.

Communications

Gdynia Radio, operating on VHF Ch 26, provides public correspondence facilities and weather forecasts.

There is an operator-controlled call office at the main post office, but without knowledge of Polish or Russian it is almost impossible to use. It is more convenient either to go to the Orbis Hotel or to use Gdynia Radio on VHF Ch 26.

The Orbis Hotel can send facsimile and telex messages.

Travel

The railway station is about fifteen minutes' walk from the harbour. Trains to Gdańsk, 20km away, are frequent and a single ticket cost about 10p in 1990. There are also good train services to Szczecin and Berlin.

The one-way taxi fare to Gdańsk was £3 in 1990 and a return trip, including waiting time, cost £8. Gdańsk has international and national air connections.

General facilities

Currency can be exchanged at the Orbis Hotel, adjacent to the yacht harbour and not difficult to find.

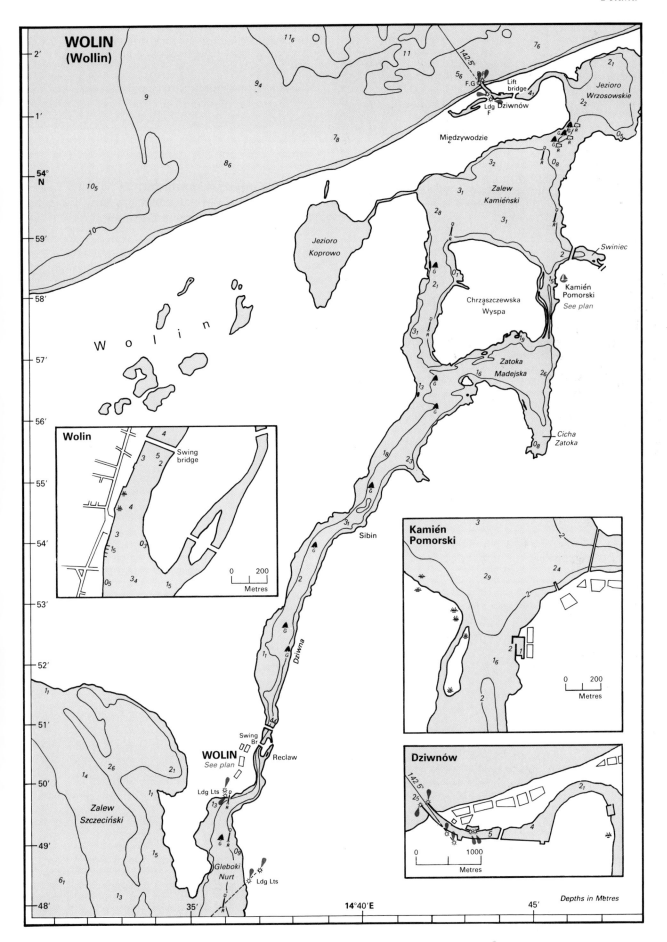

The yacht club at Trzebież.

Fishing boats at Trzebież.

Nowe Warpno (Neuwarp) 53°44'N 14°17'E
Charming fishing village on southwest side of Zalew Szczeciński, just inside border with Germany.

The coast eastwards from Świnoujście

Dziwnów (Dievenow) 54°01'N 14°44'E (See plan)
Fishing port at mouth of river Dziwna. Buoyed channel to Wolin, 1·7–2·3m deep.

Kamién Pomorski (Lammin) 53°58'N 14°46'E
(See plan). Minor commercial port in Zalew Kamienski, 3M inland from Dziwnów.

Kołobrzeg (Kolberg) 54°11'N 15°33'E
Seaside town on the coast 50M east of Świnoujście. Fishing harbour. Lighthouse. Population 25,000.

Port Darłowo (Rügenwalde) 54°27'N 16°23'E
Minor port 1½M upstream of drawbridge (opens on request) at mouth of river Wieprza, 35M east of Kołobrzeg. Depth 4m. Lighthouse at entrance.

Port Ustka (Stolpmünde) 54°35'N 16°51'E
Small commercial port 25M east of Darłowo. Uncomfortable, possibly dangerous in strong onshore winds. Lighthouse.

Port Łeba (Leba) 54°46'N 17°33'E
Commercial port at mouth of river Łeba. Normally 3m depth, but can vary widely, perhaps to as little as 2m.

See caution above about the Hel Peninsula

Władysławowo (Großendorf) 54°48'N 18°25'E
Fishing port with depths 2·5–5m. Sound as you approach.

Hel 54°36'N 18°49'E
Fishing port at extremity of Mierzeja Helska peninsula. Depth 3·7m.

Gulf of Gdańsk

Jastarnia (Heisternest) 54°42'N 18°41'E
Fishing harbour with yacht moorings. Depth 4·5m. Entrance faces south.

Puck (Putzig) 54°43'N 18°25'E
Fishing and yachting harbour. Depth 3m.

Gdańsk (Danzig) 54°21'N 18°39'E
Historic city with a population of 400,000. Major port and shipbuilding centre. No facilities for yachts. 25 minutes by train from Gdynia.

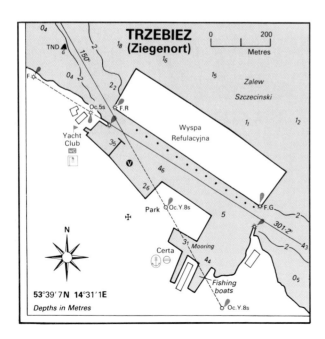

TRZEBIEZ
(Ziegenort)

0   200
Metres

Zalew
Szczecinski

Yacht
Club

Wyspa
Refulacyjna

Park

Certa

Mooring

Fishing
boats

N

53°39'7N 14°31'1E
Depths in Metres

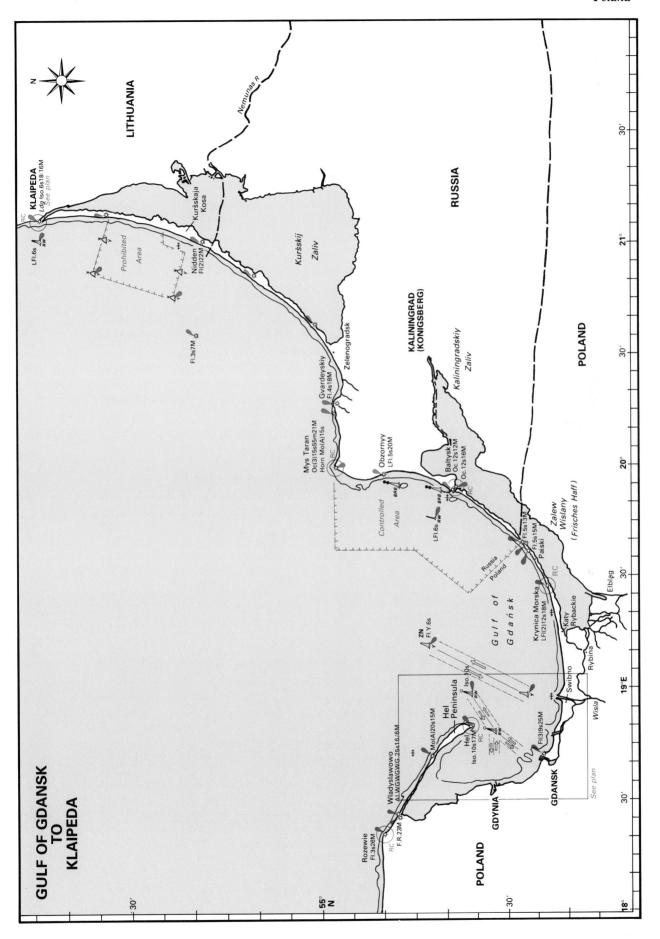

GULF OF GDANSK
TO
KLAIPEDA

KLAIPEDA
Ldg Iso.6s18·16M
See plan

RC

LFl.6s
RW

Prohibited
Area

Fl.3s7M

Nidden
Fl(2)22M

Kurśskaja
Kosa

LITHUANIA

Nemunas R

N

Zelenogradsk

Kurśskij
Zaliv

Gvardeyskiy
Fl.4s18M

Mys Taran
Oc(3)15s55m21M
Horn Mo(A)15s

RC

Obzornyy
LFl.5s20M

Controlled
Area

LFl.6s
RW

BRB

BRB

Baltysk
Oc.12s12M
Oc.12s16M

RC

KALININGRAD
(KONIGSBERG)

Kaliningradskiy
Zaliv

RUSSIA

Fl.5s13M

Fl.5s15M
Palski

Russia
Poland

Krynica Morska
LFl(2)12s18M

RC

Katy
Rybackie

Zalew
Wislany
(*Frisches Haff*)

Elbląg

POLAND

*Gulf of
Gdańsk*

ZN
Fl.Y.6s

Iso.10s

RW

Swibno

Rybina

Wisla

Hel
Peninsula

Mo(A)20s15M

Hel
Iso.10s17M

RC

Fl(3)9s25M

See plan

GDANSK

GDYNIA

Wladyslawowo
Al.WG.WG.WG.25s16/6M

Rozewie
Fl.3s26M

RC

F.R.23M

POLAND

**55°
N**

30'

30'

30'

30'

30'

18°

19°E

20°

30'

21°

30'

Górki Wschodnie 54°21'N 18°48'E
Fishing village 1½M upstream from mouth of the
Wisła Smiala, one of the branches of the Wisła delta.
Depth 2·8m.

Świbno (Schiewenhorst) 54°20'N 18°56'E
Fishing village at the mouth of Przekop Wisły, the
main branch of the Wisła delta. Depth 2m.

III. The Baltic States
Lithuania, Latvia and Estonia

The Gulf of Rīga and the Estonian islands offer interesting opportunities for off the beaten track cruising, and the proximity of the ports to each other means that the area can be covered on a day-sailing basis. The old ports of the Hanseatic League, Tallinn and Rīga, are interesting and visiting them by sea is particularly apposite. Material conditions are of a relatively low standard, but the warmhearted people are anxious to meet foreign visitors and to relate to the rest of the world. Acquaintanceship is made easier by the common language of the sea.

The coast is generally low and backed by dunes or low hills, often wooded. The approaches vary between steep-to on the more exposed parts of the coast and shoal around the Estonian islands and in the Gulf of Rīga. With the exception of Tallinn, which has modern yachting facilities created for the 1980 Olympic Games, facilities for yachts are somewhat primitive, though much development is taking place. Offshore, aids to navigation are scarce. Many cruising yachtsmen may prefer these conditions to those of more highly developed areas.

The countries

The three countries have minor hills, many marshes and lakes and much timber. The landscape has been 'done over' by glaciation and is marked with clays, gravels and other sediments overlying the bedrock, the debris of retreating glaciers. It is not exciting but has the advantage of emptiness. Mineral resources are scant and forestry, agriculture and dairy farming are important; much effort has been put into draining swamps. All three states have developed some industry. Two thirds of Lithuania's population is urban and it has heavy engineering, shipbuilding, light engineering, chemical engineering and some electronics. Three quarters of the Latvians live in towns; Latvia was the USSR's prime source of railway coaches and telephone exchanges, and provided wool, paper and mineral fertilisers. Estonia's economy depends more on the countryside than those of the other two, but unlike them, Estonia has high quality shale, exports gas to St Petersburg and is not so dependent as the others on wood and peat for fuel. Some oil is produced but all depend on foreign oil supplies.

History

Local history is complex. At the southern end, an early element was antagonism between the heathen Prussians of Lithuania and the Poles. In the 12th century the Poles sought help from the Order of Teutonic Knights, who established themselves in Lithuania and set about the conversion of the Prussians. In the north, the Danes as early as 1093 had contact with the Finnish tribes who lived in Estonia and by the 13th century had founded such towns as Tallinn (1219). From Lübeck, founded in 1143, German traders started to break into the Scandinavian monopoly of the Baltic. They established trading communities in Gotland and, encouraged by the Teutonic Knights, along the shores of the Baltic. The goal was Novgorod, south of St Petersburg, used by the Scandinavians as the source of the fur, honey, wax, pitch, tar, charcoal and so forth demanded by western Europe. The Germans also extended into Norway, blocking Dutch and English trade, and into Sweden; the Teutonic Knights bought out the Danes in Estonia and by the early part of the 13th century the Baltic had become a German lake. On the way, individual German trading towns recognised their need for common policies and defence against piracy, and after small beginnings, in the middle of the 14th century the Hanseatic League emerged. Meanwhile, in the country, the Lithuanians merged with the Poles, Roman Catholicism was established in Lithuania and in 1410 the Lithuanians and Poles defeated the Knights, who subsequently disappeared from the scene.

The last meeting of the Hanseatic League was in 1669, but long before that its position had been weakened by the trading and political activities of other countries, principally the Danes, the Dutch and the British, as well as by less manageable hazards such as the herring leaving the Baltic. The Swedes became involved in parts of all three countries in the 16th and 17th centuries, and were replaced in the 18th century by the Russians, who took control of the whole area. In 1914, the Germans, whose territory then bordered Lithuania, took it over together with part of Latvia. Immediately after the 1917 revolution, soviets were established in Russian Latvia and Estonia and the Germans reacted by invading both areas. Following the 1918 armistice the Germans were obliged to withdraw and again soviets were established. In 1919, the Soviets in Lithuania were thrown out by nationalist Lutheran forces in alliance with Polish and British-officered German troops, those in Latvia by local forces with the aid of the British navy and the German army, and those in Estonia by local forces and the British navy (which collected a Victoria Cross in an action at Tallinn). The democratic republics thus established soon gave way to right-wing dictatorships, Lithuania in 1926 and the other two in 1934. The Soviet-German agreement of 1939, which carved up Poland, also assigned Estonia, Latvia and the greater part of Lithuania to the Soviet sphere of influence, and they were taken over and included in the USSR. Almost immediately they were overrun by Germany. After the end of the Second World War, the USSR tried several techniques to consolidate its hold on the three countries; for instance, settling Russian nationals (who secured the best accommodation and the best jobs) in them, and imposing the Russian language upon them. Both of these policies have contributed to the present difficulties. In 1990 the three opted for an existence independent of the USSR, which has now itself disappeared. All now face serious problems in reorganising their economies, with administrations unused to independence and social institutions designed for another regime.

An inconvenient remnant is the existence of the Russian enclave around Kaliningrad, which has no territorial connection with Russia. Passage past Baltysk, the naval base at the entrance to the canal leading to Kaliningrad, was forbidden to yachts in 1991 but may now be possible.

The people, the church and languages

In approximate terms, in 1987 Lithuania had a population of 3·7 million of whom 9% were Russian and 8% Poles; Latvia, 2·7 million of whom 54% were Latvian and 33% Russian; Estonia, 1·6 million of whom 28% were Russian, 2·5% Ukrainian and 1·6% Belorussian. Just under half of the 5·4 million indigenous inhabitants of the three countries taken as a whole are said to be Roman Catholic. In 1956 the Lithuanian Lutherans numbered 215,000 and the Latvian 600,000. Figures for Estonia are obscure, but Roman Catholicism is more firmly established in the southwest of the area and the Lutheran and Orthodox Catholic Churches are stronger in the northeast. The influence of all churches was, of course, overlaid by the atheist approach of the former USSR.

The languages are several and difficult: Lithuanian and Latvian (or Lettish), which relate to Slavonic languages, and Estonian, which relates to Finnish, are the main indigenous languages. The best alternatives are Russian, then German, then English. Polish is a possibility in Lithuania and Finnish is widely understood in Estonia

Money

The three states inherited the Russian rouble and are scrapping it as fast as they can. Lithuania is issuing coupons until it can introduce the lita, scheduled for late 1992. Latvia has issued its own rouble at par with the Russian rouble. Estonia has issued the kroon (which rhymes with prawn) which for citizens is changed at the rate of 50 Russian roubles to one kroon. Take deutschmarks, US dollars or, in Estonia, Finnish marks.

Credit cards can be used only in the shops and hotels which exist in most major towns for the benefit of tourists.

Shopping

There is little to be bought except household goods and basic foodstuffs, the latter mainly from the markets. Foodstuffs are very cheap by Western standards, but they are in short supply and queuing is standard. A certain amount of fresh produce is brought to the markets in the summer months by the growers.

Hotels and restaurants

Rīga and Tallinn have good hotels and restaurants. In other places mentioned, both are scarce and when found not of a high standard.

Yacht clubs

See the note about yacht clubs in the Russian section.

Yacht services and chandlery

The price of moorings in most of the yacht harbours in the Baltic States is variable and clubs are in the process of formulating their pricing policies. A going rate of about $10 a night is gradually emerging.

The price of diesel, which can be obtained only through a yacht club (except in Tallinn, where there is a fuel berth), is negotiable. Generally the price is about the same as the Finnish price.

It may be possible for a yacht club to arrange for propane cylinders to be refilled, but butane is unobtainable.

Communications

Except in tourist hotels, at some yacht clubs, and through certain privileged business people, direct dialling to overseas destinations is impossible. International calls may be made from private telephones through the operator, but delays of several hours are normal. Many yacht clubs now have facsimile and / or telex facilities. Mail is unreliable, letters normally taking around four weeks for delivery to or from the UK.

The use of VHF has not been sorted out. During the period when movement was controlled by the USSR, VHF was used for speaking to shore stations and patrol boats and for emergencies. Use for other purposes created difficulties. No doubt this situation will change, as the Baltic States establish facilities and services in line with European standards.

Travel

Direct flights are available to Tallinn, Rīga and Vilnius from various western European airports. Alternatively Tallinn can be reached by train from St Petersburg which has good air connections.

It is not difficult to reach the Baltic States by rail. It is possible to travel direct to Vilnius from Warsaw and to reach Rīga by changing at Vilnius. Tallinn can be reached via Warsaw and St Petersburg; the journey from London takes 3½ interesting days.

Ferries run from Tallinn and Rīga to Helsinki.

Time

In the three Baltic States time is two hours ahead of UT in winter and three hours ahead from the last Sunday in March until the Saturday before the last Sunday in September

Formalities

Lithuania

Visas are not required for UK citizens.

In London, the Lithuanian Embassy is at 70 Essex Villas, W8 7BP, ☎ 071-937 1588.

The port of entry is Klaipěda.

The flag is a horizontal tricolour: yellow, green, red.

Latvia

Visas are not required for UK citizens.

In London, the Latvian Embassy is at 72 Queensborough Terrace, W2 3SP, ☎ 071-727 1698.

Ports of entry are Rīga, Ventspils and Liepāja.

The flag is a horizontal tricolour: maroon, white, maroon.

Estonia

Visas are not required for UK citizens.

In London, the Estonian Embassy is at 18 Chepstow Villas, W11 2RB, ☎ 071-229 6700 and can process an application within two days. In Helsinki the Estum Agency can issue a tourist visa in a matter of hours.

The flag is a horizontal tricolour: blue, black and white.

Navigation

British Hydrographic Office charts are sufficient for visiting the major ports. However, they do not adequately cover the interesting area around the Estonian islands, where Russian charts are necessary, though even they leave much to be desired. Although there are no tides there are unpredictable currents. Decca in this area is unreliable.

Russian charts can be obtained through a friendly yachtsman after arrival in Latvia or Estonia, or alternatively from the Estum Agency in Helsinki (see page 10).

Avoid military areas such as Baltysk, in the Russian enclave south of Lithuania, and Paldiski and Loksa, in Estonia. Enquire about restrictions at the port of entry.

Cruising areas

The Estonian islands of Saaremaa and Hiiumaa, together with the islands in the Gulf of Rīga, offer most interest, and it is in these smaller and less-visited harbours that personal contacts flourish best. Before independence in 1991 visits were permitted only to the major ports. Restrictions were relaxed in 1991 and doubtless this process will continue. Several ports in the sections headed 'other places' have since been visited by correspondents, but some information is based on local club information. The local yacht clubs say that all may be visited, but this needs to be taken with a grain of salt and the visitor should enquire at the port of entry about the current situation.

Lithuania

Klaipėda

55°43'N 21°08'E

Distances

Gdynia 115M, Liepāja 48M, Ventspils 110M.

Charts and guides

Admiralty chart *2288*
German chart *1441*
Baltic Pilot Volume II (NP 19)

Lights

Approach

1. **Nidden** 55°18'·2N 21°00'·8E Fl(2)5·8s77m22M Red round tower, 29m
2. **Yuodkrante** 55°33'·5N 21°07'·2E LFl.8s68m18M White metal square framework tower, 20m
3. **Klaipėda** Ldg Lts 092·5° *Front* 55°43'·7N 21°05'·6E LFl.8s68m18M White ♦ and ■, black stripe, on black framework tower, 27m
   Rear 305m from front 55°43'·7N 21°05'·9E Iso.6s44m 18M White round tower, black bands, black stripe, 40m. RC 312·5kHz *KA* (─··─/·─) 120M
4. **Sventoji** 56°01'·5N 21°05'·4E Fl(3)15s42m17M Red rectangle, white stripe on square metal framework tower, 39m

Entrance

5. **North mole head** 55°43'·8N 21°04'·9E Fl.R.3s22m 2M Red square framework tower, 19m
6. **South mole head** 55°43'·6N 21°05'E Fl.G.3s21m1M Green square framework tower, 18m

See chart for inner harbour lights.

General

Klaipėda, (German: Memel) is a pleasant, friendly town, and not without charm. It was founded in 1252 and taken over by the Teutonic Knights who fortified it in 1404. Since then its ownership has been in constant dispute. Its industry was established by the Germans and it has a large port and shipbuilding complex along the Morskoy Canal which leads to Kurskiy Zalev, a large inland sea separated from the sea by a narrow spit.

Approach

The town and the harbour entrance are clearly visible from seaward and the entrance, heavily used by commercial shipping, is well marked for entry at any time. Discoloured water from the Kurskiy Zalev may be seen well out to sea.

It is important to keep to the centre of the channel at the entrance to the river as the remains of a wrecked ship lie to one side and there is also a danger of general industrial debris in the shallows on either side.

Anchorage

Anchoring is not permitted.

Berthing

Following customs clearance (see below), yachts may proceed further up the river to the attractive yacht harbour clearly seen from the river. It is in rural surroundings on the west bank, about half a mile south of the ferry.

During normal hours, a member or an official of the yacht club will indicate which berth to take and assist with mooring lines. Mooring is bows-to with stern lines to posts.

Formalities

The visiting yacht may be met by a launch and directed to the 'Winter Harbour', one of the main commercial docks on the east bank of the Morskoy canal just before the ferry, for clearance. If this does not happen, go to the yacht club and enquire.

General facilities

Water and electricity are available at each berth in the yacht club. There are rudimentary showers and toilets.

The town centre is on the opposite side of the river to the yacht club, and it is necessary to cross on the ferry, a few minutes' walk from the yacht club. Once across, the shopping area is a further five minutes' walk and, as in all parts of the former USSR, supplies of most foodstuffs are difficult to obtain. During the summer, private enterprise traders in the market can supply basic commodities at prices which are cheap to Westerners but often prohibitive to the local population.

There are a few restaurants in the town but it is necessary to make a reservation; this is best done with the aid of a club official.

Yachting services

Supplies of fuel and propane are not easily available, but might be organised by one of the club staff or the professional skipper of one of the local yachts.

Facilities for repairs are limited, but if necessary emergency repairs could probably be arranged through the yacht club. Few materials are available, however, and spare parts are virtually impossible to obtain.

Communications

The main post office handles mail and, theoretically, provides an operator-controlled telephone service, including international calls. However, without fluent Lithuanian or Russian it is almost impossible to use the service.

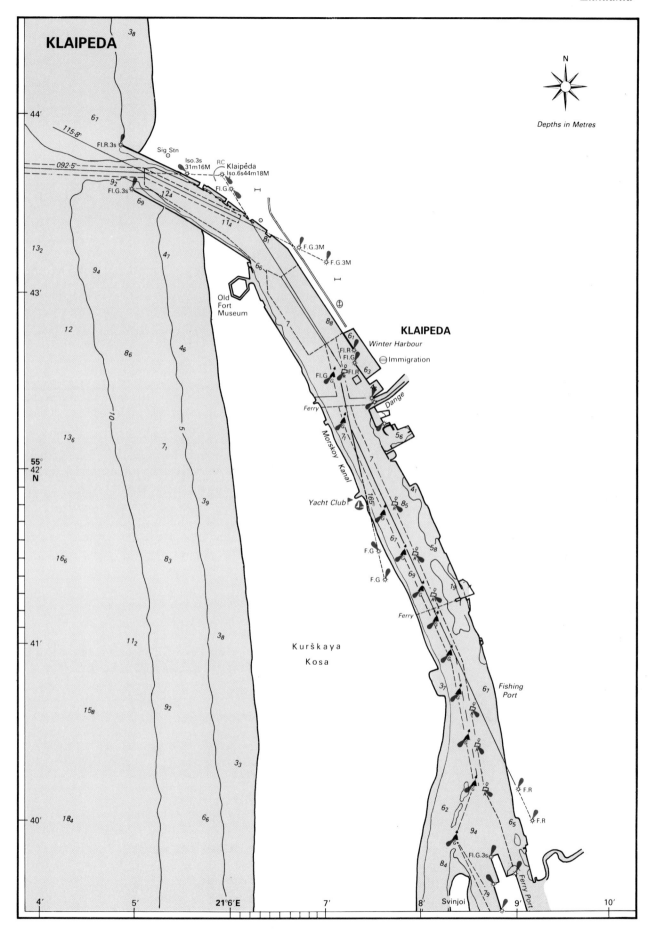

KLAIPEDA

3_8

N

Depths in Metres

—44'

6_7

115·8

Fl.R.3s ☼

Sig Stn ○

092·5

Iso.3s
31m16M

RC
Klaipėda
Iso.6s44m18M ☼

9_2
Fl.G.3s ☼

12_4

Fl.G ☼

6_9

11_4

⊣

13_2

9_4

4_7

8_1

F.G.3M ☼

—43'

6_6

F.G.3M ☼

12

Old
Fort
Museum

8_6

4_6

8_8

KLAIPEDA

7

6_1

Winter Harbour

Fl.R ☼
Fl.G ☼

⊖ Immigration

Fl.G

Fl.R

6_3

Dange

—*10*

13_6

5

Ferry

7_1

5_6

7

7_1

**55°
42'
N**

3_9

Morskoy Kanal

4_1

8_3

Yacht Club ▶

16·5

8_5

6_7

F.G

5_8

F.G

6_9

1_9

—41'

11_2

Ferry

**K u r š k a y a
K o s a**

3_8

15_8

9_2

3_7

6_7

*Fishing
Port*

3_3

6_2

F.R

—40'

18_4

6_6

6_5

F.R

9_4

8_4

Fl.G.3s ☼

7_9

Svinjoi

Ferry Port

4'   5'   **21°6'E**   7'   8'   9'   10'

The Baltic Sea

Travel

Buses to Rīga and other nearby towns. Taxis are available, but language may be a problem.

Tourism

There is an interesting maritime museum and aquarium on the west bank of the river not far from the yacht club. An old three-master is moored permanently near the centre of the town. Amber used to be worked in Klaipėda and it is worth keeping an eye out for it.

Other places

Kurskiy Zaliv

Depths are 12·5m in the north, deeper in the south. The east shore is low and wooded, and includes the delta of the Nemunas, which forms the border between Lithuania and the Russian enclave which separates it from Poland. The west shore, which is the east side of the spit Kurškaya Kosa, has many minor headlands and bays. There is an inland waterway route for shallow-draught boats linking Klaipėda with Kaliningrad.

Latvia

Liepāja

56°31'N 21°01'E

Distances

Klaipėda 65M, Ventspils 62M.

Charts and guides

Admiralty chart *2288*
Baltic Pilot Volume II (NP 19)

Lights

1. **Bernāti** 56°22'·9N 20°59'·5E Iso.4s41m15M Metal framework tower, yellow gallery, 21m
2. **Liepāja** 56°31'·1N 20°59'·5E Iso.6s32m16M Red round tower, white bands, 30m 000°-vis-180° RC 312·5kHz *LB* (·—··/—···) 120M
3. **Akmenrags** 56°50'N 21°03'·6E Mo(A)10s38m18M Red round stone tower, 37m 000°-vis- 225° RC 312·5kHz *AK* (·—/—·—) 100M

General

Liepāja (German: Libau), the third major port in Latvia, is basically a grain and timber port, but it has a shipyard, a naval base and a fishing harbour. It is mentioned here as a possible stopover.

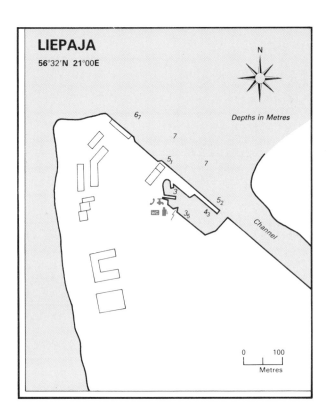

Approach

Liepāja light[2] is about 1M southeast of the harbour, which has three entrances; the middle one is marked by leading lights (not recorded) and buoys.

Berthing

In the fishing harbour inside the entrance on the south side, 3·5m.

General facilities

Water, fuel, toilets.

Communications

Call *Liepāja 31* on VHF Ch 11 or 12, but it will be surprising if the call is answered in English.

Travel

Domestic airport.

Ventspils

57°24'N 21°33'E

Distances

Liepāja 62M, Rīga 110M, Pärnu 117M.

Charts and guides

Admiralty chart *2223*
German chart *1431*
Baltic Pilot Volume II (NP 19)

The fishing dock at Ventspils.

Lights

Approach

1. **Užava** 57°12'·6N 21°25'E Fl(3)15s44m18M White round stone tower on red building, 19m Racon 035°-165° 10M
2. **Ventspils** Ldg Lts 143·6° 53°23'·7N 21°32'·6E Iso.R.3s 28m14M *Front* Red rectangle, white stripe on red framework tower, 25m. Visible only on leading line of 143·6°, 24 hours. RC 309kHz *WW* (- -/·- -) 100M *Rear* 0·5M from front 57°23'·3N 21°33'·2E Iso.R.3s45m 15M Red rectangle, white stripe on square red framework tower, 35m. 084°-vis-204°, 24 hours. Also experimental laser light 2Fl.R(hor)14M
3. **Bãušnieki** 57°27'·8N 21°37'·4E Iso.4s55m15M White truncated pyramid, red bands, 26m Racon 065°-170° 15M
4. **Oviši** 57°34'·3N 21°42'·8E LFL.7·5s38m18M Horn (2)30s White round stone tower, 37m 010°-vis-222° Racon 220°-052° 9M
5. **Irbenskiy** 57°45'N 21°43'·5E Fl(2)10s37m17M Black base, white bands, yellow tower, 35m Racon 020°-125° 12M RC 285·5kHz 35M
6. **Sõrve** 57°55'N 22°03'·6E Fl(2)30s52m19M White round tower, black top RC 306kHz *SY* (···/-·- -) 100M Racon 300°-070° 14M

Entrance
See chart.

General
Founded in 1343 but with a castle dating from 1290, Ventspils (German: Windau) is now a small and somewhat plain industrial town with a population of 27,000. It is an oil port, handles grain and timber and has a fishing harbour. It is included chiefly as a possible stopover.

Approach
The approach is by a straight buoyed channel leading to the harbour entrance. It is not desirable to deviate from the channel, as there are a number of dangerous wrecks in this vicinity.

Entry is straightforward by day or night.

Anchorage
Anchoring in the channel is not permitted.

Berthing
There is no yacht harbour as such at Ventspils. The few yachts which use the port moor at the far end of the fishing dock.

Mooring is alongside a clean, tidy quay with tractor-tyre fenders. It is as well to keep as clear of the miscellaneous commercial vessels as possible as their skippers may not be enthusiastic about accommodating yachtsmen.

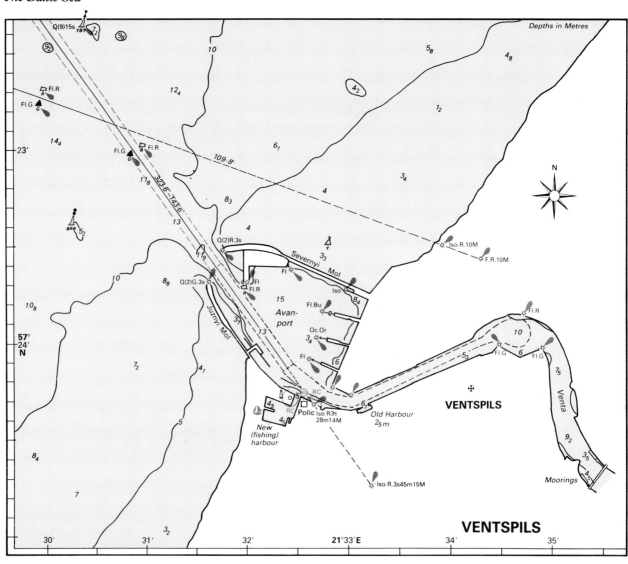

The Baltic Sea

Depths in Metres

VENTSPILS

VENTSPILS

Formalities

The customs and border guards are situated in a square building on the corner of the entrance to a fishing dock to starboard about half a mile inside the harbour. It is best to turn into the dock entrance and moor at a rough concrete quay to port for clearance.

General facilities

Electricity, cold showers, toilets and rubbish bins. A small modern hotel approximately 100 metres from the quayside.

The nearest shops are in the town centre some fifteen minutes' walk away.

Yachting services

There is no fuel, no gas and there are no repair facilities.

Communications

Telecommunications facilities are, to all intents and purposes, non-existent.

Domestic airport. Slow bus and train to Rīga.

Rīga

56°58'N 24°06'E

Distances

Ventspils 110M, Pärnu 85M, Hanko 170M.

Charts and guides

Admiralty charts *2215* and *2256*
German charts *1411* and *1421*
Russian chart *454*
Baltic Pilot Volume II (NP 19)

Lights

Approach

1. **Mãersrags** 57°22'·3N 23°07'·6E Iso.6s26m15M White concrete tower, 19m 130°-vis-345° RC 291·5 kHz *MR* (−−/·−−) 15M
2. **Engure** 57°10'N 23°13'·9E Fl(2)6s26m15M White framework tower, red top, 19m
3. **Ragciems** 57°02'·4N 23°29'·6E Iso.2s37m16M Square metal framework tower, red triangle, 30m 095°-vis-330°

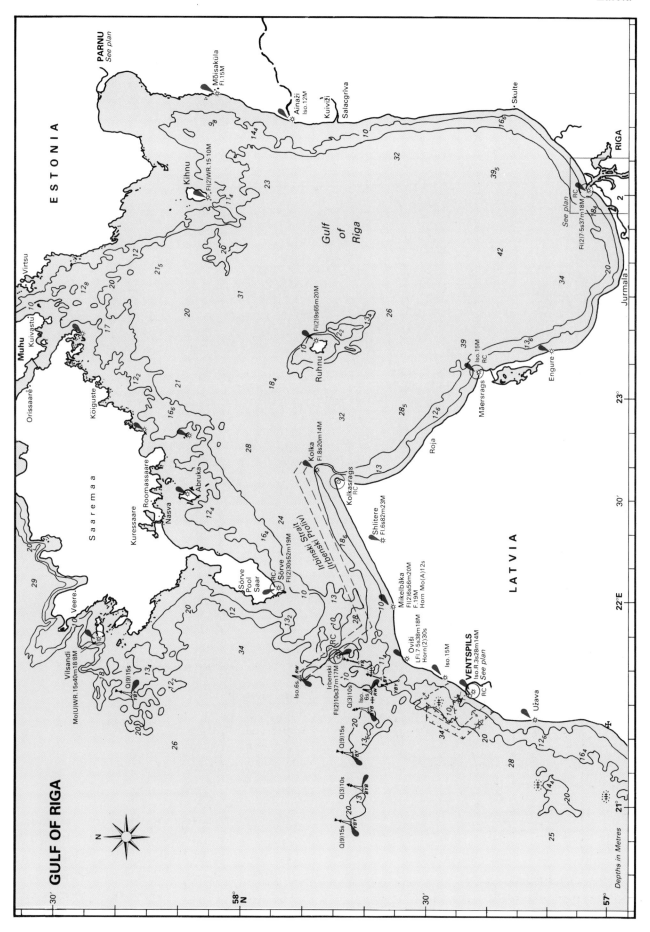

GULF OF RIGA

N

PARNU
See plan

E S T O N I A

Mõisaküla
Fl.15M

Ainaži
Iso.12M
Kuiviži
Salacgrīva

Skulte

Kihnu
Fl(2)WR.15.10M

Virtsu

Muhu

Kuivastu 10

Orissaare

*Gulf
of
Riga*

Fl(2)9s65m20M

Ruhnu

32

39₅

See plan
RC
Fl(2)7.5s37m18M

RIGA

2

18₄

Jūrmala

13₆

Engure

Iso.15M
RC
Mērsrags

39

Saaremaa

Köiguste

Roja

28₅

Roja 12₆

Kuressaare
Roomassaare
Nasva
Abruka

32

Kolka
Fl.8s20m14M
Kolkasrags
RC

13

Shlitere
Fl.6s82m23M

Sõrve
Pool
Saar

Sõrve
Fl(2)30s52m19M

RC

Irbinski Strait
(Irbenski Proliv)

18₆

Mikelbāka
Fl(2)6s56m20M
F.19M
Horn Mo(A)12s

L A T V I A

Veere

Vilsandi
Mo(U)WR.15s40m18.8M

Q(9)15s

Iso.6s
RC

Irbenski
Fl(2)10s37m17M
Q(3)10s

RW
10

RW

Oviši
L.Fl.7.5s38m18M
Horn(2)30s

Iso.15M

VENTSPILS
Iso.R.3s28m14M
See plan
RC

Užava

Q(9)15s

Q(3)10s
BYB

Q(9)15s

Depths in Metres

58°
N

30'

30'

23°

30'

22°E

23°

30'

21°

57°

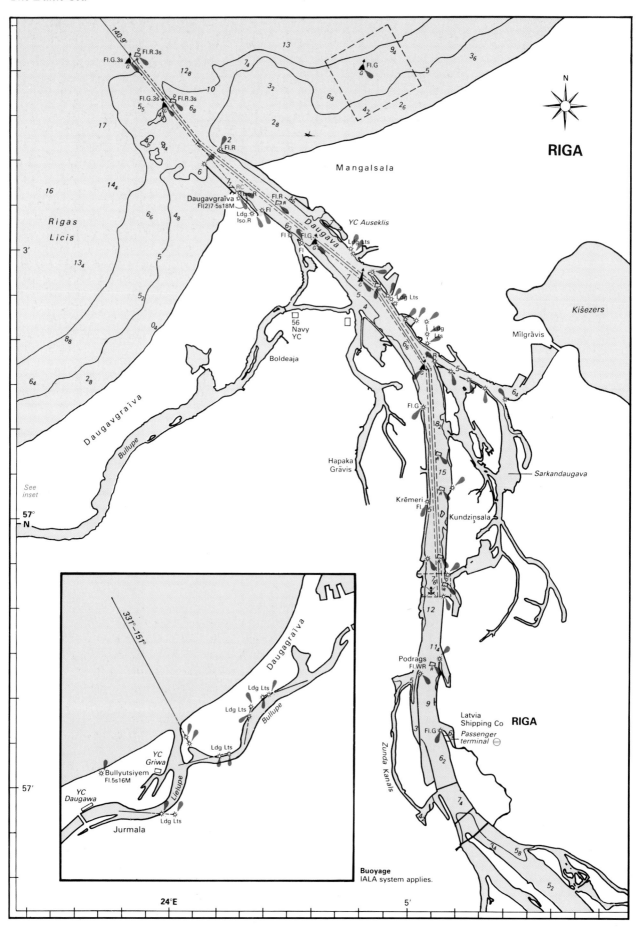

RIGA

Buoyage
IALA system applies.

October Bridge, Rīga, at night.

4. **Bullyutsiyem** 57°00'N 23°53'·6E Fl.5s36m16M
   White truncated pyramid, red top, 28m
5. **Daugagrāiva** 57°03'·6N 24°01'·4E Fl(2)7·5s37m18M
   Round white concrete tower, black bands, balcony,
   35m 035°-vis-245° Racon 265°-035° 15M RC
   286·5kHz *DG* (—··/——·) 30M

Entrance

6. **Mangalśala. West mole head** 57°03'·9N 24°00'·8E
   Fl.G.3s16m3M White metal framework tower, 13m
   East mole head 57°04'·1N 24°01'E Fl.R.3s8m4M
   Round red metal tower with balcony, 7m
7. **Ldg Lts** 140·9° *Front* 57°03'·6N 24°01'·4E
   Iso.R.5s20m 11M White daymark, red stripe, red
   framework tower, 15m
   Rear 590m from front 57°03'·4N 24°01'·8E
   Iso.R.5s29m 11M White base, red stripe, square metal
   framework, 27m. Leading lights visible only on line of
   140·9°, 24 hours.

General

Rīga is the capital city of Latvia and has a
population of about 800,000. It lies on the river
Daugava, about seven miles from the sea. There is a
busy port along the banks of the river between the
city centre and the sea and a considerable amount of
industry outside the central area. The old town,
situated near the centre of the city, is extremely
picturesque. The newer city centre is spaciously laid
out and the shopping centre seems to have more in
common with West European capitals than with
East European cities.

Approach

The wide river mouth, with powerful leading lights,
presents no entry problems at any time of the day.

The river itself is wide and well marked and
normally has an outgoing current of about two
knots.

Anchorage

Yachts are not allowed to anchor in the river.

Berthing

There is a yacht harbour on the west side of the river
about one mile from the sea, but this is a
considerable distance from the city centre. Foreign
yachts normally stay at the Latvian Shipping
Company Yacht Club, inside the Andreyevski
harbour behind the passenger terminal (Sea
Station), where the customs clearance point is
located. Mooring is bows to the quay with stern line
to buoy.

The Latvian Shipping Company Yacht Club is the
home of the Latvian Union of Cruising Yachts.

Formalities

A foreign yacht may be intercepted by a launch on
arrival at the river mouth and escorted silently to the
Andreyevski harbour, the basin on the east side of
the river eight miles upstream, where customs
clearance and passport control take place. If this
does not happen, go to the Latvian Shipping
Company Yacht Club and enquire.

General facilities

Water, electricity and rubbish disposal facilities are provided on the quay. The toilet and shower facilities are modest.

The city centre, with better shopping facilities than most cities of the Baltic states, is a five-minute tram ride from the yacht club. There is a foreign-currency shop in the Hotel Latvia.

Restaurants, some of them very good, abound. It is usually possible to get a table at the excellent restaurant in the Hotel Rīga without booking, but at smaller restaurants it is essential to book for an evening meal during the earlier part of the day.

Roubles can be purchased at banks and hotels at official rates.

The yacht club has a commercial manager, who for a modest fee in foreign currency will arrange excursions, car hire (not self-drive), theatre tickets and restaurants.

Yachting services

Fuel can be obtained via the director of the yacht club, who can also arrange for repairs and for propane cylinders to be refilled. Butane is not available. There is no chandlery.

Communications

The main post office has all facilities, but the telephone system is almost impossible to use without good knowledge of either Russian or Latvian.

Direct flights from Stockholm and København. Trains to Moscow, St Petersburg, Tallinn and Vilnius, and good bus services to most nearby towns.

Taxis can be hired at the main hotels and in the street.

Tourism

Rīga was founded in 1158 and joined the Hanseatic League in 1282; up to 1914 it had been variously possessed by the Poles (1581), the Swedes (1621 – they allowed a measure of self government), and the Russians (1710). The old town, on the east bank between Gorki and Suvorova Avenues, has many buildings remaining from Hanseatic times; St Peter's Church with its famous spire and the castle of the Teutonic Knights are outstanding features.

The rolling countryside around Rīga has many places of historic interest within easy reach. A popular beach resort, Jāurmala, with its own yacht harbour, is ten miles northwest of the city centre (see below).

Segulda castle, near Rīga.

Rīga

Other places

Roja 57°30'N 22°48'E
A fishing harbour with fuel, water, shopping, toilets.
2·5–5m. VHF Ch 10, callsign *Roja 52*.

Mãersrags 57°22'N 23°14'E
A fishing harbour. 5m. Water, fuel, shopping,
toilets. VHF Ch 10, callsign *Mãersrags 52*.

Engure 57°10'N 23°14'E
A fishing harbour with a yacht club. 2–3·5m. Water,
fuel, electricity, shopping, toilets. VHF Ch 10, callsign *Engure 52*.

Jãurmala 57°00'N 22°58'E
4m. A resort and fishing harbour along the coast a
few miles west of Rīga with two yacht clubs, Griwa
and Daugawa, both on the north shore of the river.
Water, fuel, electricity, toilets, shopping. VHF Ch
10, callsign *Jãurmala 52*.

Auda 57°03'N 24°04'E
4–6m. On the northeast side of the river at the
entrance to Rīga. Fishing harbour and yacht club
Auseklis. Bus No 24 to Rīga. Shopping, water, fuel,
electricity, toilets. VHF Ch 10, callsign *Rīga 52*.

Skulte 57°N 19'E 24°24'E
4m. A fishing harbour with water, fuel, toilet. VHF
Ch 12, callsign *Zvejniekciems 52* (for the bold).

Salacgrīva 57°45'N 24°21'E
4m. A fishing harbour. Shopping, water, fuel,
electricity, toilets. VHF Ch 12 , callsign *Salacgrīva
52*.

Kuiviži 57°47'N 24°20'E
3m. A fishing harbour, shopping, water, fuel, toilet.
VHF Ch 12.

Estonia

General

Ports which are supposed to maintain customs and
immigration facilities are Pärnu, Dirhami, Nasva,
Lehtma, Tallinn/Pirita and Narva. Possibly
Haapsalu will also be added. Once cleared in, it is
not necessary to clear out for another port within
Estonia, but it is most advisable to ask the harbour
office of the port you are leaving to notify the next
port of your visit. Clearance must of course be
obtained before leaving territorial waters.

Pärnu

58°23'N 24°29'E

Distances

Rīga 85M, Tallinn 75M, Hanko 130M.

Charts and guides

Admiralty chart *2215*
Russian chart *453*
Baltic Pilot Volume II (NP 19)
Harbours and lights on the Estonian Coast. Annually
produced by Eesti Avamerepur Jetamisliit (Estonian
Yachting Association). Available in Tallinn.

Lights

1. **Mys Pikkana** 58°06'·1N 23°58'·7E Fl(2)WR.12s28m
   15/10M Round white metal tower, 32m 262°-W-225°-
   R- 262°
2. **Sorgu Saar** 58°11'N 24°12'·4E Iso.WR.6s19m7/3M
   Round red brick tower, 16m 101°-W-342°-R-101°
3. **Ldg Lts** 023·9° *Front* 58°22'·8N 24°28'·1E Iso.R.6s
   16m10M White rectangle, black stripe, square metal
   framework, 15m. Visible only on leading line of 023·9°
   Rear 820m from front 58°23'·1N 24°28'·4E Iso.R.6s
   21m11M White rectangle, black stripe, square metal
   framework, 20m
4. **East breakwater head** 58°22'N 24°28'E Fl.G.3s5m
   1M White mast, black bands, concrete base, 4m
5. **West breakwater head** 58°22'·1N 24°27'·9E Fl.Y.3s
   5m1M White mast, black bands, concrete base, 4m

General

Pärnu is an attractive and friendly small town and
holiday resort, in the extreme northeast corner of
the Gulf of Rīga, with a friendly yacht club. It is a
port of entry and a fishing base.

Pärnu Yacht Club.

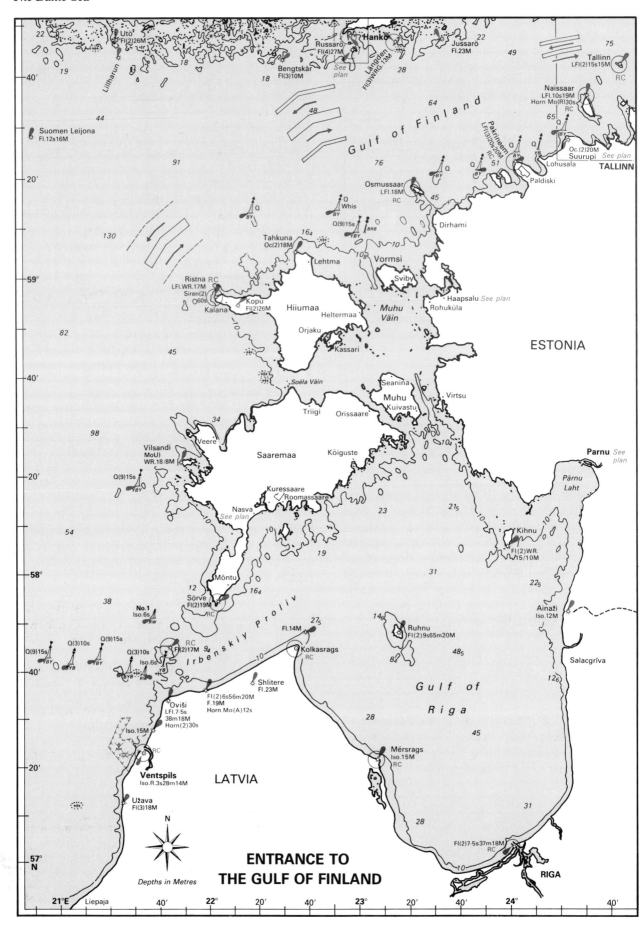

Utö
Fl(2)26M
22
19
18
Lillharun
44
Suomen Leijona
Fl.12s16M
91
130
Russarö
Fl(4)27M
Hankö
Bengtskär
Fl(3)10M
18
See plan
Långden
Fl(3)WRG.13M
Jussarö
Fl.23M
49
22
48
Gulf of Finland
64
76
75
Tallinn
LFl(2)15s15M
RC
Naissaar
LFl.10s19M
Horn Mo(R)30s
RC
65
Q
Pakrineem
LFl(3)20s20M
RC
51
Q
BY
Q
BY
Q
Y.B
Q
BY
Oc.(2)20M
Suurupi
Lohusala
See plan
TALLINN
Paldiski
Osmussaar
LFl.18M
RC
45
Dirhami
Q
Whis
Q(9)15s
Y.B
BRB
Tahkuna
Oc(2)18M
16₄
Lehtma
10₆
10
Vormsi
Sviby
Haapsalu See plan
Rohuküla
Ristna RC
LFl.WR.17M
Siren(2)
Q60s
Kopu
Fl(2)26M
Kalana
Hiiumaa
Heltermaa
Muhu
Väin
ESTONIA
82
10
Orjaku
45
Kassari
Soëla Väin
Seanina
Virtsu
40'
Triigi
Muhu
Kuivastu
34
Orissaare
98
Veere
Saaremaa
Kõiguste
10₄
Pärnu See plan
Vilsandi
(MoU)
WR.18/8M
Q(9)15s
Y.B.Y
Kuressaare
Roomassaare
Nasva
See plan
23
21₅
Pärnu
Laht
Kihnu
Fl(2)WR.
15/10M
10
54
19
31
22₅
Möntu
16₄
Sörve
Fl(2)19M
RC
12
Irbenskiy Proliv
Ruhnu
Fl(2)9s65m20M
14₆
Ainaži
Iso.12M
No.1
Iso.6s
RW
38
Fl.14M
27₅
Q(9)15s
Y.B.Y
Q(3)10s
Y.B.Y
Q(9)15s
RC
Fl(2)17M
Iso.6s
B.Y.B
Q(3)10s
Iso.6s
B.Y.B
Y.B
RW
9₄
10
Kolkasrags
RC
84
48₅
126
Salacgrīva
Shlitere
Fl.23M
Gulf of
Riga
Oviši
LFl.7·5s
38m18M
Horn(2)30s
Fl(2)6s56m20M
F.19M
Horn Mo(A)12s
28
45
Iso.15M
RC
Mērsrags
Iso.15M
RC
Ventspils
Iso.R.3s28m14M
LATVIA
28
31
Užava
Fl(3)18M
N
Fl(2)7·5s37m18M
RC
57°
N
Depths in Metres
**ENTRANCE TO
THE GULF OF FINLAND**
10
RIGA
21°E Liepaja 40' **22°** 20' 40' **23°** 20' 40' **24°** 40'

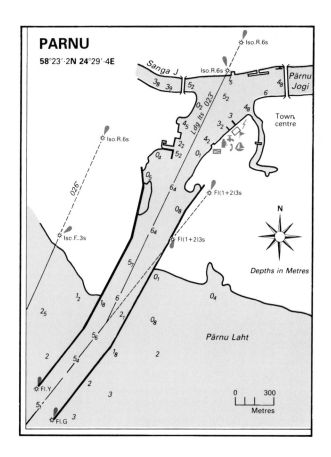

PARNU

58°23'·2N 24°29'·4E

Depths in Metres

Approach

The approach is along a fairway 30 miles in length, leading from a position 6M southwest of Mys Pikkana[1], on Kihnu, to the entrance of Pärnu harbour; in the daytime, Sorgu Saar light[2] may be difficult to spot. When in sight of the shore the first[3] of three pairs of leading lights will be seen. It should be noted that the television tower, visible for many miles out to sea, is well to the east of the harbour entrance; it is misleading to steer towards it.

Anchorage

It is not advisable to anchor in the region of Pärnu.

Berthing

Berth at the Pärnu Yacht Club on the east bank of the river just inside the entrance. Mooring is bows to pontoon and stern line to buoy. The water is 3–4m deep everywhere in the yacht club area.

Formalities

Customs and immigration.

General facilities

Water and electricity are supplied to each berth, and there are good showers and toilets ashore. There is a small wooden clubhouse with a bar which serves excellent snacks. A new two-storey clubhouse is under construction.

The shopping centre is about ten minutes' walk away from the yacht club. The Pärnu Hotel in the town centre has a small hard-currency shop, mainly selling drinks, and there is a bank opposite the hotel. There are several good restaurants.

Yachting services

Fuel can be obtained by arrangement with the club manager, but chandlery and gas are not obtainable.

Communications

Telephone calls inside Estonia may be made from the club manager's office, ☎ (7) 0144-441-948, but international calls are almost impossible to make. There is, however, a facsimile machine at the commodore's business address in the town, *Fax* (7) 0144-441-028.

There is a regular coach service to Tallinn, a two-hour journey.

Tallinn

59°27'N 24°45'E

Distances

Parnu 75M, Hanko 60M, Helsinki 45M.

Charts and guides

Admiralty charts *2227* and *2248*
German chart *157*
Russian chart *1149*
Baltic Pilot Volume III (NP 20)

Lights

Approach

1. **Piksaäre Ots** 59°36'·2N 24°30'·8E LFl.10s47m19M Horn Mo(R)30s North end of Naissaar. Octagonal white concrete tower, red top, 45m 025°-vis-355° RC 294·5 kHz *NG* (–·/––·) 75M
2. **Tallinn** 59°42'·7N 24°44'·1E Fl(2)15s29m15M Red and black column, blue and white bands, 31m RC 300·5kHz *TN* (–/–·) 25M
3. **Ldg Lts** 159·1° *Front* 59°26'·2N 24°48'·1E Iso.WG.3s 49m19/13M Conical red tower on building, 18m 143°-G-156°-W-165°
   Rear 0·6M from front 59°25'·7N 24°48'·5E Iso.6s80m 23M Round white stone tower, black top, 40m 123·5°-vis-187·5°

Entrance
Pirita Jöji

4. **Pirita south breakwater head** 59°28'·2N 24°49'·2E Fl.G.3s6m1M Green metal column with gallery, 5m
5. **Pirita north breakwater head** 59°28'·2N 24°49'·3E Fl.R.3s6m2M Red metal column with gallery, 5m

The Baltic Sea

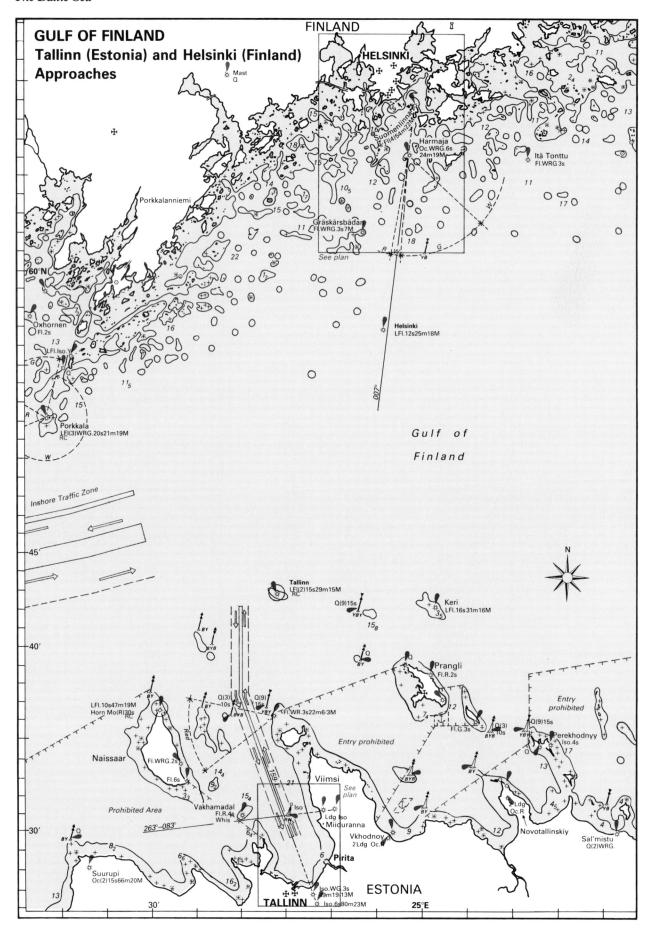

GULF OF FINLAND
Tallinn (Estonia) and Helsinki (Finland)
Approaches

88

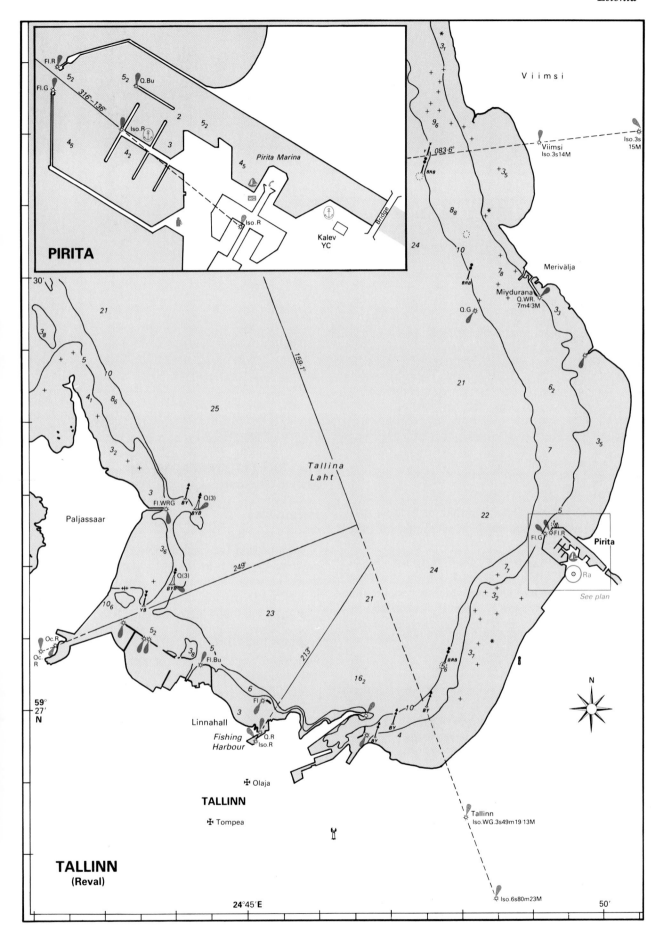

PIRITA

Fl.R
5₂
Fl.G
316°-136°
4₅
5₂ Q.Bu
4₂
Iso.R
3
2
5₂
4₅
Pirita Marina
Iso.R
Bridge
Kalev
YC

V i i m s i

3₁
9₆
083·6°
Y
BRB
Iso.3s
15M
Viimsi
Iso.3s14M
3₅
8₈
24
10
Merivälja
BRB
7₈
Miydurana
Q.WR.
7m4/3M
3₃
Q.G

21
6₂

30'
21
3₈
5
10
4₁
8₆
25
3₂
159.1°
3
Fl.WRG
BY
Q(3)
BYB
Paljassaar
3₆
3
Q(3)
BYB
249°
23
YB
Oc.R
5₂
Oc.
R
3₈
5
Fl.Bu
6
Fl
213°
16₂
10₆
Linnahall
3
Fishing
Harbour
Q.R
Iso.R
10
BY
BY
4
✠ Olaja

Tallina
Laht

22
5
Pirita
1₈
Fl.R
Fl.G
Ra
See plan
7₇
3₂
24
7
3₅
7
3₂
BRB
5₂
3₇

N

TALLINN

✠ Tompea

Tallinn
Iso.WG.3s49m19·13M

TALLINN
(Reval)

59°
27'
N

24°45'E

Iso.6s80m23M

50'

89

The main harbour at Pirita Marina, Tallinn.

General

Tallinn, the capital of the Republic of Estonia, has about 400,000 inhabitants. It is an important port and industrial centre.

The yacht harbour is at Pirita, 8km to the east of the city. Pirita Marina was built for the yachting Olympics in 1980, and has subsequently become the main yachting centre for Estonia. A new marina is due to open in 1993 in Tallinn itself, near to the port.

Approach

In 1975 the western approach south of Naissaar was closed to shipping, and in 1991 it was still obligatory to approach from the north. From Tallinn lighthouse[2] follow the centre of the main shipping route down the centre of the Gulf of Tallinn, using the leading lights[3] immediately to the east of the city until the Pirita breakwater lights are picked up in the vicinity of the television tower.

The harbour entrance is conspicuous and there are no offlying hazards.

Berthing

After clearing customs, yachts may continue into the harbour to find moorings (bows-to with stern line to buoy) at one of three yacht clubs: the old-established Kalev Yacht Club ☎ (7) 0142-239-154

Fax (7) 0142-239-028, the Navy Club or Pirita Marina (see chart).

Formalities

When entering the outer harbour follow the 'Customs' sign (in English) and moor alongside the customs post immediately to starboard inside the inner harbour. Clearance is usually efficient and quick, but if arriving at night it may be necessary to wait until the following morning.

General facilities

Whichever yacht club is chosen, all berths have water and electricity easily available and there are plenty of rubbish skips.

Toilets, showers and saunas are available at both the Kalev Club and Pirita Marina, and they both have pleasant snack bars. The nearby Hotel Sport has dining facilities, a travel bureau, a bank and a hairdresser. It also has an Olympic-size indoor swimming pool.

Buses leave every few minutes for Tallinn and its banks, hotels and restaurants. It has relatively good shopping facilities, but goods are far from plentiful. Luxury goods not obtainable in the local shops can be bought at tourist shops in the main hotels for prices roughly corresponding to UK prices.

There is an excellent open-air market near the Olympia Hotel where fresh produce can be obtained during the summer months.

Yachting services

Fuel is readily available at a filling station operated by the Finnish company, Neste.

Propane cylinders can be refilled by arrangement with the Kalev Yacht Club, which also has extensive workshop facilities and skilled shipwrights. Many materials, however, are in short supply and spare parts have to be brought in from Helsinki.

There is a sail loft near the Kalev Club.

Weather forecasts in English can be received on VHF from Helsinki Radio and its satellites at 0733 and 1933 UT. See page 109.

The main building of Pirita Marina, Tallinn. Originally built for the 1980 Olympics, but now privatised.

The old Hanseatic town of Tallinn.

Communications

Telephone calls to overseas destinations can be made at the main hotels or by VHF on Finnish channels.

The Hotel Sport and the Kalev Yacht Club have facsimile machines.

International flights to Stockholm, Moscow and St Petersburg. Good train services to Moscow, St Petersburg and Rīga. Buses to St Petersburg, Rīga and many destinations inside Estonia.

Several ferries each day between Tallinn and Helsinki.

Tourism

Tallinn was founded by Waldemar II of Denmark in 1219. It became a Hanseatic town, shared in the later Swedish-Russian cycle and in 1710 was annexed by Peter the Great, who in 1713 founded the naval harbour. The old, upper town (Domberg) has the castle and cathedral, the palace built by Peter for Catherine and other buildings of interest. There are many cultural activities, especially music and dance.

Narva-Yyesuu

59°28'N 28°02'E

Distances

Tallinn 105M, St Petersburg 110M.

Charts and guides

Admiralty chart *2264*
Finnish chart *901*

Lights

1. **Reka Narva** 59°28'N 28°02'·7E Fl(2)12s34m17M White round concrete tower, red band, black gallery.
2. **Outer Ldg Lts** 105°, characteristics unlisted, 17m and 8m both on 5m tripod with white triangular daymark, the front one with a red stripe. Their position varies with the shifts in the channel.
3. **Inner Ldg Lts** 162°, characteristics unlisted, 18m and 11m, the rear on a column 8m with white rectangular daymark with a red stripe, the front on a pyramid with a similar daymark.

General

Narva-Yyesuu (also spelt Jõesuu) is a fishing and commercial harbour on the River Narva which forms the border between Estonia and Russia. It is a port of entry/exit and a convenient stop between Tallinn and St Petersburg.

Approach.

Make for Reka Narva and pick up the approach buoy about 2M northwest of the light. Follow the outer leading marks until about ¼M from the land

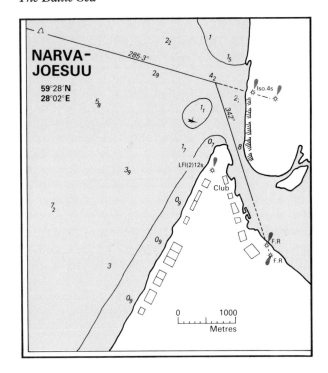

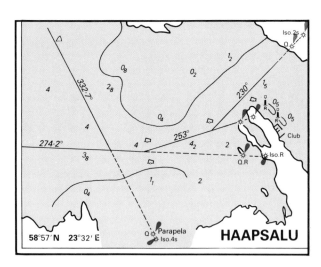

and then switch to the inner leading marks. The harbour is on the west bank under the lighthouse; the east bank is Russian.

Berthing
Berth at the south end of the first basin. This basin houses the Ahto Yacht Club.

Formalities
Customs and immigration.

Facilities
Water, sauna, WCs, shower. Restaurant, food store.

Communications
Buses. Post office.

Other places

Haapsalu
58°57'N 23°32'E

Charts
Admiralty chart *2241*
Finnish chart *944*
Russian charts *23011, 22011, 25025* and *2202*

Lights
Two sets of unlisted leading lights: see sketch.

General
Haapsalu is on a small peninsula on which stands the ruin of an old castle with a high tower. It is a pleasant old town of about 15,000 inhabitants, with a medieval history. At the end of the 19th century it was a popular resort for the wealthy of St Petersburg, and their grand wooden villas still dominate the scenery. There are several museums and the shopping is of decent local standards. It is the Estonian centre for ice yachting.

Approach
From the north the main channel lies between Vormsi and Hiiumaa islands; the channel between Vormsi and the mainland is silting and has reportedly only 1·5m. Approach Haapsalu from the west along a marked channel. Call harbour control, *Haapsalu 32*, on VHF Ch 10 or 16. The approach is tricky and the marks are indistinct.

Berthing
Haapsalu Yacht Club, which has its own jetties, is in Taaga Bay next to the commercial harbour. It is fairly well protected, though winds from north through east can cause some swell. Berth at the visitors' berths, either inside or south of the southernmost jetty, bows to jetty, stern to mooring buoy. 2·5–3·5m. 1992 all-in fees were 50 Finnish marks per day, irrespective of size, cash on the nail.

Facilities
Showers, WC, water, electricity. The fee includes local telephone calls and the security guard. Hotel, café.

Communications
Ferries to Estonian ports. Railway.

Dirhami

59°12'N 23°30'E

Lights

1. **Osmussaar NW point** 59°18'·3N 23°23'E LFl.10s 39m18M Black tower, white bands, 35m
2. **Pöösaspea** 59°13'·9N 23°31'·8E Fl.3s17m6M Red framework tower, white bands, 16m
3. Unlisted leading lights

Charts

Admiralty chart *2241*
Finnish chart *944*

General

A fishing harbour on the mainland inside the island of Osmussaar and situated between the headlands of Pöösaspea and Dirhami. It is useful as a port of entry and customs and immigration are said to maintain a 24-hour service. There are no yachting facilities as such, and the harbour authorities do not like yachts staying overnight; they do not, however, charge for yachts which enter only for clearance and then leave.

Approach

From the entrance buoy 1·3M off Pöösaspea follow the green leading lights on 170°. The fairway is only 40–60m wide. Call the harbourmaster, *Dirhami 32*, on VHF Ch 10 or 16.

Mooring

Bows to the breakwater quay with stern anchor. 4m, sand, good holding.

Miiduranna

59°30'N 24°49'E

Lights

Unlisted molehead lights, white and red.

General

A former fishing harbour sheltered by a breakwater and located 2M north of Pirita on the east shore of Tallinn bay.

Approach

Enter from the southwest through the gap in the breakwater. Call harbour control, *Miiduranna 32*, on VHF Ch 10.

Berthing

At the visitors' berth, bows to quay, stern to mooring buoy. 4m.

Facilities

Showers, WC, electricity, water. Local telephone calls and the security guard are included in the daily rate of 40 Finnish marks. Café and canteen. Slip for hauling out. Winter storage. Repair facilities geared towards fishing boats – visitors are not allowed to enter the workshops, but engine and rigging repairs and wood and metal work can be undertaken.

Other places

Virtsu 58°35'N 23°31'E
3–5m inside. Stern buoys, ladders. Ferry wharf, water, fuel, shopping, toilet. VHF Ch 11.

Rohuküla 58°55'N 23°26'E
An artificial ferry harbour, 3m. Fuel, water, some provisions.

Kihnu

Kihnu Harbour

58°08'N 24°01'E

Charts

Admiralty *2215*
Russian *25037* which includes a Kihnu Harbour insert, described as completely wrong and a real wrecker.

Lights

1. **Mys Pikkana** 58°06'·1N 23°58'·7E Fl(2)WR.12s28m 15-10M White round metal tower, 32m 262°-W-225°-R-262°
2. **Pier head** 58°08'·8N 24°01'·9E Q.6m5M White metal column, concrete base

General

A small island in the approaches to Pärnu with a permanent population of about 20 families engaged in farming and fishing. It is a popular weekend call of the Pärnu Yacht Club. The manmade harbour is at the northeast corner; it is protected by a large area of reeds immediately to the north, though east to northeast winds can produce a nasty chop.

Approach

Kihnu is surrounded by shallows which in most places extend two miles offshore, though in the northwest corner the reef extends 5 miles. There is a tricky passage round the north side of the island which should only be attempted in good visibility. The easiest approach is to round the south side and follow the east coast at a suitable distance offshore until the north tip of the island bears west. Turn towards it, close with care and identify the leading marks on 270°. Stick closely to the line; the approach is strewn with rocks and wrecks.

Mooring

Go alongside at the head of the basin or alongside another vessel.

Facilities

Water, WC. Bar/canteen ten minutes' walk. Otherwise nothing but beaches and pine and juniper forest. The old lighthouse was built by the British.

Saaremaa

Nasva

58°13'N 22°23'E

General

Nasva, on the south side of the island, is the port for Kuressaare, the capital, 18km away. Saaremaa has one of the highest standards of living in Estonia, derived from its international fishing industry, and besides fortifications and museums, Kuressaare has reasonable shops and good inns (wild boar is sometimes available on the menu).

Approach

Locate the entrance buoy at 58°11'·6N 22°23'·4E and identify the leading marks on 013°, two on shore behind the head of the pier and one at the head of the pier. The channel is dredged to 4m and goes close to the head of the pier.

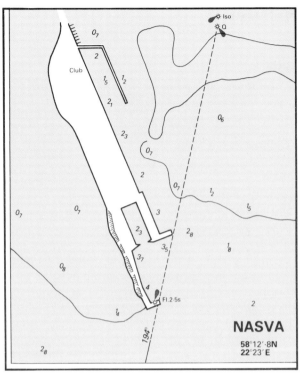

NASVA
58°12'·8N
22°23'E

Berthing

Pass the first entrance and go about 100m up the east side of the mole to the inner basin (see chart). 2·5m.

Facilities

Water, showers, sauna, WC, electricity.

Communications

Car and bicycle hire.

Other places

Møntu 57°57'N 22°08'E
Mole with 3–5m, small harbour with 2m.

Köiguste Laht 58°20'N 23°00'E
Fishing pier with 3m.

Orisaare 58°34'N 23°05'E
The harbour, with depths of 2–2·5m, is near the town of Orisaare.

Veere 58°27'N 22°05'E
Natural anchorage in quiet bay with small jetty. Good shelter.

Muhu

Kuivastu 58°35'N 23°24'E
Stone pier with 3–5m alongside. Used by ferries, but there should be room.

Nasva yacht harbour, island of Saaremaa.

Hiiumaa

Lehtma

59°04'N 22°42'E

Lights

1. **Köpu** 58°55'·2N 22°12'·3E Fl(2)10s102m26M White square round tower, 36m
2. **Tahkuna Nina** 59°05'·8N 22°35'·4E Oc(2)15s43m 18M White round tower, 43m

General

A small shelter on the north side of Hiiumaa with big plans for expansion, including a marina, customs and immigration, etc. Although the last two may be in position in 1992, the first will not materialise for some years. There are woods with wild boar and beautiful beaches, some near the harbour; tours can be arranged to Köpu, where a light has been established since 1499, and to Suuremöisalinna Castle. The closest town, Kärdlä, is 13km away; it has about 3000 inhabitants, a lot of parks and virtually no industry.

Approach

Approach on the leading marks on 272° and keep close to the breakwater. Protection from the south is from a submerged reef which curves into the harbour inside the breakwater.

Berth

Go alongside at the inner end of the pier near the harbour authority building; the harbourmaster will direct you to a visitor's mooring, bows to quay, stern to mooring buoy or anchor. Good holding in sand or clay.

Facilities

Washrooms, WC, sauna. Minor repairs.

Old farm on the island of Saaremaa.

The Baltic Sea

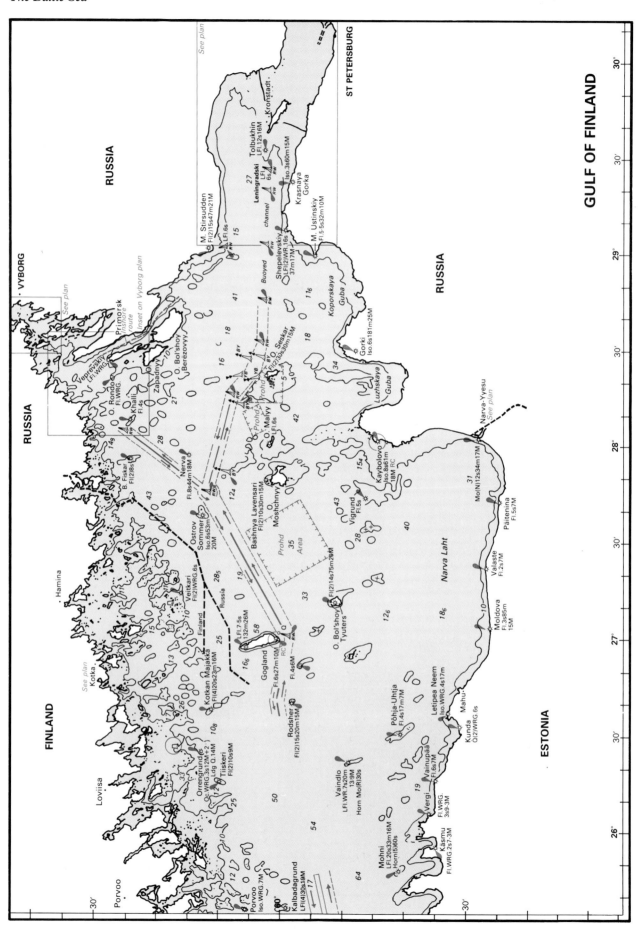

GULF OF FINLAND

96

IV. Russia

Cruising areas

The attractions of a cruise to this part of Russia are mainly concerned with the wealth of interest which exists in St Petersburg, but there are several other possibilities.

The sea area between St Petersburg and Kronstadt, inside the artificial sea wall built from Kronstadt to the mainland shore to the north of St Petersburg, is a popular sailing area for Russian yachtsmen. It is generally shallow and is crisscrossed by a number of *farvarters* – fairways – well marked by buoys. It makes for an interesting day sail to take on board one of the many willing Russians from either of the major yacht clubs and to meander across to Petrodvoryets (the Summer Palace) or Strelna – or to view the splendours of St Petersburg from the water. This is even more attractive if done at night, when the bridges are opened.

Vyborg, about 85 miles to the northwest of St Petersburg, can now be visited. It is close to the start of the Finnish-administered Saimaa Canal, which can only be approached through Russian territorial waters and which leads to a most attractive lake region in Finland, also famous for its annual opera festival. The approach to both is described below.

Much further away is Kaliningrad (German: Königsberg). It is isolated from Russia by Belarus and sandwiched between Poland and Lithuania, and is mentioned in this section simply because it is part of Russia. Kaliningrad, formerly a cultural centre of Prussia, is well inland and entered via a sea canal from Baltysk. In 1991 this passage stayed closed to foreign yachts, but the speed of change is such that it may now be open. For shallow-draught boats it may be possible to cross the border into Poland from Kaliningrad through the Zalew Wisłany. There are also inland waterways between Kaliningrad and Klaipēda in Lithuania, used by commercial shipping.

The great inland waterways are opening up to foreign yachts, providing the opportunity of voyaging both to the White Sea in the north and through the heartlands of Russia to the Black Sea in the south.

In many countries there are good facilities for boat and crew, but visitors are largely left to their own devices by the local population. In Russia it is the opposite. There are few home comforts for boat or crew, but the people are warm hearted, genuinely pleased to see visiting yachtsmen. Russians are anxious to meet visitors and are proud to show them the buildings, the art treasures and the culture they have inherited, but the subject uppermost in their minds is their current position and their relationship with the West.

The people

Little more need be said except to point out that even within the borders of what is now Russia, there are many groups with customs, habits and languages quite different from those of the northwestern Russian; the Russian Federation contains, for instance, 16 autonomous republics, 5 autonomous regions and 10 autonomous areas, all based on ethnic differences. Members of these groups may be met at any time, besides nationals of republics lying outside the Russian Federation.

With the abolition of communism as the state orthodoxy, the Russian Orthodox Church has been trying to re-establish its position in local life and appears to have gained considerable support, though there are no figures to measure its extent.

Private enterprise street traders in St Petersburg.

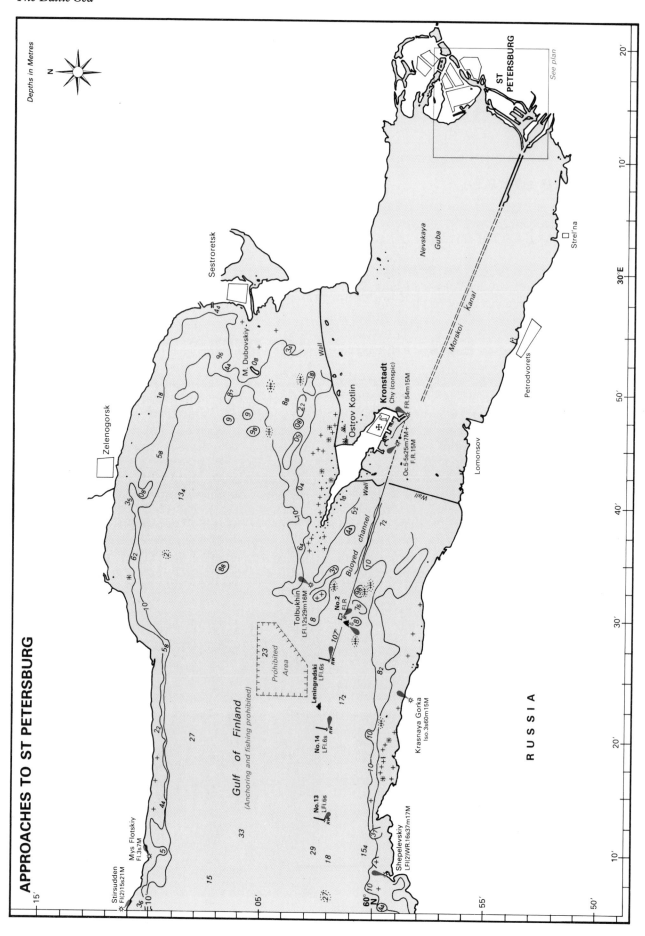

APPROACHES TO ST PETERSBURG

Depths in Metres

N

Stirsudden
Fl(2)15s21M

Mys Flotskiy
Fl.3s7M

Zelenogorsk

Sestroretsk

M. Dubovskiy

Wall

Ostrov Kotlin

Kronstadt
Chy (conspic)
F.R.54m15M

Nevskaya
Guba

Morskoi   Kanal

ST
PETERSBURG

See plan

Strel'na

Gulf of Finland
(Anchoring and fishing prohibited)

Prohibited
Area

Leningradski
I.Fl.6s

No.14
I.Fl.6s

No.13
I.Fl.bs

Tolbukhin
L.Fl.12s29m16M

No.2
Fl.R

Buoyed channel

Wall

Wall

Oc.5.5s25m7M+
F.R.15M

Lomonsov

Petrodvorets

Krasnaya Gorka
Iso.3s60m15M

Shepelevskiy
L.Fl(2)WR.16s37m17M

R U S S I A

98

The military port of Kronstadt. The numbers are for checking compasses.

The economy

Beside being a centre for the arts, St Petersburg is home to a wide range of major industries – steel works, shipbuilding, mechanical equipment, heavy electrical engineering and so forth – as well as lighter industry such as timber processing, textiles and electrical. With minor exceptions, its only local fuel is some oil shale and peat, and its only mineral bauxite; its land grows timber and flax and not much else. Fuel, food and other raw materials have to be brought from outside. There is a nuclear power station of doubtful integrity 50M west at Sosnovy Bor.

State tourist office

Some visitors to Russian waters have made arrangements through Inflot, the official Russian import/export agency. The services provided by Inflot to yachtsmen have proved expensive and unnecessary. Similarly, the services Intourist can provide have not been found relevant to yachtsmen.

Money

Inflation is sharp. Transactions are in cash – even the army sells interviews for dollars. Roubles are necessary for most purchases. Some tourists obtain them on the street, though the practice may not be within the letter of the law. Visa cards may be used in certain St Petersburg banks to obtain hard currency, but not roubles. Traveller's cheques may be used to obtain roubles but not hard currency. The best plan is to buy roubles on the street or from a bank for dollars, Finnish marks or deutschmarks which have either been brought in or, such is the

Old man at the River Yacht Club, St Petersburg.

system, obtained from the bank itself with a Visa card.

Credit cards are accepted only at hard-currency shops, tourist hotels and restaurants.

Shopping

Apart from basic foodstuffs, there is little to buy for roubles. Abolition of price controls has resulted in basic commodities appearing on the stalls at prices which seem exorbitant to a Russian wage earner but cheap to a Westerner. In the state shops prices are only a fraction of those in the markets, but only a very restricted range of goods is available and long queues are the norm.

There are several Beriozka shops selling luxury goods (but not usually foodstuffs) for foreign currency at prices similar to those in the UK.

Hotels and restaurants

There are many hotels and restaurants. The more modern ones are essentially geared to foreign currency and are not cheap.

Yacht clubs

In Russia, clubs remain owned by organisations such as town councils, local business enterprises, trade unions or the military, but many are being privatised. They employ full-time staff for administrative and technical work. They frequently have their own boatyard facilities including sailmaking. There is virtually no private ownership of yachts, and the larger yachts have full-time paid captains. People wishing to sail apply to clubs for places on boats, but in practice the captains choose members of the crew and keep them as permanent. How the clubs will adjust to a market economy remains to be seen.

Yacht services and chandlery

Mooring costs are about the same as those in Scandinavia, and diesel fuel, if available, generally costs about the same as it does in Finland.

Yacht clubs can normally arrange for propane bottles to be refilled but not exchanged. It takes some days.

Chandlery is virtually unobtainable: most Russian yachtsmen purchase their equipment from Finland or other Western countries.

Weather forecasts, if available, are from the yacht clubs. There is no VHF forecast service.

Formalities

All visitors to Russia must have a valid visa before arrival. The Russian consulate in London (5 Kensington Palace Gardens, W8, *Fax* 071-229 3215) has not changed the system of the old USSR and the procedure can take as long as three months. For help, try Select, 102 Millfield Avenue, London E17 ☎ 081-523 3504.

Yachts are required to obtain clearance at each port entered, but as there are only two accessible major Russian ports in the Gulf of Finland this means in practice either St Petersburg or Vyborg.

The customs and immigration procedures on arrival are on the whole less onerous than those in many countries of the West. Normally yachts are boarded by two or three officials who tend to be concerned more with the appropriate forms than with inspecting the boat. Their main concerns are drugs and weapons.

Surveillance is maintained over both foreign and Russian yachts, and most yachts will from time to time be visited by a patrol boat. Normally a patrol vessel will approach to within 50m or so and ask on VHF Ch 16 for the name and nationality of the yacht, the number of people on board and the last and next ports of call. The first time this happens can be frightening, especially if the patrol vessel approaches without lights on a dark night and then without warning focuses a powerful searchlight on the yacht. However, given the language problems, patrol vessel captains are not usually aggressive unless they perceive that the yacht is being uncooperative.

There are no specific rules restricting the temporary importation of yachts for wintering or repairs.

The Russian flag is a horizontal tricolour, white over blue over red.

Navigation

The *Baltic Pilot Volume III (NP 20)* provides detailed information, but is designed for use by large ships.

Finnish charts of the area are useful.

Decca, using the two-station chain in Finland, is not very reliable on the Russian coast.

Time

St Petersburg and Moscow are both three hours ahead of UT in winter and four hours ahead from the last Sunday in March until the Saturday before the last Sunday in September.

Communications

International calls can usually be made during office hours from the two major yacht clubs, or from the tourist hotels but at greater cost. Few private lines have direct dialling facilities, and international calls may take several hours (or even days) to make.

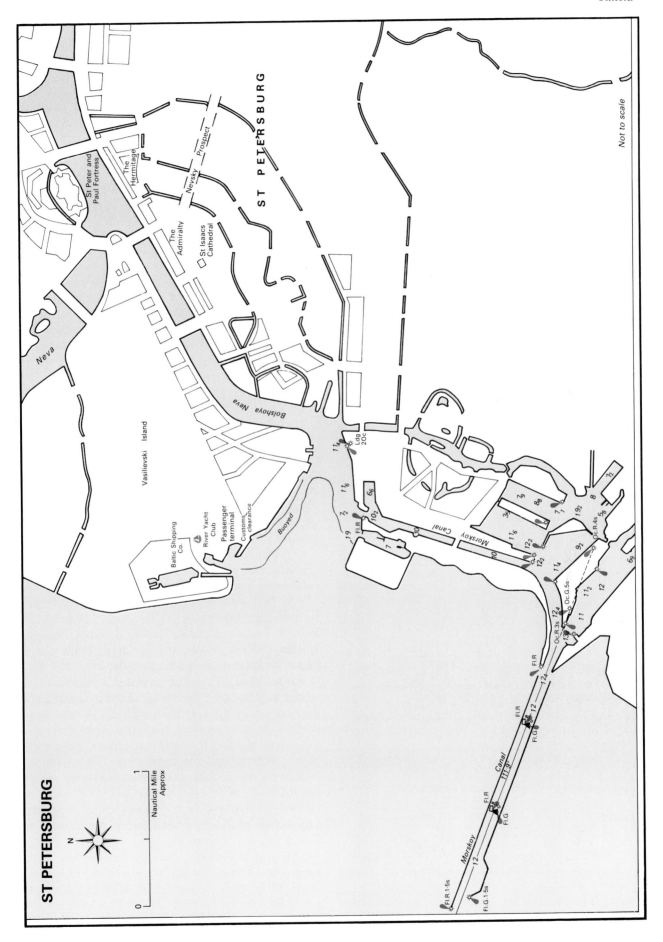

ST PETERSBURG

All large towns have major operator-controlled long-distance telephone call offices. The procedure is very complicated, and without fluent Russian it is almost impossible to use them.

The major yacht clubs have facsimile and telex facilities. Telex is fast and effective but facsimile is frequently subject to delay.

Mail is unreliable and slow. A letter between the UK and St Petersburg usually takes 4–6 weeks. Some UK based express delivery organisations now undertake delivery and collection in major cities in Russia.

There is no public correspondence service in English on Russian VHF. It is possible, however, to use it for talking to patrol vessels and for port operations.

Travel

There are regular flights to St Petersburg from most European centres.

The journey by train from London to St Petersburg takes 2–3 days. There are also good train services from Helsinki.

Bus services operate to Helsinki and Tallinn and ferry services to Stockholm.

St Petersburg

59°56'N 30°18'E

Distances

Helsinki 170M, Tallinn 180M.

Charts and guides

Admiralty charts *2264* and *2395*
Finnish chart *901*
Baltic Pilot Volume III (NP 20)

Lights

1. **Shepelevskiy** 59°59'·1N 29°07'·6E LFl(2)WR.16s 37m17M Round white stone tower, red bands, 36m 053°-R-100°-W-265°-R-280°
2. **Krasnaya Gorka** 59°58'·3N 29°23'·2E Iso.3s60m 15M Red rectangle, white stripe on red metal framework tower, 38m
3. **Tolbukhin** 60°02'·6N 29°32'·6E LFl.12s29m16M Round white stone tower and building, 30m
4. **Leningradski** lightbuoy 60°02'N 29°26'E

General

St Petersburg, with four million inhabitants, is the second largest city in Russia. It is built on a complex of waterways, and is a grand and a spacious city. It is justifiably recognised as the cultural capital of Russia: few cities in the world have art galleries, concert halls, museums and theatres which can compare with those of St Petersburg.

No visitor to St Petersburg should miss the Hermitage (the Winter Palace), which undoubtedly contains one of the world's most important collections of art treasures, nor the Russian Museum, actually an art gallery. The Peter and Paul Fortress, the cruiser *Aurora*, St Isaac's Cathedral, the Admiralty, Chesma Church, Kazanski Cathedral, Smolny Cathedral, the St Petersburg Philharmonia and the Kirov Theatre, to name only a few, all demand attention. And of course a few miles outside the city is the resplendent Petrodvoryets, well worth a visit by Meteor jet foil or even a day sail in the company of one of the Russians who will befriend you at the yacht club.

Behind the prestigious buildings and squares is another city: a sad city, worn out after decades of inadequate care, with poor quality housing, dirty streets, decrepit transport, buildings seemingly forever under repair and people standing for hours in the food queues. Yet there is a mood of optimism, a hope that things will get better. Foreign yachtsmen, especially yachtsmen from western Europe, are still few and far between. In consequence, they receive a warm welcome, and even if the facilities at the yacht clubs are still embryonic, this is more than offset by the helpfulness and the friendliness of the people.

History

After returning to Russia from his study of industry in western Europe, Peter the Great (1672-1725) sought to give Russia secure access to the west, which meant access to the Baltic. It was necessary for him to break the power of the Swedes, who then dominated the Baltic, and in 1700 he began the war which lasted until 1721. By 1702, he already felt sufficiently confident to start building his fortress city at the mouth of the Neva, and his position was further consolidated in 1709, after the Battle of Poltava, when Sweden ceded Latvia, Estonia, Karelia and part of Finland to Russia. Peter took a direct personal share in the development of the city. It was founded on a swamp, isolated from sources of labour and building materials. Mortality among the pressed labour was high. Not only the workers were pressed; the nobility were obliged to establish houses in the new city which, in 1713, became the capital of Russia and remained so until 1918. The construction of the Baltic fleet was started, foreign shipping was encouraged to use the port and St Petersburg overtook Novgorod as the trade centre. With the appearance of Russia on the Baltic, the balance of power in north Europe changed completely, but St Petersburg has always been vulnerable; the most serious attempt on its life was made in the Second World War, when it was besieged by the Germans indirectly assisted by the Finns, but held out despite very considerable privation.

The Peter and Paul Fortress, St Petersburg.

Part of the St Petersburg skyline: the Admiralty and, right, St Isaac's Cathedral.

Ever since its foundation, St Petersburg has been a collecting centre for the arts. Exploration of its museums and palaces alone is more than sufficient motive for making it a port of call.

Approach

In the Gulf of Finland, approach south of Gogland and beware the separation lanes. From the Leningradski lightbuoy, at 60°01'·6N 29°26'E to the west of Kronstadt, the approach is via the main shipping channel along the well lit and well buoyed Morskoy Canal into the main port area, where the canal swings to the north and joins the estuary of the Bolshoya Neva. Care must be taken where the channel winds past the military port of Kronstadt, but otherwise there are no navigational problems by day or by night.

Arriving at the estuary of the Bolshoya Neva, it is necessary to turn to starboard (i.e. upstream) before turning to port into a short buoyed channel leading to the passenger terminal for customs clearance.

It is possible to leave the Morskoy Canal at buoy No. 34, three miles to the northeast of the famous Tsars' Summer Palace at Petrodvoryets, and take a direct route northeast to the entrance to the river Neva along one of several buoyed channels much used by Meteor high speed jet foils, but these fairways are not marked on British charts, and unless a Russian chart is available, this is not recommended.

Anchorage

Anchoring is not prohibited outside the port area, the buoyed channels and the military areas around Kronstadt, but there are no anchorages as such.

Berthing

Visiting yachts will find it best to go to one of three yacht clubs:

The River Yacht Club (ex-Central Yacht Club)
The Baltic Shipping Company Yacht Club
The Navy Yacht Club (VMF)

After clearance, the customs officers will ask which club you wish to visit, and will telephone for a (free) pilot to be sent to guide you to the correct place.

The River Yacht Club, on Vasilievski Island not far from the passenger terminal, has permanently supervised moorings and is about 35 minutes from the city centre by bus or trolley bus.

The Baltic Shipping Company Club, a mile further north, has perhaps marginally better facilities but is less convenient for the city centre.

The Navy Club is very close to the passenger terminal, but hitherto has been very little used by visiting yachts.

Russian yacht clubs are becoming aware of the commercial opportunities of attracting yachts from overseas, and formal pricing policies are emerging.

Charges in the region of £5 to £10 per day are becoming the norm; for example, the Central Yacht Club's charges were $1 per metre in 1992.

Formalities

The berth used for clearance of yachts is at 59°55'·5N 30°14'·4E and is a low concrete quay at right angles to the channel, just before the Sea Station – the main terminal for passenger ships. The building marked 'Customs' on chart *2395* should be ignored.

In the daytime, at some point along the Morskoy Canal yachts may be met by a military launch and silently escorted to the passenger terminal.

Clearance is usually relaxed and friendly. One of the customs officers or border guards who will come on board will usually be able to speak a little English.

General facilities

Water, electricity and rubbish disposal facilities are available at all three clubs.

The Baltic Shipping Club has adequate toilets and showers, and the River Club is in the process of modernising its toilet facilities.

Shopping facilities are in all three cases some distance away, usually involving a bus ride or cycle trip. There is, however, an excellent private enterprise market on Vasiliyevski Island, not far from the River Yacht Club, where most essential foodstuffs can be bought without queuing, at prices which, although still cheap to Western visitors, are high for the local population.

City tours and guided visits to the many museums, art galleries and churches can usually be arranged for modest fees through the yacht clubs. Tickets for the Kirov Theatre are extremely difficult to obtain through official channels, but are easily purchased for a few dollars immediately before the performance from the black market dealers operating openly outside the theatre. Performances at the famous Philharmonia and other concert halls can usually be booked at the box office, even without significant knowledge of the language.

Yachting services

There are no filling stations; fuel can be obtained only by arrangement with club officers, and supplies are not guaranteed.

Gas is, as always in Russia, a problem. Propane cylinders can usually be refilled through the auspices of the yacht clubs.

Basic repairs can be arranged at the main yacht clubs, which have well equipped, if old fashioned, workshops. All spare parts, however, must be imported. Electronic skills are almost non-existent. The River Club has a sizeable sailmaking loft.

Communications

The yacht clubs are equipped with telephone, facsimile and telex facilities, and communication with the West is usually possible.

Travel

Taxis are available everywhere, but taxi drivers are well attuned to the presence of foreign tourists and usually demand payment in foreign currency. For major journeys it is as well to arrange taxis through the yacht club to avoid being charged excessive prices.

Vyborg

(**Viipuri** – Finnish)

60°42'N 28°45'E

Distances

Helsinki 125M, St Petersburg 85M.

Charts

Admiralty *2264* and *1090*
Finnish *13, 14, 140* and *141*

Lights

1. **Povorotnyy** 60°34'·5N 28°25'·6E Fl.WRG.1·5s18m7-2M White octagonal tower, red lantern, 13m Shore-G-359°-W-009°-R-020°-G-029°-W-231° 239°-G-249°-W-255°-R-270°
2. **Ostrov Igrivyy** Southeast buoy 60°35'N 28°28'·75E Q(6)+LFl.15s Yellow and black pillar

Note There are five sets of leading lights to take a vessel through the Vysotsk narrows into the buoyed channel leading to the junction of the Saimaa canal approach with the Vyborg final approach; see chart.

3. **Saymenskiy** 60°41'·9N 28°42'·8N Iso.Y.2s8m3M White column, red stripe, 4m. Consult text.

General

Vyborg was for centuries Finland's second most important town and cultural centre. It was held by Peter the Great for a short period as part of his programme to consolidate his grip on St Petersburg, but despite Russia's subsequent efforts to extend her influence over Keralia in the 18th and 19th centuries, Vyborg itself only passed to the Russians again after the Second World War. It is a commercial port dealing in timber, fish, agriculture, cement and ironware. It is of no great significance except for its proximity to the Saimaa canal; it is of interest here in that context and because it is one of the few Russian ports open to foreign yachts.

Approach

See plan page 96.
There are three routes to Povorotnyy[1]:

- The inshore route along the Finnish coast from Kotka or Hamina. The Finnish charts are essential for this passage. Finnish emigration and customs checks are carried out at the coast guard station at Santio Island (60°27'·5N 26°43'·5E). In 1992 this passage was closed to foreign yachts.
- The big-ship route south of Gogland to the Sommers roundabout (60°11'·5N 28°46'·2E), on between Bol'shoy Fiskar (60°24'·7N 27°56'·7E Fl2(W)8s) and Khalli (60°24'·3N 28°08'·4E Fl(W)4s), then past Rondo (60°27'·4N 28°21'·6E FlWRG.1·5s) northwards to Povorotnyy. It is possible for a small boat to deviate from the main route, but good charts are necessary. If leaving Finland, emigration and customs are at Haapasaari (60°17'·2N 27°11'·5N).
- The inshore route from St Petersburg, the Proliv B'yerkësund (Koiviston Salmi in Finnish), leading east of the three wooded islands of Ostrov Bol'shoy Berëzovyy, Ostrov Zapadnyy Berëzovyy and Ostrov Severnyy Berëzovyy.

After Povorotnyy pilotage is compulsory for all vessels; vessels may be led in groups. The route lies through the narrows of Vysotsk, a considerable commercial town where Russian immigration and customs are based, and then up an intermittently buoyed channel to Saymenskiy light[3], which not only marks the junction with the Saimaa canal but is also the front light for two sets of leading lights; see chart. Past Saymenskiy, a buoyed channel leads into Vyborg. At least 12 hours' notice of arrival at the pilot station, to be confirmed 2 hours before arriving, is required by the Vyborg port section of Inflot, Box 40, Vyborg, *Telex* 99-6412-1521 (no fax listed); they may also be contacted on VHF Ch 16 for discussion in Russian or English on VHF Ch 11. The information required is the name of the boat, its length, speed and time of arrival, and the name of the person requiring the service. The pilot station is on Vihrevoj (60°34'N 28°26'E), and big ships are normally boarded about 1M WSW of Mayachnyy (the island with light 1 at its north tip), but yachts may collect northwest of Ostrov Igrivyy.

Communications

Main-line railway between Helsinki and St Petersburg.

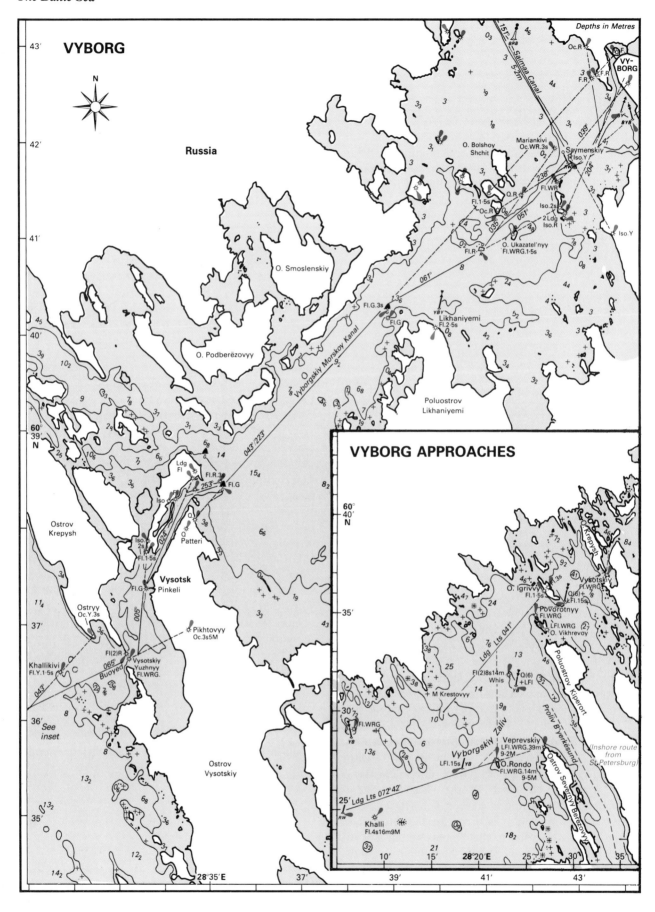

VYBORG

N

Russia

Depths in Metres

VYBORG APPROACHES

V. Finland

Finland, or Suomi, has the best cruising grounds in the Baltic and is one of the most socially advanced countries in the world. Sailing is a well established sport and facilities are excellent everywhere. The combination is a very good reason to pay a visit.

In this account, the Finnish version of place names has been used westwards to Turku (Swedish: Åbo) and the Swedish version thereafter.

The country

The name Suomi means the land of lakes and fens. A narrow coastal plain which supports limited farming is backed by a rocky plateau some 100m above sea level, containing thousands of lakes draining through rapids into the Gulf of Bothnia and Lake Ladoga. The plateau is forested and is mainly inhabited by wildlife. A third physical region is the uplands area of the far north, where the continuous low temperature makes all life difficult to sustain.

On the fringe of the highly indented Baltic coastline is a string of thousands of islands, at their most dense at the western end: Turku and the remarkable Åland islands.

A brief history

Finland was part of the kingdom of Sweden from 1154 to 1809, when it was invaded by Russia. At first, when it was a grand duchy in the Russian empire, Finland was treated liberally, but at the end of the century a Greater Russia chauvinistic movement resulted in the suppression of Finnish institutions. In the First World War the Finnish students surreptitiously turned to Germany for military training and formed a so-called Jäger battalion. At the time of the Russian revolution of 1917, all parties in Finland were agreed that Finland should be independent, but after they had taken advantage of the new Soviet constitution to make it so by a unilateral declaration, the division between the socialists, who wanted close ties with the USSR, and the conservatives, who wanted complete independence, led to civil war. As on the other shore of the Baltic, one side was supported by the USSR, the other by Germany. In the event, the conservatives, with the superior leadership of Mannerheim and the support of the Jägers, won. In the interwar period great economic and social progress was achieved and a sound democratic system consolidated, but Finland was unable to reduce the USSR's fear for the security of her western flank – a fear not lessened by the long memory of the damage done to Russian interests by the British navy operating in Finland during the Crimean War. In 1939 the USSR followed up her demand for a frontier adjustment and a base in Finland by invasion, and she forced a settlement in 1940. With the intervention of the Germans, hostilities soon restarted and the Finns, who were again rallied under Mannerheim, recaptured their territory only to be thrown out once more when the tide turned against Germany. During this period a small British force was for a time sent to help the Finns. An armistice in October 1944 settled the present Karelian border, west of its original line, which had Vyborg placed in Finland. For the last 45 years the Finns have been balancing between their democratic instincts and the necessity of horse trading with their powerful neighbour, an act which they have judged very finely whilst working actively to promote better relations between East and West.

The people

With a population of 5 million, Finland is a parliamentary democracy, with a president elected for six years and a single-chamber 200-seat parliament, elected every four years by proportional representation. In 1906, it was the first European country to grant women the vote. There are two national churches: Lutheran and Orthodox. One in six Finns attends university. 93% of Finns speak Finnish as their native tongue and 7% of them are Swedish speaking, mostly around Åland. Finnish, an agglutinative language related to Hungarian, is very difficult; Swedish is easier. Excellent English is spoken widely.

Åland, an ancient realm of 6,000 islands and skerries, and the oldest inhabited part of Finland, is a semi-autonomous province of Finland. Its population of 23,000 speak Swedish as their native tongue. It has its own parliament, flies its own flag, prints its own stamps and registers its own ships. Its citizens do not have to do military service as other Finnish citizens have to, and they are exempt from national taxation.

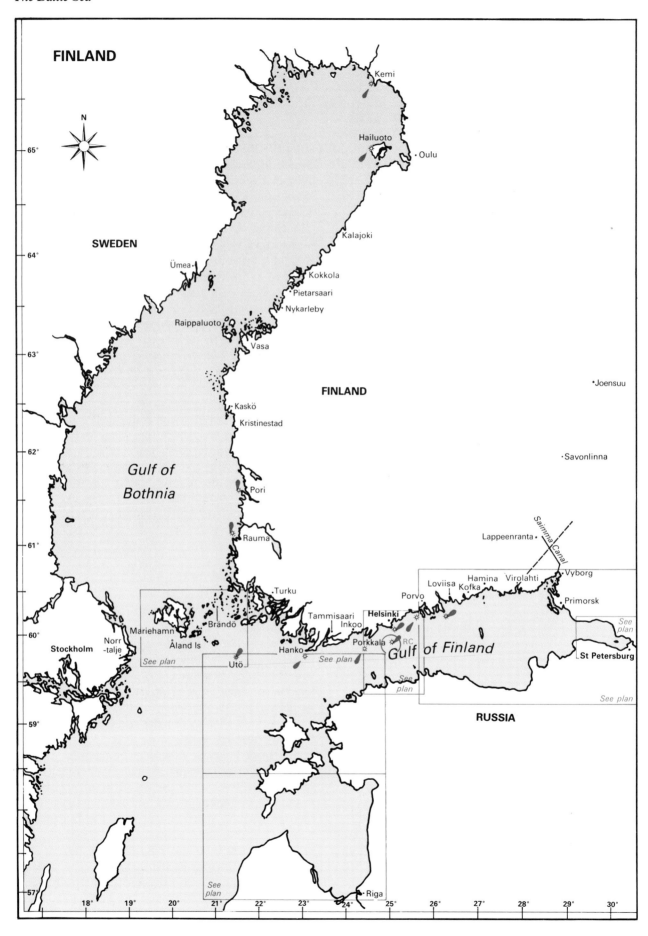

FINLAND

N

SWEDEN

FINLAND

·Joensuu

·Savonlinna

Kemi

Hailuoto   ·Oulu

Kalajoki

Ümea·   Kokkola
·Pietarsaari
·Nykarleby
Raippaluoto·
Vasa

Kaskö
Kristinestad

Gulf of Bothnia

Pori

Rauma

Lappeenranta·   Saimaa Canal

Vyborg
Virolahti
Loviisa Hamina
Porvo Kofka Primorsk
Helsinki
Turku
Tammisaari
Inkoo
Mariehamn   Brändö   Porkkala   RC   *Gulf of Finland*   *See plan*
Stockholm   Norr-talje   Åland Is   Hanko   *See plan*   St Petersburg
See plan   Utö

See plan

RUSSIA

See plan

See plan   Riga

The culture and history of the Åland islands are closely bound up with the sea and shipping. In the 19th century Åland dominated the world grain-shipping trade, and its remaining sailing traders, owned by Gustaf Erikson, were still in commission in 1945; the four-masted barque *Pommern* in the West Harbour at Mariehamn is a memorial to this era.

The economy

Finland's highly export-orientated market economy is based on private ownership. The chief natural resource is wood, and its derivatives – paper, paper board, wood pulp, veneers, plywood and timber – are important to the economy; there is a smaller but significant agricultural industry. There is much high-tech industry, producing electrical equipment, machinery and transport equipment (Finland leads the world in the design and construction of ice-breakers). A small volume product, but one of interest to sailors, is Stockholm tar, dry distilled from pine logs during a five-day smoulder in a covered tar pit. Natural resources apart from timber include copper, iron and nickel; a quarter of Finnish electricity is derived from water power. Finns have a standard of living matched by few other countries, but Finland is dependent upon world trade, and has been particularly affected by developments in the former USSR, which used to take about 20% of her exports.

Money

The currency of Finland is the Finnish mark (finmark).

Traveller's cheques, Eurocheques and major credit cards are widely accepted.

Shopping

Food is plentiful, and there are excellent, well stocked supermarkets everywhere. Prices are about 30–40% higher than those in England, except that fish (perhaps the most notable speciality of Finland) costs somewhat less than it does in the UK.

Beer can be bought in supermarkets and is not particularly expensive, but has an alcohol content of 2·8–3%. Full-strength beer (4·7–5·8%), wines and spirits can be bought only at branches of ALKO, the state alcohol company, at prices about 50% higher than UK prices.

Yacht clubs

The principal club is Nylandska Jaktklubben (NJK) which has extensive premises in Helsinki. It owns a number of islands and anchorages where its members carefully guard their privacy, and appropriate enquiries should be made at the club if a visit to one of these places is contemplated.

The Finnish Cruising Club (Sjöbjörnarna – Sea Bears) also owns islands and anchorages, and its rules forbid use by non-members.

Yacht services and chandlery

There are numerous good boatyards, and chandlery is easy to obtain.

Mooring fees are considerably lower than those in England, and diesel for use in boats is also relatively cheap. Butane is unobtainable but it may be possible to have propane cylinders refilled.

English-language weather forecasts are broadcast twice daily by each station, Helsinki at 0733 and 1933 UT and Mariehamn at 0833 and 2033 UT.

Communications

Most Finnish telephone kiosks can be used for dialling numbers in other countries. The international exchange access code is 990, followed by 44 for calls to the UK.

In Helsinki, weather reports and news in English can be obtained by dialling 040. News in English is also broadcast by VHF stations at 2155.

There are facsimile and telex facilities at commercial bureaux and at most large post offices.

Letters take about 4–5 days to or from the United Kingdom. It is essential to quote the correct postal index (post code) when addressing letters to Finland.

Travel

Helsinki has good communications by air with all parts of Europe, and Mariehamn and Turku can be reached from Stockholm. There are competitive ferry services linking Helsinki with Turku, Mariehamn, Stockholm and many other destinations, including Tallinn in Estonia. The rail/ferry and coach/ferry services to western Europe are good, as is the rail service within Finland.

Time

Finnish time is 2 hours ahead of UT in winter and 3 hours ahead in summer.

Formalities

The coastguard service is the combined customs and immigration authority. Its boats and helicopters are dark green with a diagonal orange and white stripe. Their boats make contact by radio (Ch 16) or by coming alongside and shouting. Coastguard officers are friendly but thorough in their dealings with visiting yachts.

Yachts are required to go to frontier guard stations which are often on small islands, see below. If a yacht has not been intercepted it should call on VHF Ch 16 when close to the coast and seek instructions.

The coastguard normally ask for details of the expected route in Finnish waters and expect to be informed of significant changes of plan. They should be contacted for outward clearance immediately prior to departure from the country.

If in transit to Russia or the Baltic States and carrying large supplies of duty-free drinks, the coastguard should be told. Excess liquor will be sealed in bond aboard for the duration of the stay in Finland.

A yacht may remain in Finland without penalty for one year provided that the owner does not leave the country. It may, however, be left to winter if a bank bond, possibly 10–20% of the value of the yacht, is produced, and providing work is to be done on it. The amount of the bond is negotiated with customs and is against default of conditions laid down by them. An owner leaving a boat in Finland without making appropriate arrangements with customs may be charged 22% of the value of the boat as assessed by customs and fined 22% of the same value in lieu of prosecution.

The Finnish flag is white with a blue Scandinavian cross.

The Åland flag is blue with a red cross on a yellow cross. Even Finnish yachts wear this courtesy flag when west of Skiftet, the sound dividing the Åland from the Finnish archipelago.

UK representation

British Embassy Itainen Puistotie 17, 00140 Helsinki ☎ (358) 0-90 66 13 42 *Fax* (358) 0-90 66 13 42 *Telex* 121122.

Turku British Consulate Turun Kauppakamari, Puollalankatu 1, Turku ☎ (358) 21-50 14 40 *Telex* 62114.

Mariehamn British Consulate Södragatan 16 B4, 22100 Mariehamn ☎ (358) 16620 28439 *Fax* (358) 16901.

Finnish Embassy in London 32 Grosvenor Gardens SW1W 0DH ☎ 071-235 9531.

Navigation

Although Admiralty charts are very good for navigating at sea, it is essential to obtain Finnish charts to enjoy the delights of cruising inside the archipelago. These can be bought as individual charts or in book form (in which case a considerable amount of additional detail and useful information is provided) and are very easily available, not only at each of the main Finnish ports, but also in Sweden and from Kapitän Stegmann and Company, the chart agent at the Holtenau lock on the Kiel Canal. These charts make navigation straightforward in the many channels. The channels have both obvious leading marks and black-and-white spar buoys with cardinal stripes but no topmarks. However, Finnish charts are based on Russian surveys of the 19th century and are less reliable in areas outside the marked channels.

Admiralty *Baltic Pilot Volume III (NP 20)* covers the southern part of Finland in great detail, but the written description of the channels is so involved that the information is sometimes difficult to interpret quickly. It also lacks much of the practical information required by yachtsmen. Nevertheless, it is an extremely useful publication to have on board.

There are no other English-language pilot guides to Finnish waters for yachtsmen.

Decca coverage of the Finnish coast is not completely reliable. It relies on a chain with only two slaves. It is reportedly sensitive to fog or rain. West of Hanko master and slave are in line, with resulting poor fixes, and from Utö westwards it is better to use the Baltic chain.

Coast radio

Finland's VHF coast radio stations are extremely well organised and convenient to use. There are two stations: Helsinki and Mariehamn, each with a number of remotely controlled transmitters. All parts of the coastline have excellent coverage. There are good public correspondence facilities, the procedure being to call on the working frequency rather than on VHF Ch 16. For details see page 7, or the books of Finnish charts, which contain maps showing the layout and channel details of the stations.

Frontier guard stations

Calling channel for all is 16. Working hours are 0800–2000 every day.

Frontier station	Fairway
Santio or Hurppu 60°27'·5N 27°43'·5E	Coastal fairway leading past Santio.
Haapasaari 60°17'N 27°11'·5E	Fairway leading past Haapasaari.
Boistö 60°19'·5N 26°30'E	Fairway leading from Tainio lighthouse past Orrengrund.
Pirttisaari 60°10'N 25°26'·5E	Fairway leading past Porvoo lighthouse.
Suomenlinna 60°09'N 24°59'E	Fairway leading from Helsinki lighthouse past Harmaja.
Bågaskär 59°57'N 24°01'E	Fairways leading past Porkkala lighthouse and Sömmaro.

Amongst the Finnish islands.

Amongst the Finnish islands the channels are extremely well marked.

Hanko 59°48'·5N 22°55'E	Fairways leading past Russarö.
Fagerhölm 60°06'·5N 21°42'·5E	Fairway leading from Üto past Fagerhölm.
Kökar 59°56'N 20°52'E	Fairway leading past Kökarsören.
Storklubb 59°58'N 20°56'·5E	Fairway leading from Nyhamn and Üto past Storklubb.
Mariehamn 60°05'N 19°56'E	Fairways leading past Körsö or Nyhamn.
Enskär 60°13'N 19°19'·5E	Fairway leading past Signilskär; fairways leading west of Eckerö past Sälskär.

Cruising areas

Cruising in Finland means meandering amid tree-clad islands, with clear, tideless and sheltered waters, colourful villages, yachting marinas, secluded anchorages, warm summer days, rich and fertile land and fragrant forests carpeted with pine needles. The people are extremely friendly and wildlife abounds: wild swans, eider, deer, sea trout, turbot and many other species. There is a special satisfaction in being able to navigate in complete confidence through the myriad channels between the islands, often only a matter of feet from the rocks, with the use of the Finnish charts. The Åland Islands, a favourite cruising ground for yachtsmen from Sweden and Finland, are of particular interest, not only because of their beauty, but also because of their connection with the sailing traders.

A separate cruising ground is the Saimaa Lake area, an immense landlocked complex of lakes entered through the Saimaa Canal. The Saimaa Canal starts near Vyborg, and runs through territory secured by the Russians in 1944 and leased back to the Finns in 1963 in return for the undertaking by the latter of the upkeep of the canal. The Saimaa lakes are a favourite cruising ground for local yachtsmen, especially at the time of the opera festival in July, but little visited by foreign yachts. The Board of Management of the Saimaa Canal issues a well produced booklet of instructions for small-boat traffic in the Saimaa Canal.

The Gulf of Bothnia extends for some 350 miles. On the Finnish side the Skärgård continues to a point just south of Rauma. It starts again about 10 miles south of Vasa and runs some 50 miles to Pietarsaari (Swedish: Jakobstad), home of Swan Yachts. In between the coast is flat, and beyond Pietarsaari it becomes lonely. Rauma and Pietarsaari can carry out repairs and provide stores and fuel; other places worth visiting are Nystad, Kristinestad, Kaskö, Vasa and Karleby (north of Pietarsaari).

Saimaa

Charts and guides

Finnish chart *Volumes L and M 240.*
Saimaan Kanavan Kartasto Viipuri − Lappeen ranta 1:10,000 (Finnish chart of the canal).
Saimaa Matkailukardda (touring map at 1:250,000 of the entire system).
Venematkailu Annual magazine covering lakeland harbours and facilities, with good aerial photographs.

General

Saimaa, a beautiful lake area famous for its opera season, is reached through the Saimaa Canal, which is operated by the Finns under an agreement with the Russians. The lakes are the highway for a great timber trade; log rafts, made up from felled timber piled on the ice during the winter and cleared from the south as the ice melts, are frequently met as they are moved under tow at an unstoppable knot or two. The area is also famous for the production of Stockholm tar.

The lakes are navigable for deep-draught yachts with fixed masts for some 200M to Kuopio and Joensuu. There is free sailing on the larger bodies of water, but there are many sheltered and often tortuous leads. The area is very well marked and even the smallest leads have transits. Savonlinna, a bottleneck through which all the routes pass, is the seat of the opera festival each July. It is a good communications centre and is convenient for crew changes.

Approach

See Vyborg (page 105) for the approach to the entrance of the canal. Two weeks' notice of arrival is required by the board of management of the Saimaa Canal, Itäinen kanavatie 2, SF 53420, Lappeen-ranta, Finland, ☎ (358) 53-85170 and *Fax* (358) 53-6259210. Pilotage and canal dues are modest. A Russian visa is not necessary unless Vyborg is to be visited. Inbound convoys are on Wednesday, Friday and Sunday; outbound on Tuesday, Thursday and Saturday; at other times a pilot may be engaged at extra cost. The Russian pilot joins the convoy at Vihrevoj island and leaves it at the frontier at Nuijamaa. There are strict regulations about safety equipment to be carried; the board of management produce a booklet of instructions in English for small-boat traffic which includes details of both Finnish and Russian formalities.

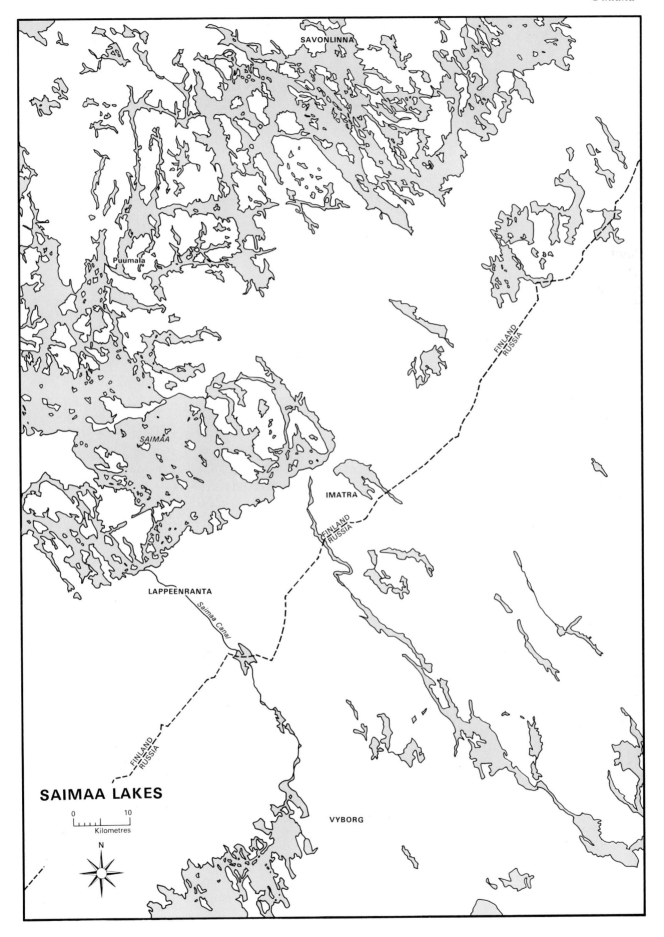

SAVONLINNA

Puumala

SAIMAA

FINLAND
RUSSIA

IMATRA

FINLAND
RUSSIA

LAPPEENRANTA

Saimaa Canal

FINLAND
RUSSIA

SAIMAA LAKES

0   10
Kilometres

N

VYBORG

Lake harbours

Lappeenranta

61°04'N 28°11'E

General

A centre for the timber processing industry near the head of the canal. It is a friendly town with several well sheltered yacht harbours. A tour of the paper mill is interesting, and the old military area on a hill overlooking the harbour has a good museum where the old Majrska tea room is worthwhile.

Approach

The approach is through the commercial port and quite complicated; the Saimaa chart booklet has details. The overhead clearance shown on the cables is nearer 18m than the 12m indicated; taller masts have to make a detour.

Berthing

There are two municipal guest harbours; the first, on the starboard hand when entering, has all facilities but is a good hike from town. The second, at the limit of navigation into town, is more conveniently and most attractively placed. In both harbours moor bows-to with a line to a buoy.

Facilities

Both harbours have water and electricity at the berths and toilets, showers and sauna ashore. The first harbour has a washing machine and a restaurant.

Imatra

61°13'N 28°43'E

General

A small town on the Vuoski, the only river flowing out of the southern lakes into Lake Ladoga, over the border in Russia. There are spectacular rapids; a hydroelectric station just south of the town helps control lake levels. The sluices are opened at set times daily as a tourist attraction.

Approach

Straightforward.

Berthing

Guest docks on the east side of the bay with 2m or more at all berths. Moor bows to dock with a stern line to a buoy.

Formalities

Book in at the hotel on the hilltop over the dock.

Facilities

Water and electricity at the berths. Toilets and showers in the hotel. Shopping at hotel for ordinary food requirements.

Fuel at the marina at the south end of the bay.

Puumala

61°31'N 28°11'E

General

A small town through which all traffic passes.

Approach

Straightforward.

Berthing

Alongside at the municipal quay in more than 3m, or at a small yacht dock controlled by the adjacent garage.

Formalities

If in the yacht dock, ask at the garage.

Facilities

Good supermarket five minutes' walk up the hill. Banks and small shops. Cheapest fuel in Finland.

Savonlinna

61°52'N 28°54'E

General

Savonlinna is a good turning point for a short cruise in the lakes, and can be reached in two days from the canal or equally after a week's pottering.

It is a charming small tourist town straddling several islands, forming a bridge across the Saimaa lakes, and home of the famous July opera festival which is held in the castle. It is also the home of many of the old boats still in use, which, though now converted from steam to diesel, still lend their own grace to the scene. There is an interesting maritime museum.

Approach

Straightforward.

Berthing

- Harri Westburg, on the west side of town. A dull area but handy for shops. Bows-to with stern buoys.
- Koulukadun, attractively placed adjacent to the castle. Will accommodate boats up to 18m.
- Casinon, north of the town and requiring an inconvenient passage for sailboats through opening bridges. A bit cramped for the bigger boats. Bows-to with stern buoys.

Facilities

There is a good daily open market on the quay.

Harri Westburg Water, electricity, fuel, small chandlery. Café.

Koulukadun Water and electricity on the docks. Toilet, showers in the hotel at 100m. Free cars for shopping and movement to and from the bus and the railway station and the airport.

Casinon All facilities in the nearby Casino hotel.

Other places

Punkaharju 61°45'N 29°25'E

A series of ridges formed by glacial action. Passage from the southwest through some of the most attractive leads in the lakes. Home of the Retretti underground art centre and concert hall.

Kuopio 62°50'N 27°40'E

A large modern town in a beautiful area at the northwest limit of navigation for boats with fixed masts of more than 12·5m.

Joensuu 62°35'N 29°45'E

A small sedate town at the northeast limit of navigation for boats with fixed masts of more than 12·5m

Kotka

60°28'N 26°27'E

Distances

Helsinki 60M, Vyborg 60M, St Petersburg 110M.

Charts and guides

Admiralty charts *2357, 2393, 503*
Finnish charts *Volume A*, charts *901, 902, 14*
Baltic Pilot Volume III (NP 20)

Lights
Approach

1. Kotkan Majakka 60°10'·3N 26°39'·2E Fl(4)20s23m 16M Yellow metal column, blue band, helicopter platform

Entrance

2. Lelleri 60°24'N 26°58'·5E Fl(2)WRG.5s5m7M Lantern on concrete base, white to the S, red to the N 144°-G-167°-W-174°-R-244°-G-330·5°-W-336°-R-354°

General

Kotka is a small town and an important port. It is a useful point of departure from Finland to St Petersburg or Vyborg.

Approach

The inshore approach from Helsinki passes north of the island of Kaunissaari Fagerö, then follows leading marks west of the islands of Varissaari and Pieri Varissaari. From the southeast the approach is close east of the islands of Haapasaari and Lelleri, then follows a series of well marked channels leading east of Varissaari and Pieri Varissaari.

Anchorage

It is not practicable to anchor in the immediate vicinity of Kotka.

Berthing

The yacht harbour is at Sapokanpalahti (60°27'·4N 26°57'·3E), immediately west of the causeway leading to Kuusinen island. It is best initially to moor alongside the fuel berth for berthing instructions.

Formalities

If coming from the west it is likely that clearance will already have been obtained. Coming from Russia, however, clearance should be obtained at the island of Haapasaari, about 12M southeast of Kotka.

Facilities

Water, electricity, toilets and showers are available.

The shopping centre, where most food requirements can be met, is about ten minutes' walk from the yacht harbour. There are also banks, restaurants and hotels in the town.

Yachting services

Fuel and some small items of chandlery can be bought at the fuelling berth.

Weather forecasts are broadcast at 0733 and 1933 UT by Helsinki radio on VHF Ch 25 and 27.

Communications

Telephone and postal services in the town. Helsinki radio handles public correspondence on VHF Ch 25 and 27.

Travel

Good coach and rail connections to Helsinki, whence there are good connections to all parts of western Europe.

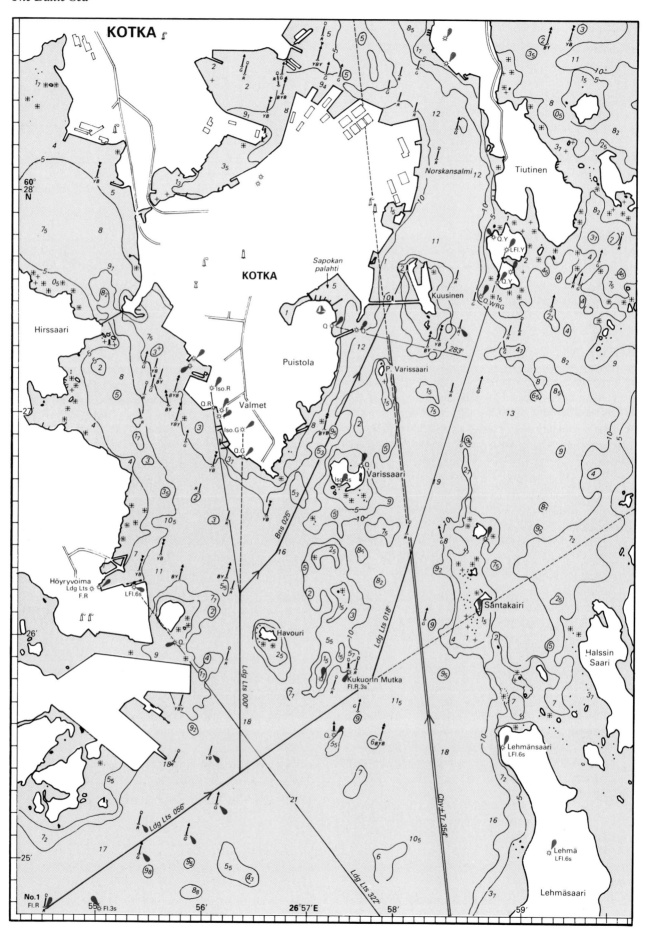

Helsinki

(Helsingfors)

60°10'N 24°57'E

Distances

Tallinn 48M, St Petersburg 170M, Hanko 70M.

Charts and guides

Admiralty charts *2248* and *2224*
Finnish charts *Volume B*, charts *719, 18*
Baltic Pilot Volume III (NP 20)

Lights

1. **Helsinki** 59°56'·9N 24°55'·7E LFl.12s25m18M White tower, red top, three galleries, aluminium lantern, 25m Racon all round 13M
2. **Harmaja** Ldg Lts 007° *Front* 60°06'·3N 24°58'·7E Oc.WRG.6s24m19M Red round tower, white band, square base 004·5°-W-010·5°-R-168°-G-187°-W-193°-R-212°-W-250°-R-260°-W-312°-G-004·5° Racon all round 9-15M
   Suomenlinna church *Rear* 2·6M from front 60°08'·9N 24°59'·4E Fl(4)15s54m22M Cupola on church tower. Racon all round 14-17M

General

Helsinki, the capital of Finland, has a population of over 500,000. It is a prosperous, well planned and pleasant city with the relaxed and friendly atmosphere typical of most major Scandinavian capitals. Nearly everyone speaks fluent English and the standard of living is as high as that anywhere in the world. The shopping centre is expensive and has high-class shops of every description. There are excellent outdoor and indoor markets close to the harbour.

The historic buildings, such as the cathedral and the university in the old part of the city, are aesthetically and historically pleasing – but perhaps it is the wide-ranging examples of modern architecture in the centre which contribute most to the atmosphere of life and excitement which the city exudes.

South Harbour (Eteläsatama), the main harbour for passenger ships and yachts, is conveniently close to the city centre and is always full of interest and activity.

Approach

Helsinki is surrounded by water on three sides, and there are many possible approaches through the hundreds of nearby islands. However, although local yachtsmen appear to navigate freely in these waters with impunity, the visitor is advised to use only the main routes indicated, at least until familiar with local hazards. Large ships have little difficulty in entering, even at night, but yachts unfamiliar with the local geography are recommended to enter only in daylight.

Whichever approach is used, it is essential to be equipped with Admiralty chart *2224*, Finnish chart *18* or, best of all, *Volume B* of the Finnish detailed charts. See plan on page 88.

From south This is the main approach from the open sea. From Helsinki light, the channel is the main shipping route and lies in a generally northerly direction, with Harmaja lighthouse in line with Suomenlinna church. It then passes close east of the Harmaja light, but yachts should not attempt to follow the main shipping channel between the islands of Susisaari and Vallisaari. It is better to keep west of the island of Susisaari and enter South Harbour by the southern entrance, between the islands of Sarkkä and Lansi Mustasaari and west of Luoto island. The channel is well marked by buoys, beacons and leading lights.

From west The inshore passage through the islands from the west passes between the islands of Melkki and Tiirakari, and thence continues in a generally northeasterly direction, also to enter South Harbour through the southern entrance.

This approach is very clearly marked, but it is easy to be confused by the plethora of beacons, lights and leading marks. Suomenlinna church tower is a useful landmark throughout the approach.

From east A third deep-water channel for vessels using the inshore route from the east passes south of the islands of Santahamina and Vallisaari, joining the main channel from the south approximately one mile north of the Harmaja light.

Formalities

After inbound yachts have passed close to the east of the Harmaja lighthouse, a coastguard launch normally intercepts them with instructions on where to put in for clearance. Until 1991, clearance was carried out in North Harbour (Pohjoissatama), but there is now a clearance point specially for yachts, situated in a deep but narrow rocky inlet on the west side of Suomenlinna island, at 60°08'·8N 24°59'·1E. Normal working hours are 0800–2000, but the point is open 24 hours.

If a coastguard launch does not materialise on approaching Suomenlinna, or if the time of arrival is outside the above times, contact the coastguard via VHF Ch 16 to ask for instructions.

Anchorage

Although there are few official restrictions on anchoring in the Helsinki area, in practice it is almost impossible as it is difficult to find an anchorage which does not involve landing on private property.

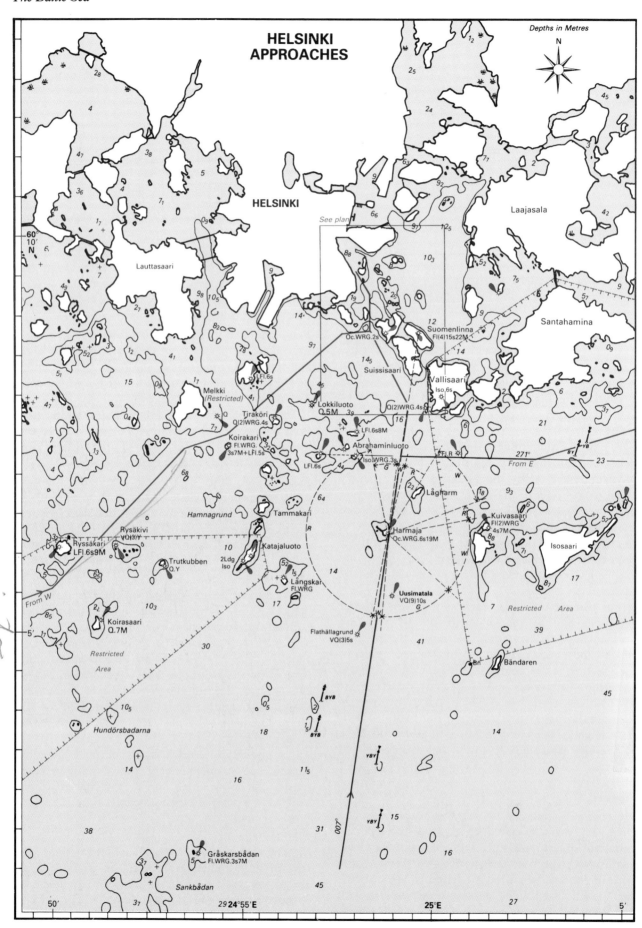

The Baltic Sea

HELSINKI
APPROACHES

Depths in Metres

N

HELSINKI

See plan

Laajasala

Lauttasaari

60°
10'
N

Santahamina

Suomenlinna
Fl(4)15s22M

Suissisaari

Vallisaari
Iso.6s

Melkki
(Restricted)

LFl.6s

Tiraköri
Q(2)WRG.4s

Q

Lokkiluoto
Q.5M

Q(2)WRG.4s

Koirakari
Fl.WRG.
3s7M+LFl.5s

LFl.6s8M

Abrahaminluoto

Iso.WRG.3s

LFl.6s

Fl.R

271°
From E

23

BY
YB

Lågharm

Hamnagrund

Tammakari

Kuivasaari
Fl(2)WRG
4s7M

Rysäkivi
VQ(3)Y

Ryssäkari
LFl.6s9M

Harmaja
Oc.WRG.6s19M

Isosaari

Katajaluoto

From W

Trutkubben
Q.Y

2Ldg
Iso

Långskar
Fl.WRG

Koirasaari
Q.7M

*Restricted
Area*

Uusimatala
VQ(9)10s
G

Restricted   Area

Flathällagrund
VQ(3)5s

Bn
Bändaren

Hundörsbadarna

BYB

007°

BYB

YBY

YBY

Gråskarsbådan
Fl.WRG.3s7M

Sankbådan

50'
29 **24°55'E**
25°E
5'

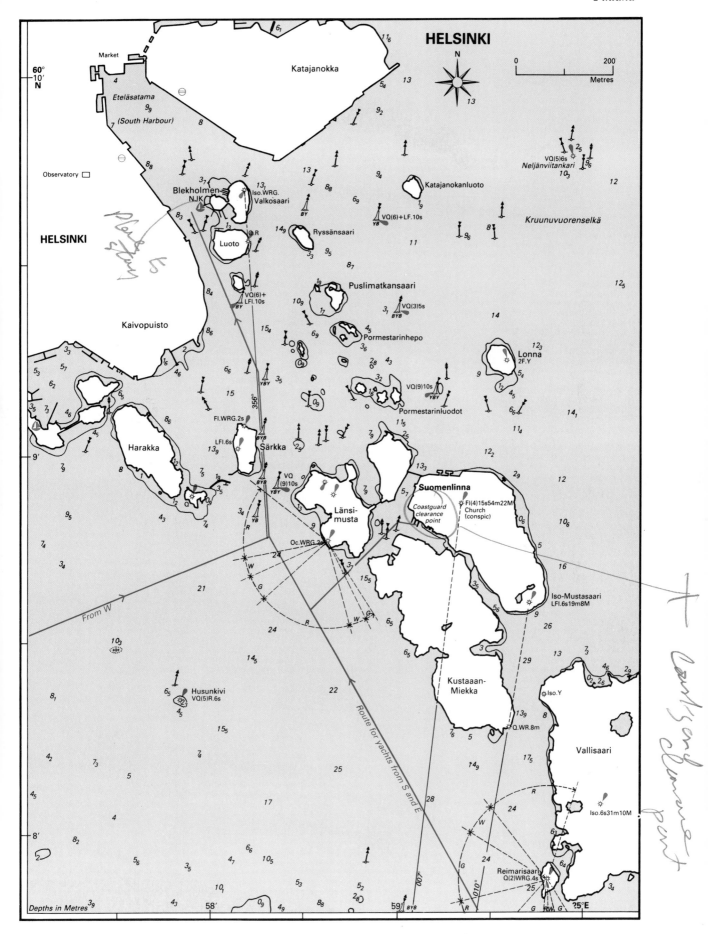

HELSINKI

Market

Katajanokka

Etelässatama
(South Harbour)

Observatory

Blekholmen
NJK
Valkosaari
Iso.WRG.

Luoto

Ryssänsaari

HELSINKI

Kaivopuisto

Katajanokanluoto

VQ(6)+LF.10s

Kruunuvuorenselkä

VQ(5)6s
Neljänviitankari

Puslimatkansaari

VQ(3)5s

Pormestarinhepo

VQ(9)10s

Lonna
2F.Y

Pormestarinluodot

VQ(6)+
LFI.10s

Harakka

FI.WRG.2s
LFI.6s
Särkka

Länsi-
musta

Suomenlinna

Coastguard
clearance
point

FI(4)15s54m22M
Church
(conspic)

Iso-Mustasaari
LFI.6s19m8M

VQ
(9)10s

Oc.WRG.2s

From W

Route for yachts from S and E

Husunkivi
VQ(5)R.6s

Kustaaan-
Miekka

Iso.Y

Q.WR.8m

Vallisaari

Iso.6s31m10M

Reimarisaari
Q(2)WRG.4s

Entering South Harbour, Helsinki. The NJK club is to the right.

NJK, the oldest yacht club in Finland, on the island of Blekholmen in South Harbour, Helsinki.

Berthing

There are about fifteen yacht harbours and clubs in the immediate vicinity of Helsinki, but the visitor will normally find it most convenient to head for the attractive NJK club, the oldest yacht club in Finland, on the tiny island of Blekholmer (60°09'·6N 24°58'E) in South Harbour. It has a large visitors' pontoon with 3m depth all round it, and can accommodate yachts of up to around 20 tonnes. A two-minute ferry journey (every 20 minutes) connects with the mainland.

The HSS Yacht Club (60°09'·2N 24°57'·5E) is also convenient for the city centre, and has excellent facilities including fuel and launderette.

Large yachts, with special permission from the Helsinki harbour office, can moor alongside the quay in the northeast corner of South Harbour, but there are no facilities.

There is also a yacht basin, designed for shopping stops, close to the covered market in the northwest corner of South Harbour. It is suitable only for small boats, and has a time limit of 2 hours.

General facilities

Water, electricity, shower and toilet facilities are all provided at the NJK club, and there are public telephones and an excellent restaurant overlooking the harbour.

The open-air and covered markets situated on the north side of South Harbour can satisfy most needs, although it is perhaps for their wide variety of fish, fresh vegetables and fruit that they are most famous.

There are many excellent supermarkets in the main shopping centre, a few minutes' walk from the markets, but especially recommended are Stockmanns – the Harrods of Helsinki – and several which are open on Saturdays and Sundays underneath the main railway station.

Low alcohol beer can be bought in the supermarkets, but other alcoholic drinks can be purchased only from ALKO, the state-owned liquor store. There is a branch a few minutes' walk from the harbour. Prices approach double UK prices.

There is a tourist information office at the end of the harbour, and there are also banks, restaurants and hotels in the vicinity.

Yachting services

Fuel is readily available at several quayside filling stations.

Propane bottles with standard (international) fittings may be refillable. Try the Esso main depot at Degerö (Laajasalo), Shell Tullinpuomi, 116 Mannerheimintie (☎ (358) 0-413477), or Julius Tallberg & Co, ☎ (358) 0-826122.

There is a well stocked chandlery, O.Y. Maritim, overlooking the harbour, and a very large hardware and ironmongery store, Renlund, about five minutes' walk from the harbour.

Sailmakers and a wide range of engineering services can be located by enquiring at the NJK office.

Helsinki Radio broadcasts excellent English-language weather forecasts for all sea areas at 0733 and 1933 UT on all VHF working channels.

Communications

International telephone calls can be made without difficulty through Helsinki Radio and from all public telephones.

Telex and facsimile services are available at the main post office near the main railway station.

Travel

There are good rail, air and coach services between Helsinki and all major European cities.

Hanko

(Hangö)

59°49'·2N 22°58'·3E

Distances

Turku 50M, Mariehamn 100M, Rīga 170M, Tallinn 60M, Helsinki 70M.

Charts and guides

Admiralty charts *3898, 2331* and *523*
Finnish charts *Volume B,* charts *728, 21* or *22*
Baltic Pilot Volume III (NP 20)

Lights

1. **Bengtskär** 59°43'·4N 22°30'·1E Fl(3)15s51m10M Round granite tower and building. Wind generator 46m
2. **Russarö** 59°46'N 22°57'·1E Fl(4)45s34m27M Red octagonal tower, 21m 174°-vis-115°
3. **Djubkobben** Ldg Lts 327° *Front* 59°48'·4N 22°58'·2E Fl.3s8m11M, by day 8M, Red rectangle, yellow stripe, on framework tower
   Rear 59°49'·1 22°57'·2E LFl.12s22m11M, by day 9M, Red rectangle, yellow stripe, on framework tower
   Both Visible arc by night 324·5°-329·5°, by day 321·5°-332·5°
4. **Hankoneimi** Ldg Lts 319° *Front* 59°49'·3N 22°55'·6E Q.Y.17m6M Red rectangle, yellow stripe, on framework tower
   Rear 59°49'·4N 22°55'·4E LFl.Y.6s26m9M Red rectangle, yellow stripe, on framework tower
   Both Visible arc 315°-323°

General

The pleasant town of Hanko, population 12,000, was founded in 1874 and owes its prosperity mainly to the fact that its port is closed by ice for shorter periods in winter than other Finnish ports. It is also popular as a holiday resort and tourist centre.

The Baltic Sea

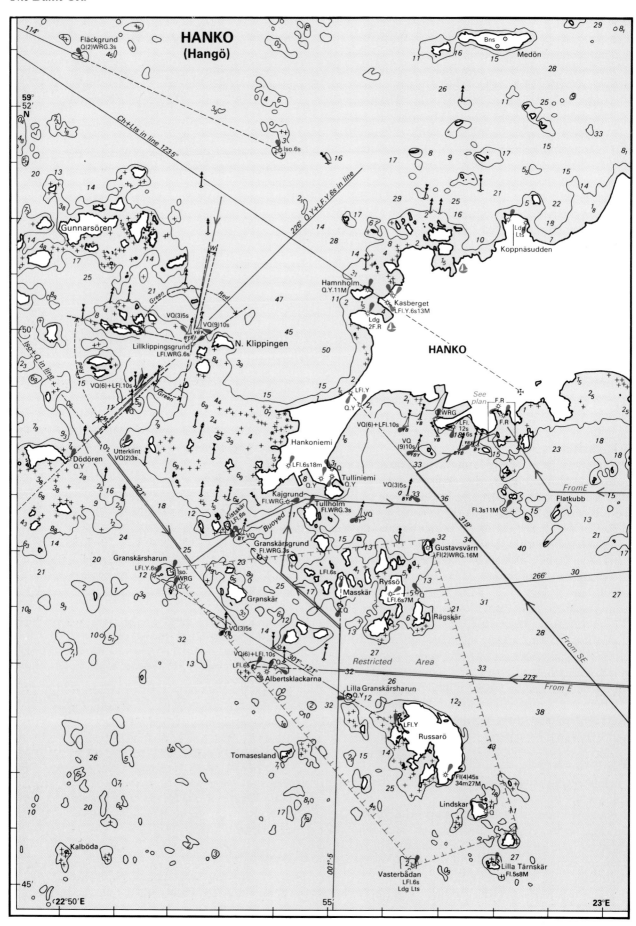

122

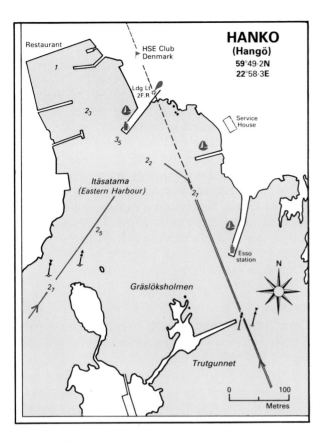

HANKO
(Hangö)
59°49·2N
22°58·3E

Approach

The waters immediately around Hanko contain many hazards. However, the area is well marked with leading marks, buoys and beacons and, using one of the detailed charts (it is best to use *Volume B* of the books of detailed charts of Finnish waters), navigation in daylight is a great deal easier than appears at first sight. It is recommended that entry by night should not be attempted until familiar with the waters.

From southeast From No. 1 east cardinal beacon, approximately 4 miles southeast of Russarö lighthouse, steer 327° with Djubkobben leading lights[3] in line and then turn onto the Hankoneimi leading lights[4] on 319°. The channel is marked by further east and west cardinal beacons, numbered 3, 4 and 5.

About 300m before reaching Maejerfelt islet, three cardinal marks (east, west and north) will come roughly in line on a heading of 060°, about ½M off. Turn on to 060°, leave all the east marks to port and the west and north marks to starboard, and enter the harbour by its southwest entrance, which passes immediately south of Drottningberget and, although very narrow, is well marked.

From east The beautiful inshore passage from Helsinki to Hanko passes close north of the islands of Mulan and Andalskär, and leads directly to the well marked southeast entrance of Eastern Harbour. The route is clearly shown on Finnish detailed charts.

Its Eastern Harbour (Itäsatama) is the yacht harbour, accommodating 250 boats.

From northwest Arriving at Hanko through the islands from Turku or Utö, the route passes close south of Fläckgrund lighthouse, 5 miles northwest of the town, and follows a somewhat circuitous path through a number of well marked channels to arrive at the southwest entrance to Eastern Harbour.

It is essential to be equipped with the Finnish detailed charts for navigation in this area.

Anchorage

Although there are few restrictions on anchoring, the depth of the water and the nature of the bottom make it impractical to consider anchoring off in the vicinity of the town.

Berthing

Whilst local yachts may choose to moor in other places, it is recommended that visiting yachts without local knowledge should use Hanko Eastern Harbour (59°49'·2N 22°58'·3E), a first-class, modern yacht harbour with good facilities and excellent shelter.

Entry is either by the narrow channel from the southwest or by the main entrance from the southeast. Both are well marked. Mooring is bows-to with stern to pickup buoy. In the south end of the harbour the private marina Itämeren Portti (Gate to the Baltic) has a visitors' pontoon and good facilities, and is a good place to leave a boat for a day or two.

Mooring fees include electricity and free use of showers and saunas from 0700 to 1200 and from 1900 to 2100.

Formalities

If entering Finland, contact the coastguard on VHF Ch 16 when approaching the port.

General facilities

The facilities of Eastern Harbour include water, electricity, toilets, showers, saunas, laundry, solarium, cafeteria and three restaurants.

General provisions may be bought from a mobile shop or from the wide variety of shops in the town centre, approximately 1km away.

The town centre has a tourist office, banks, hotels and additional restaurants.

Yachting services

There is a fuelling station in the harbour.

Repair facilities are limited. It is best, if time allows, to seek engineering services, sail repairs and chandlery in Helsinki. However, in case of emergency the harbour office will advise on where repairs can be effected. There is a yacht chandlery.

A videotext weather forecast is displayed in the window of the harbour office, and Helsinki Radio has a remote transmitting station at Hanko, broadcasting excellent English-language weather forecasts on VHF Ch 3, 25 and 86 at 0733 and 1933 UT.

Communications

All public telephones provide international call facilities. Helsinki Radio, through its satellite transmitter at Hanko, takes public correspondence on VHF Ch 3, 25 and 86.

The harbour office can be contacted via VHF Ch 68.

Hanko is served by the Finnish railway system, and international travel can be arranged via Helsinki or Turku.

Turku

(Åbo)

60°20'·2N 22°14'·3E

Distances

Mariehamn 75M, Hanko 50M.

Charts and guides

Admiralty charts *2297, 3897* and *3899*
Finnish charts *Volume D*, charts *25, 26* and *27*
Baltic Pilot Volume III (NP 20)

Lights

1. **Lillharun** 59°43'·6N 21°24'·2E Fl.WRG.7s17m10M Black concrete tower 262°-G-340°-W-045°-R-101°-G-148°-W-156°-R-172° Racon all round 12M. Wind generator
2. **Utö** 59°46'·9N 21°22'·3E Fl.12s40m26M Centre of island. Square white granite tower, red stripes, 24m
3. **Bokullankivi** 59°50'·8N 21°25'·4E Fl.WRG.4s9m9M White tower, black band 009°-G-050°-W-054°-R-165°-G-232·5°-W-236·5°-R-009° Racon all round 10M
4. **Lövskär** 60°13'·2N 21°43'·6E Q.WRG.7m5M Framework tower 197°-G-254°-W-258°-R-000°-W-197°
5. **Petäis** 60°14'·3N 21°48'·1E Fl.WRG.3s6m4M Black concrete base, white lantern 030°-G-051°-W-055°-R-130°-G-209°-W-230°-R-240°
6. **Orhisaari** 60°16'·5N 22°00'E Fl.WRG.18m8M White metal framework tower, concrete base 019°-G-073°-W-158°-G-210°-W-217°-R-232°-G-246°-W-266°-R-284°
7. **Rajakari** 60°22'·7N 22°06'E Fl.WRG.13m11M Red and white round concrete tower 166°-G-172°-W-173°-R-194°-G-203·5°-W-205°-R-257°-G-016°-W-024·5°-R-031°

General

Turku (Swedish: Åbo), the capital of Finland until the early 19th century, is the country's third largest city, with a population of about 160,000. It is also one of the most important ports in Finland, handling oil, containers and other freight, together with busy ferry services to Stockholm.

The modern city, built on a grid pattern, was rebuilt in 1827 after the old town was virtually wiped out by fire. The 700-year-old cathedral, gutted by the fire, has been completely restored.

Turku Castle, which stands near the mouth of the Aurajoki river, dates back to the 13th century. It now houses an important museum. There is also an extensive maritime museum, and a large collection of maritime books in the university library.

Approach

The picturesque approach channel to Turku is some 50 miles long, entering the archipelago at Utö and leading through the islands generally in a north-easterly direction. Its appearance on the chart may seem somewhat fearsome, but it is a well marked channel with a minimum depth of 10m, regularly used by large ships. By day, using the detailed Finnish charts which are essential, there is little difficulty; movement by night needs experience. As can be seen from the charts, there is a network of channels amongst the islands and there are various ways to approach Turku. The main route from Utö light is north, then northeast past Bokullankivi light and again north to Lövskär, where it joins the 13m channel, much used by large ferries both by night and by day. There are many places suitable for an overnight anchorage in pleasant surroundings, if time allows.

Anchorages

In Turku itself, most possible anchorages involve trespassing on private ground. Away from Turku there are many picturesque locations which can be used for an overnight anchorage in good weather.

Berthing

There are several well equipped marinas outside Turku, but visiting yachts will undoubtedly find it best to moor at the small yacht harbour near the town centre in the Aurajoki river, just before the first bridge and directly opposite the three-master *Swan of Finland (Suomen Jontsen)*. Should there be no spaces, a place can usually be found on the outside of one of the charter vessels moored along the quayside.

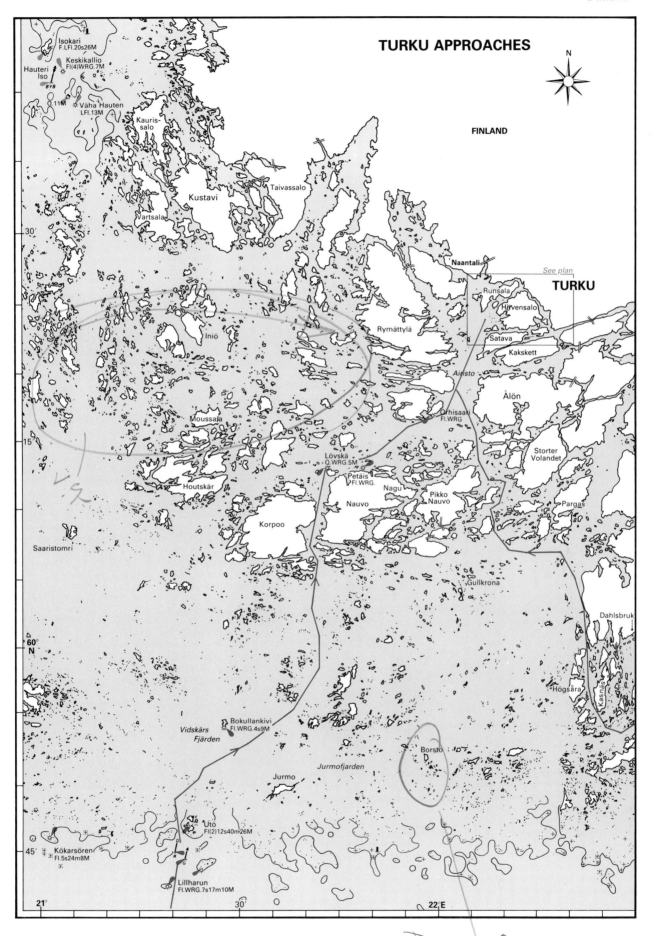

Finland

TURKU APPROACHES

N

FINLAND

TURKU

See plan

Naantali

Runsala

Hirvensalo

Satava

Kakskett

Ålön

Storter
Volandet

Pargas

Ainsto

Rymättylä

Orhisaari
Fl.WRG

Iniö

Moussala

Lövskä
Q.WRG.5M

Petäis
Fl.WRG.

Nagu

Pikko
Nauvo

Nauvo

Houtskär

Korpoo

Saaristomri

Gullkrona

Dahlsbruk

Högsåra

Kasnäs

Isokari
F.LFl.20s26M

Keskikallio
Fl(4)WRG.7M

Hauteri
Iso
BYB

Q.11M

Väha Hauten
LFl.13M

Kauris-
salo

Kustavi

Vartsala

Taivassalo

60°
N

Vidskärs
Fjärden

Bokullankivi
Fl.WRG.4s9M

Borstö

Jurmofjarden

Jurmo

Utö
Fl(2)12s40m26M

Kökarsören
Fl.5s24m8M

Lillharun
Fl.WRG.7s17m10M

21°

30'

22°E

125

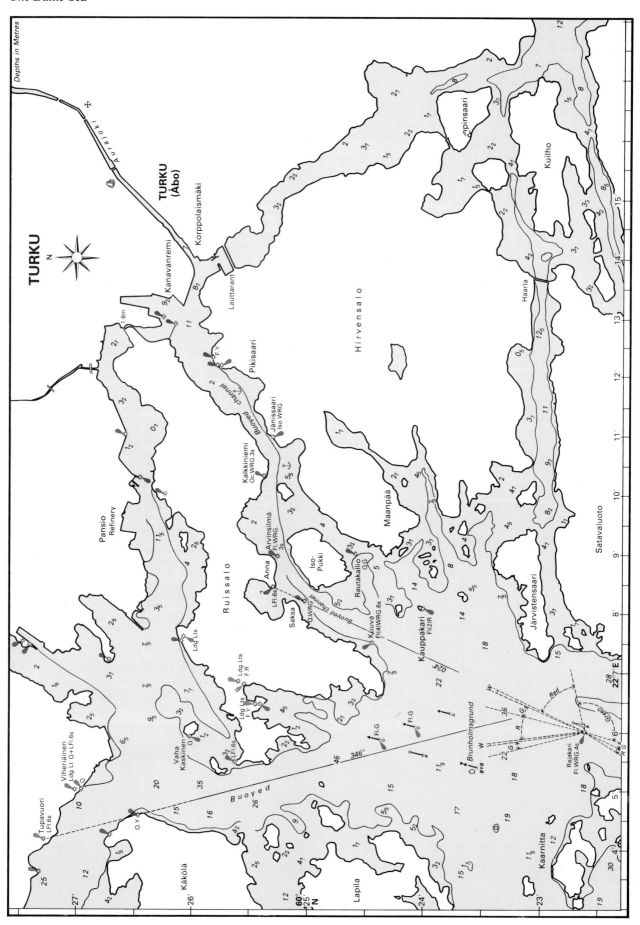

Yachts and historic ships at Turku.

Formalities

If Turku is the first port of call in Finland, clearance can be obtained at one of the frontier guard stations listed above, page 110.

General facilities

Neither water nor electricity is available to visiting yachts as a matter of course. However, by negotiation with the skipper of one of the charter vessels, both can usually be obtained.

There are no toilets or showers.

There are several good supermarkets within easy walking distance of the quay, and most supplies can be obtained without difficulty.

There is a tourist information office in the town, and there is a wide choice of banks, restaurants and hotels.

Yachting services

There is no fuelling berth for yachts, but there is one of the largest yacht chandleries in Finland. Propane cylinders can be refilled with difficulty.

In case of emergency it may be possible to find repair services, but this would have to be done by finding out what local yachtsmen do in similar circumstances.

Mariehamn transmits weather forecasts in English at 0833 and 2033 UT, and Helsinki at 0733 and 1933 UT.

Communications

There are good postal, telephone and facsimile services.

Mariehamn Radio and Helsinki Radio each have a satellite transmitting station at Turku. Mariehamn Radio operates on VHF Ch 26 and Helsinki on Ch 2.

Direct charter flights operate from Turku to Luton, but most destinations can be reached without difficulty via Helsinki.

There are regular rail/ferry and coach/ferry connections with England and most main continental cities, through Stockholm and København.

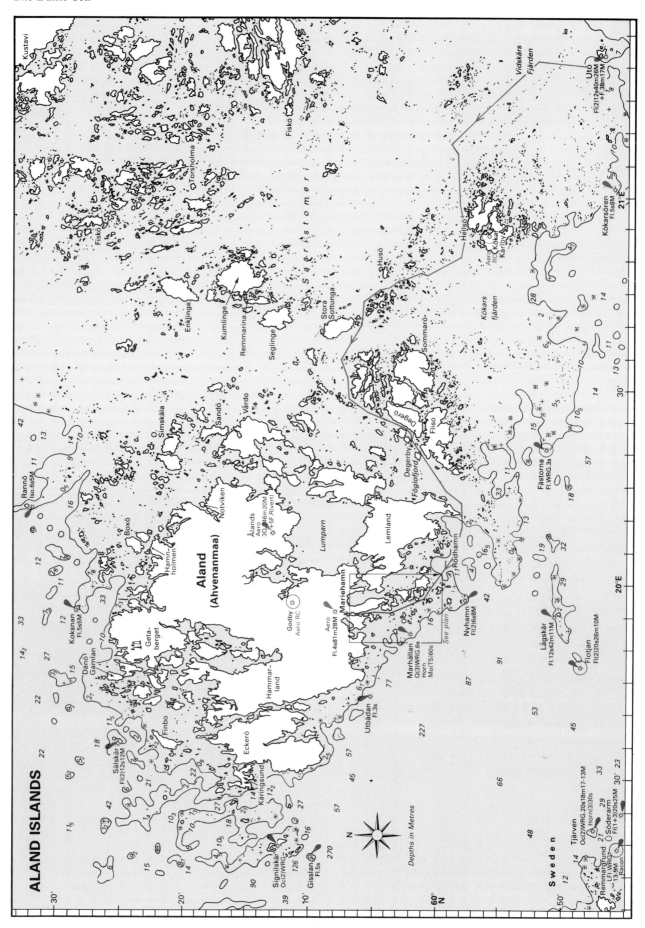

ALAND ISLANDS

Aland
(Ahvenanmaa)

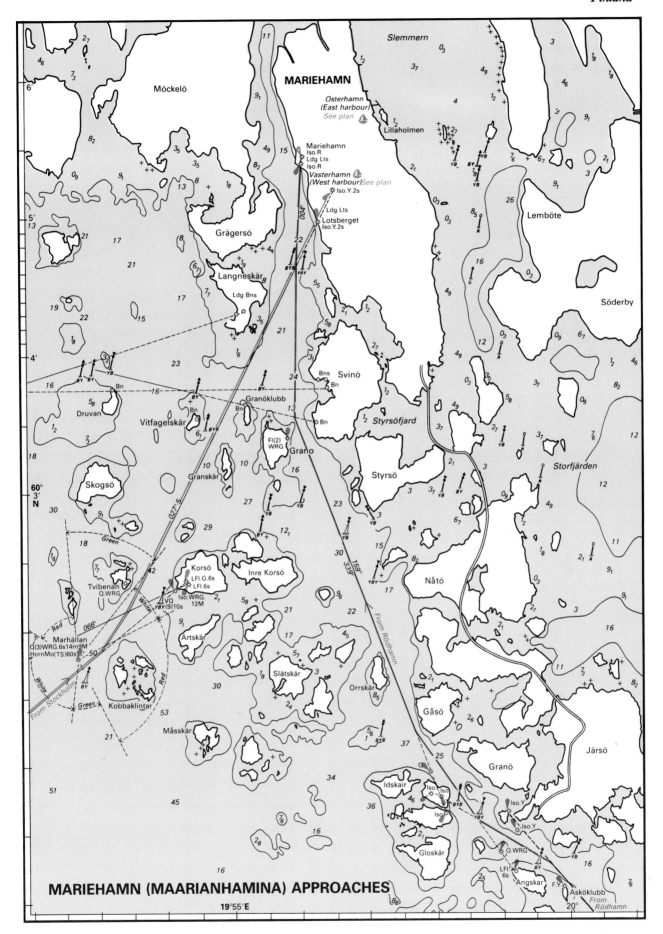

MARIEHAMN (MAARIANHAMINA) APPROACHES

19°55′E

Mariehamn

(Maarianhamina)

60°05'·9N 19°55'·6E

Distances

Stockholm 70M, Hanko 100M, Turku 75M.

Charts and guides

Admiralty charts *2297* and *3891*
Finnish charts *Volume C*, charts *903, 904* and *30*
Baltic Pilot Volume III (NP 20)

Lights

Approach
1. **Marhällan** 60°01'·9N 19°52'·5E Q(3)WRG.14m9M
   Horn Mo(TS)60s Round red tower, black band,
   floodlit 007°-W-120°-R-175°-G-219°-W-244°-R-333°-
   G-007° Racon all round 13M
2. **Nyhamn** 59°57'·5N 19°57'·5E Fl(2)6s43m8M
   Lantern on white tower with broad top. Pilot station

Entrance
3. **Lotsberget** Ldg Lts 027·5° *Front* 60°05'N 19°56'·2E
   Iso.Y.2s31m11M Red rectangle, yellow stripe, on
   metal framework tower with white lantern
   Rear 457m from front 60°05'·2N 19°56'·5E
   Iso.Y.2s51m 11M Red rectangle, yellow stripe, on
   metal framework tower.
   Both Visible arc 023°-033°

General

Mariehamn is the main town of Åland and has a
population of about 4,000. It is a modern, spacious
town with wide avenues and a good shopping
centre.

There are two yacht harbours, East Harbour and
West Harbour, but visiting yachts are likely to find
West Harbour, easily accessible from the sea, more
convenient.

If, however, it is intended to cruise the central part
of the Åland Islands, East Harbour can easily be
included on the route. It is a modern marina with
excellent facilities. It is a favoured destination for
many Finnish and Swedish yachts, and is close to
shops.

Approach

Mariehamn is normally approached either from the
southwest, from Stockholm, or from the southeast,
through the Åland Islands.

From Sweden, steer close south of Marhällan
light, then turn on to a course of 027·5° to follow
the shipping channel into the south part of the
harbour, using the Lotsberget leading lights.

For the southerly approach, follow the 6·3/7·3m
shipping channel between Järsö, Granö and Gåsö
and the islets to their southwest, and thence
continue on a course of 340° to the entrance of the
harbour.

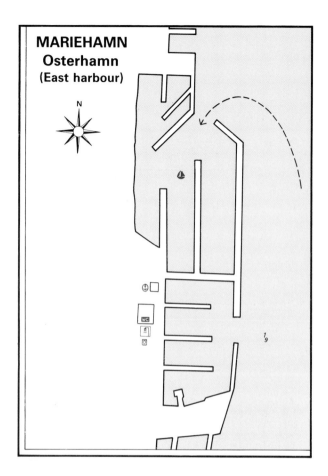

MARIEHAMN
Osterhamn
(East harbour)

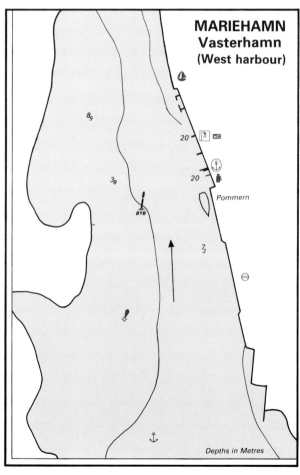

MARIEHAMN
Vasterhamn
(West harbour)

Pommern

Depths in Metres

Anchorage

There are no special restrictions on anchoring in the area of Mariehamn, but it will be difficult to find any suitable part of the shore which is not private property.

Berthing

Mooring at West Harbour is bows-to with stern to buoy. Take any vacant berth and report as soon as convenient to the harbour office near the first pontoon.

In 1992 an overnight mooring fee of £5 was charged for a yacht 12 metres long, and included free use of showers, sauna and laundry.

Formalities

When entering Åland from abroad (not Finland), contact the coastguard via the harbour office. Fly the Åland flag.

Facilities at West Harbour

There is water on each pontoon. Electricity can be obtained from domestic sockets in various buildings along the side of the harbour.

There are good shower, sauna, laundry and toilet facilities.

Bread, groceries, green groceries, fast food and other supplies can be bought in the town. The shopping centre is about ten minutes' walk from West Harbour. There is a tourist information office, together with banks, restaurants and hotels, in the town.

Yachting services

Fuel can be purchased at the fuelling berth at the yacht harbour. There is a small chandlery in the centre of Mariehamn.

Restricted repair services are available. It is better, if the situation allows, to seek engineering and other services in Stockholm or Helsinki.

Weather forecasts are broadcast daily at 0833 and 2033 UT by Mariehamn Radio.

Communications

There are numerous telephone kiosks. Postal and facsimile services are of the usual high standards expected in Finland.

Mariehamn Radio on VHF Ch 7 and 25, for public correspondence and weather forecasts.

Travel

There are regular flights and ferries from Mariehamn to Turku and Stockholm. The Åland Islands are linked by an interisland ferry service, and any island can be reached from Mariehamn without difficulty.

The west harbour at Mariehamn, the capital of the Åland islands.

Other ports

There are so many beautiful and interesting harbours to visit in Finland and it is only possible in this guide to mention a small selection of them. The following are some of the stopping places likely to be especially attractive to the visiting yachtsman.

Kuorsalo 60°28'N 27°23'·5E
Pretty bay surrounded by many coloured houses. Open to the north.

Nuokko 60°26'N 27°13'·5E
Attractive landlocked bay with narrow entrance.

Hamina 60°34'N 27°11'E
Attractive small fortified town. Guest harbour and a yacht club on the island which accepts visitors.

Kotka

Loviisa 60°27'·1N 26°14'·4E
Interesting town with two yacht harbours.

Byö 60°16'N 26°00'E
Beautiful totally enclosed lagoon with very narrow entrance. A must if only for lunch.

Pellinki 60°14'·5N 25°54'E
An attractive mini archipelago with several sheltered anchorages. Suninsalmi has a good shop and fuel dock.

Porvoo 60°23'·2N 25°40'·2E
Pleasant old town with small yacht harbour.

Helsinki

Ingå 60°02'·5N 24°00'·5E
Attractive yacht harbour in rural surroundings.

Jakobshamn 59°59'·7N 23°59'E
Isolated quayside mooring.

Barösund 59°57'·9N 23°51'·4E
Useful overnight stop on passage from Helsinki to Hanko. Small marina with single pontoon, sauna and restaurant.

Ekenäs 59°58'·6N 23°26'E
Very special. A small port 100km from Helsinki, but with an excellent train service. If time is pressing, it is worth considering leaving the boat here and visiting Helsinki by train. Good for wildlife, trees and flowers. Restaurant on piles over the water. 90% Swedish speaking. Good chandlery.

Hanko

Dahlsbruk 60°01'·2N 22°30'·6E
Interesting small town with quay.

Högsåra 59°57'·1N 22°22'·1E
Attractive island with small yacht harbour.

Kasnäs 59°55'·2N 22°24'·7E
Tree-clad island. Large marina with good facilities.

Pargas port 60°09'N 22°17'·4E
Fishing village with shops. Interesting path through woods to beach on west of island.

Airisto 60°15'·1N 22°06'·7E
Pleasant small port with large tourist hotel.

Runsala 60°25'·6N 22°09'·6E
Two agreeable yacht harbours off the main channel to Turku.

Naantali 60°28'·2N 22°01'·1E
A very nice town with two yacht harbours and a commercial harbour handling oil and ferry traffic. Many nice restaurants. A famous music festival in June.

Nagu 60°11'·6N 21°55'E
A small rural harbour situated on a tree-lined bay.

Gullkrona 60°05'·3N 22°05'·4E
Very popular fishing harbour, where it is possible to buy fresh and smoked fish. There is also a sauna.

Fishermen's boat sheds on the island of Borstö.

Nötö 59°57'·3N 21°45'·6E
Rather special: a beautiful little village with small church and shop.

Borstö 59°51'·7N 21°58'·3E
Another delightful fishing hamlet with a special variety of flat fish which is smoked in a shed by the harbour.

Jurmo 59°49'·6N 21°35'·3E
In days gone by a pirate island, completely burnt to the ground by King Gustav Wasa 500 years ago to stop the pirates' activities. There are a small church, a graveyard and a square planted forest.

Utö 59°46'·9N 21°22'·5E
Bleak island with a military establishment, a lighthouse and a small harbour. Very wild and slightly eerie, with a very special cemetery.

Karlby 59°55'·3N 20°55'E
Very attractive small natural harbour at the head of a long inlet. New marina and tourist hotel.

Hellsö 59°57'·1N 20°55'·6E
Small primitive yacht and fishing harbour. Restaurant on hillside overlooking harbour.

Husö 60°03'·9N 20°48'·5E
Natural harbour with a 50m pier on a small island. The pier has water, electricity and toilets. There are a shop, a café, and the possibility of buying smoked and fresh fish. It is possible to rent a cottage and to hire a fully equipped fishing boat. Ferry. There is also a beautiful narrow passage – the Embarsund – due westwards towards Degerby.

The picturesque island of Borstö.

The ferry pier on the island of Borstö.

Keistiö 60°22'·3N 21°21'·1E
A gem of a tiny fishing harbour.

Kustavi 60°32'·4N 21°20'·2E
Superb small harbour. Reaching it involves negotiating a very narrow but very beautiful passage.

Torsholma 60°21'·9N 21°04'·3E
Delightful small harbour.

Fiskö 60°27'·2N 20°56'·4E
Isolated and breathtaking.

Remmarina 60°15'·5N 20°44'·5E
Small fishing village with pontoon for yachts.

Seglinge 60°12'·8N 20°42'·7E
Delightful and secluded.

Notviken 60°11'·7N 19°37'·4E
Very beautiful small guest harbour on island of Eckerö. Nearby are ruins of a Russian-built fortress – destroyed in the last century – by the English.

Hamnholmen 60°22'·5N 20°05'·4E
Coastguard station and small boat harbour – off the beaten track.

Käringsund 60°14'N 19°32'·6E
Gorgeous fishing hamlet in enclosed bay on Eckerö.

Rödhamn 58°59'·1N 20°06'·4E
Quiet anchorage en route from south into Marie-hamn. An excellent overnight stop, but no shops.

Degerby 60°01'·9N 20°23'·5E
Small town with a few shops and banks. Ferry terminal – can be busy and noisy.

The small yacht and fishing harbour at Hellsö.

VI. Sweden

The eastern seaboard of Sweden is a magnificent cruising area, especially in July and August, when the air is clear, the skies are sunny, the sea is blue and the islands are green. With 300,000 registered pleasure craft, Sweden is well geared towards yachting. There are well equipped yacht harbours, interesting fishing villages and countless quiet anchorages amongst the islands.

The country

Sweden can be described in four zones, three of which are founded on ancient rocks. The northern two thirds of the country, mentioned for the sake of completeness, has mountains along the Norwegian border; eastwards it is boulder-strewn bare rock, with peat bogs and spruce, pine and birch stretching northwards until they are beaten by the climate. The land slopes down to the central lowlands, which are more hospitable, with prosperous agriculture and deciduous trees among the conifers. Stockholm and Göteborg are in this region. Southern Sweden has a central raised area with the same feel as the rocky north, bordered by a coastal lowland given over to agriculture and fishing. The fourth region, Skåne, in the extreme southwest, has the most recent rock, often covered with boulder clay, with beech and oak rather than conifers, and with wheat rather than barley and rye. The mood of Skåne is much like that of Denmark.

The coast from north of Stockholm down to Kalmar is guarded by tens of thousands of islands – the Skärgård, where the water often reaches 24°C – some inhabited, some not, some rocky and desolate and others green and fertile. It is a seductive area where the yachtsman finds it easy to linger. The southern part of the Swedish coast, from Kalmar round to Malmö, is very attractive, with an undulating coastline and a number of interesting harbours. In July and August, mosquitoes can be an irritation, especially in the remoter anchorages.

History

In the late 14th century the Swedish nobles rebelled against their king, Albrecht, and sought help from the regent of Norway and Denmark, Margaret, who, by defeating Albrecht, united the three Scandinavian kingdoms. At the Union of Kalmar, agreed in 1397, Margaret's grand-nephew Eric was elected king of the three countries. The Union of Kalmar never became law; the three countries were administered separately and indeed the Swedes resented the idea of the Union. During the 15th century Swedish nationalism steadily developed, and in 1435 parliament was established; the second oldest in the world, it lasted unaltered for five hundred years. The independence of Sweden was contested by the Danes, and there were many grim events until Gustavus Vasa, helped by Hanseatic Lübeck, established himself as king in 1523 whose successors remained in place until the 19th century. There followed the Age of Greatness, when Sweden was involved in political and military alliances and adventures for reasons which had commercial, territorial and religious constituents involving all Europe. She established her presence, with varying success and for varying periods, in Denmark, Norway, Finland, Russia, the three Baltic Republics, Poland and Germany. She also developed her copper and iron mines, and expanded economically. Towards the end of the period, Sweden had established her present boundaries with Denmark and had withdrawn from overseas adventures. In the 18th century architecture and other arts thrived. At the end of that century, the successors of Gustav Vasa proved unable to act as heads of state, and in 1810, one of Napoleon's marshalls, Bernadotte, a defector in modern terms, became by invitation Sweden's de facto leader. When the linear king, Charles XIII, died in 1818, Bernadotte took the throne as Charles XIV. Swedish history then became one of mainly social and economic development, though Sweden's last foreign territorial interest, a loose union with Norway, did not fall apart until 1906.

The people

Sweden has a population of around 8 million, and a political system which includes a hereditary monarchy and a parliamentary democracy with a universal franchise, proportional representation and a single chamber of 349 members elected every three years. The established national church is Lutheran; non-Lutherans (including 130,000 Roman Catholics) make up less than 1·5% of the population.

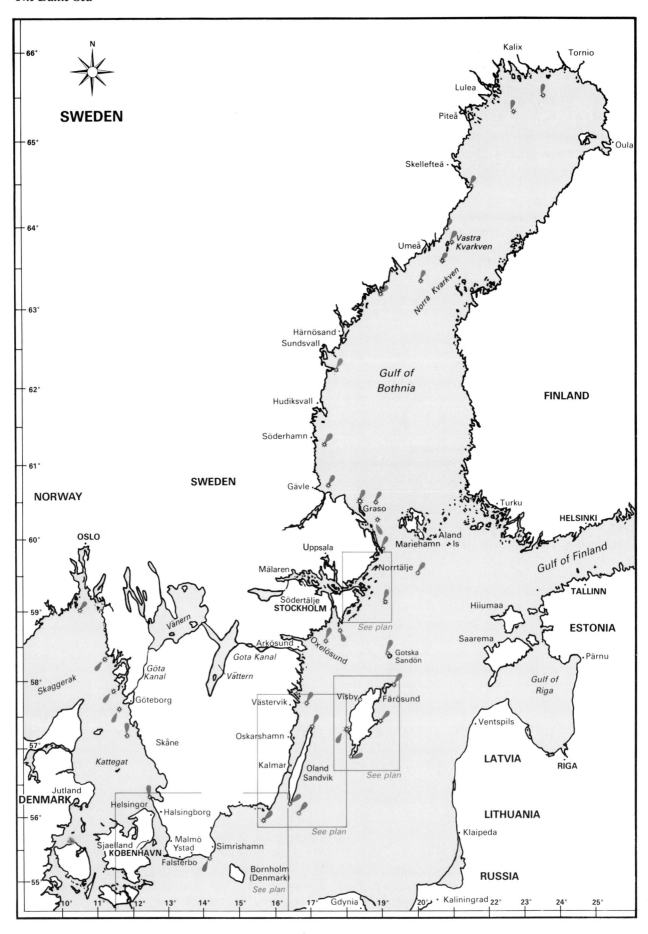

N

SWEDEN

66°

65°

64°

63°

62°

61°

60°

59°

58°

57°

56°

55°

OSLO

NORWAY

SWEDEN

Vänern

Göta
Kanal

Vättern

Skaggerak

Göteborg

Skåne

Kattegat

Jutland

DENMARK

Helsingor

· Halsingborg

Malmö
Ystad

Sjaelland
KOBENHAVN

Falsterbo

· Simrishamn

Bornholm
(Denmark)
See plan

Gdynia

Kaliningrad

RUSSIA

LITHUANIA

Klaipeda

LATVIA

RIGA

Gulf of
Riga

· Ventspils

· Pärnu

ESTONIA

Saarema

Hiiumaa

TALLINN

Gulf of Finland

HELSINKI

Turku

Aland
Mariehamn Is

Uppsala

Mälaren

Södertälje
STOCKHOLM

Arkösund

Oxelösund

See plan

Norrtälje

Gotska
Sandön

Visby

Färösund

See plan

Västervik

Oskarshamn

Kalmar

Oland
Sandvik

See plan

Gävle

Graso

Söderhamn

Hudiksvall

Härnösand
Sundsvall

*Gulf of
Bothnia*

FINLAND

Umeå

Vastra
Kvarkven

Norra Kvarkven

Skellefteä ·

Piteå

Lulea

Kalix

Tornio

Oula

10°   11°   12°   13°   14°   15°   16°   17°   18°   19°   20°   21°   22°   23°   24°   25°

Early on in the modern period, attention was paid to the welfare of all sections of the society, not just to the upper layers. Free education and poor relief started in 1807, old age pensions in 1890, employment injury insurance in 1901, and basic and disability pensions in 1914, and a list of other benefits has been added since. Total social expenditure, including health and social assistance, is now about a third of the gross national product. The results of ordinary and higher education are good – one result is a well trained work force, another an appreciation of the arts, which have also flourished in practice, and a third, conveniently, widespread skill in the English language.

Friendly but formal, the Swedes have developed a regulated society which, from Gustav Vasa onwards, has looked after its environment and has avoided the worst squalors of industrialisation.

The economy

Sweden's iron and copper began to be of real significance in European markets at the end of the 16th century, and in world terms Sweden is still a leading exporter of iron ore. Building on these and other mineral resources, Sweden has developed an advanced engineering industry now capable of handling almost any category of work from heavy engineering to electronics, which produces more than half the value of all her manufactures. Another major resource is timber, which covers more than half of the country. A quarter of it is publicly owned, a quarter is owned by companies and the rest is in private hands; it produces in all some 20% of the total value of manufactures. Sweden's lack is fuel; a little coal is mined in Skåne, but she depends on imports for oil and coal. About 45% of her electricity is produced by water power and 50% by nuclear power; only 5% is produced by thermal power stations.

Fishing is significant to the economy, but is more important on the west coast than the east.

The Swedish Tourist Association

The Swedish Tourist Association, Box 7615, S-10394 Stockholm, publishes a useful guide book in Swedish listing harbours with visitors' berths. It is issued free of charge on request.

Money

The unit of currency is the krone, divided into 100 öre. Exchange is easy, and traveller's cheques, Eurocheques and most major credit cards are widely accepted.

Shopping

The standard and cost of living are both high compared with those of the United Kingdom. Food prices are in general slightly higher than those in Denmark, but slightly lower than those in Finland. There are few commodities which cannot be obtained. Beer available generally has an alcohol content of 2·8%. Stronger alcoholic drinks are expensive and available only at Systembolaget, the state-owned chain of liquor stores.

The Swedish Institute for Arts and Crafts (Hemslöyd), founded in 1845, is still going strong, with branches in every town.

Hotels and restaurants

Many and good.

Yacht services and chandlery

Both generally excellent. Mooring fees are a little lower than they are in the UK. Diesel is readily available, but costs about twice as much as it does in the UK. *Camping Gaz* (butane) can be found as far north as Kalmar, but beyond this it is unlikely to be found.

Weather forecasts in English are given on the Stockholm VHF net radio at 0933 and 2133 UT, and gale warnings at 0133, 0533, 1333 and 1733 UT and on the Göteborg net one hour later (see *Introduction* page 6 for VHF organisation).

Communications

Direct dialling is available from all Swedish telephone kiosks. Charges are high, and it can be difficult to insert coins quickly enough to avoid disconnection. The dialling code for the international exchange is 009.

Facsimile and telex are widely available at post offices and commercial bureaux.

Letters take 3–5 days to or from the United Kingdom.

Public correspondence facilities are provided by Stockholm Radio, which covers the coast from Smygehuk in the south to Väddö in the north, and by Göteborg Radio, which covers the coast of Skåne.

Travel

Sweden is well served by bus, rail, sea and air services from the United Kingdom and all parts of the continent. Internal bus, train and air services leave little to be desired. Swedish State Railways honour the British Senior Railcard, generally giving a 30% discount on normal fares.

Scandinavian Seaways five senior citizens 50% discount

Time

Swedish time is one hour ahead of UT in winter, and two hours ahead from the last Sunday in March until the Saturday before the last Sunday in September.

Formalities

According to the letter of the law, foreign nationals, other than those from the other Nordic countries, are required to carry passports and to report to the Swedish customs immediately on arrival. The boat should carry her certificate of registration and, if this does not constitute proof of ownership, additional documentation which does so. However, advice given by customs at some ports of entry is that it is necessary to report to customs 'only if you have something to declare', and it is often difficult to find a customs officer willing to deal with a yacht. On the other hand, in the south, where drugs might be landed, yachts may be boarded by customs officers. It is perhaps best to err on the side of formality rather than risk falling foul of the authorities. Arriving from Germany or Denmark, Falsterbo, Gislövs Läge (near Trelleborg), Ystad and Simrishamn are convenient first ports of call. Arriving from Finland, it is best to seek instructions by VHF when in the vicinity of Kapellskär or Sandhamn.

A foreign national may keep a boat in Sweden for up to a year without payment of duty, provided that he stays on board. See the *Introduction* on laying up.

A right of public access means that a boat can be anchored anywhere, and that there is free access anywhere except to grounds around private dwellings. Elsewhere you may walk across private land, pick berries, flowers or mushrooms, and even pitch a tent. This freedom brings responsibilities. You must not disturb wildlife, leave litter, light fires or cause damage of any sort. Do not flush toilets in harbours or close to populated shores.

Most yacht clubs and harbours fly the ensign of their visitors. It is important that the Swedish ensign is worn in response.

The flag is blue with a yellow Scandinavian cross.

UK representation

British Embassy Skarpögatan 6-8, 115 27 Stockholm ☎ (46) 08-667 01 40 *Fax* (46) 08-662 99 89 *Telex* 19340.

Swedish Embassy in London 11 Montague Place W1H 2AL ☎ 071-724 2101.

Navigation

The *Baltic Pilot Volume II (NP 19)* covers every detail of the Swedish coast from Ystad in the south to Norrtälje in the north. It is an important and definitive publication, but often difficult to interpret, and although facilities for yachts are frequently mentioned, much of the practical information needed by yachtsmen is missing.

There is no English-language pilot specifically for yachtsmen, but the Swedish pilots are quite easy to follow; the German pilots are less so. A selection is given in *Appendix I*. Every coastal town of any size has a shop, usually a bookstore, that sells charts and pilots.

The Swedish coast is well lit and well buoyed. In the skerries, although it is possible to use large scale Admiralty charts, it is better to use Swedish charts, which are readily available and beautifully produced. They can be bought either as individual charts, or in book form as *Båtsportkort, Series A–K*. The skerries can markedly affect wind directions and strength.

There are prohibited areas and other areas variously described as controlled, protected or restricted, and it is important to obey the regulations governing them; infractions may lead to a fine on the spot. Foreigners are not allowed into prohibited areas. Foreigners may transit other areas along official routes, but may not stop and may not go ashore. At certain times of the year landing is not permitted on wildlife sanctuaries, and in some cases approach within 100m of the shore is forbidden. These areas are marked on Swedish charts (page 189 *Appendix I. Bibliography*).

Although Decca coverage is generally good, cruising in the archipelago involves navigating within metres of rocks. Eyeballing is without doubt the only satisfactory approach to the problem.

Cruising areas

The whole of the Baltic coast of Sweden north of Simrishamn offers superb cruising in relatively sheltered waters amongst the islands. Skåne, the extreme southwest, and the southern end of Gotland have a reputation for fog.

The areas which visiting yachtsmen are most likely to find attractive are:

- The Blue Coast, around Oskarshamn.
- The Stockholm archipelago.
- Lake Mälaren, immediately west of Stockholm, where many Swedes spend a lifetime cruising (but which has mosquitoes).

The Göta Canal, together with Lakes Vänern and Vättern and the Dalslands Canal, also represents an enormous cruising ground where those inclined towards the pleasures of inland waterway cruising could easily spend several years. In 1991 the dues for the main canal were around £280.

The Swedish coast of the Gulf of Bothnia is more interesting than the Finnish coast. When making a round trip, the Swedes prefer to go north up Sweden and south down Finland, possibly because the sea breeze in summer tends to become established from the southeast on the west side and from the northwest on the east side of the Gulf, but northerly winds are quite usual, sea breeze or no. North of Gävle, the coastal hills gradually get higher and ports and good anchorages fewer, and though inshore passages are sometimes possible, and there is a good cruising area between Härnösand and Umeå, the Skärgård does not begin again until Piteå, which is a long way north (65°19'N 21°30'E). The ports and their towns are generally geared towards commerce, with the exception of Umeå, which is also a university town.

Stockholm

59°20'N 18°04'E

Distances

Mariehamn 80M, Arkösund 80M, Visby 110M.

Charts and guides

Admiralty charts *2362, 3196, 3126* and *3114*

Swedish charts 71, 111, 611*, 612*, 613*, 615*, 616*, 6141, 6142*, 6143*, 6144*, 6145*, 6161*, 6171* and 6172 (* available also in book form as *Båtsportkort, Series A*)

Lights

1. **Söderarm** 59°45'·2N 19°24'·6E Fl(1+3)20s31m25M Round white stone tower, red band, floodlit, 21m
2. **Landsorts Bredgrund** 58°43'·9N 17°52'·7E Iso.WRG. 4s19m16-12M Horn(2)60s Orange tower, floodlit. For sectors see chart. Racon all round 14M
3. **Landsorts south point** 58°44'·4N 17°52'·1E Fl(1+4) 60s44m22M and F.WRG.27m14-10M White tower, red top, 25m 323·5°-G-351°-W-358°-R-023° RC 289·5kHZ *LO* (·—··/———) 50M
4. **Almagrund** 59°09'·6N 19°07'·8E LFl(3)WRG.30s 28m19-17M Black tower, red band, floodlit, helipad, 30m 045°-R-077°-G-150°-W-155°-R-180°-G-225°-W-045° RC 286·5kHz *AL* (·—/·—··) 70M Racon all round 16M

General

Stockholm, established where access to Lake Mälaren could be controlled, was founded as a town by Birger Jarl in 1250, and was especially concerned with the metalwork industry developed inland. It was an important trading centre in Hanseatic times, when half its population was German. An old town remains on the island, with the royal palace, which has medieval and renaissance street plans. Modern Stockholm, whose population is now approaching 2 million, has spread across the waterways to the mainland. It is a friendly, relaxing city with tree-

Scene on the northeastern approach to Stockholm.

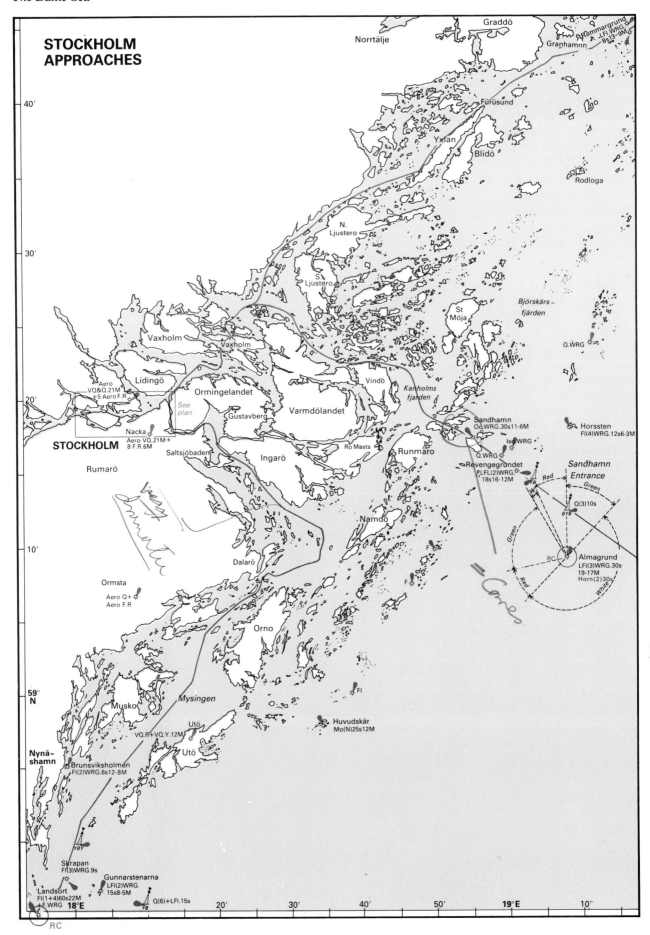

STOCKHOLM
APPROACHES

Graddö

Norrtälje

Granhamnn

Remmargrund
LFI.WRG.
8s.13-9M

40'

Fürüsund

Yxlan

Blidö

Rödloga

30'

N.
Ljusterö

S.
Ljusterö

Björskärs –
fjärden

St
Möja

Q.WRG

Vaxholm

Vaxholm

Vindö

Kanholms
fjärden

Sandhamn
Oc.WRG.30s11-6M

Horssten
FI(4)WRG.12s6-3M

Aero
VQ&Q.21M
+5 Aero F.R

Lidingö

Ormingelandet

See
plan

Varmdölandet

Isc.WRG

Q.WRG

20'

Nacka
Aero VQ.21M+
8 F.R.6M

Gustavberg

Ro Masts

Revengegrundet
LFI(2)WRG.
18s16-12M

Sandhamn
Entrance

Red

STOCKHOLM

Saltsjöbaden

Ingarö

Runmaro

Green

YB

Rumarö

Namdo

Green

Q(3)10s

BYB

10'

Dalarö

RC

Almagrund
LFI(3)WRG.30s
19-17M
Horn(2)30s

Red

White

Ormsta

Aero Q+
Aero F.R

Orno

F

Cones

FI

59°
N

Musko

Mysingen

Huvudskär
Mo(N)25s12M

FI

Utö

VQ.R+VQ.Y.12M

Utö

**Nynä-
shamn**

Brunsviksholmen
FI(2)WRG.6s12-8M

YBY

Skrapan
FI(3)WRG.9s

Gunnarstenarna
LFI(2)WRG.
15s8-5M

Q(6)+LFI.15s

Landsort
FI(1+4)60s22M
+F.WRG **18°E**

20'

30'

40'

50'

19°E

10'

YB

RC

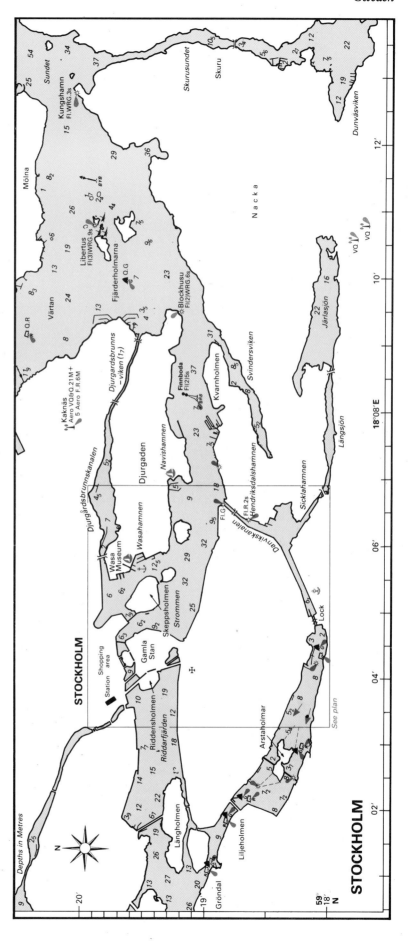

Stockholm waterfront facade.

lined squares and beautiful waterfronts blended with modern architecture, all intersected by busy waterways. It also has a great deal of cultural interest, with palaces, fine churches and historic ships, including the 17th-century man-of-war *Wasa*, raised from where she sank, top heavy, within minutes of setting out on her maiden voyage.

Approach

There are four main routes through the archipelago to Stockholm, but many diversions can be made if time allows. Such is the nature of the archipelago that it could easily provide a whole summer's enjoyment.

The northern route enters the archipelago north of Söderarm lighthouse, and continues in a southwesterly direction to Vaxholm and so into Stockholm.

Approaching from the south, the most attractive route to the yachtsman leads NNE from Landsorts lighthouse through Mysingen, winds through easily navigable channels around Dalarö, passes close by Saltsjöbaden, and then continues through the narrow channels of Baggensstäk and Skurusund to join the main shipping channel into Stockholm from the northeast.

A second route from the south enters west of Landsorts, leads through the Södertälje Kanal into Mälaren, the large inland sea to the west of

very [handwritten annotation next to "narrow"]

Stockholm, and then passes through the Hammarbyleden, which is the main link between Mälaren and Saltsjön, the main fairway leading into Stockholm from the east. This route is suitable for yachts with masts up to 26m in height, and involves two locks and a number of opening bridges.

From the east, it is probably best to start from the vicinity of Almagrund lighthouse, join the main shipping channel past Revengegrund lighthouse, and then divert through the narrow channel close in front of the famous yachting centre of Sandhamn, the Cowes of Sweden. Rejoin the main shipping channel NNW across Kanholmsfjärden, round the north of Vindö, and then close in front of the ancient town of Vaxholm and into Stockholm.

Anchorage

Anchoring is not advisable anywhere in the main harbour area.

Berthing

There are three major yacht harbours in the immediate area of Stockholm, and there are many other places where yachts seem to have found a corner in which to moor. There is also a public quay, normally used only by large yachts, with facilities geared to the requirements of larger vessels.

For the visitor with a moderately sized yacht, Wasahamnen (59°19'·5N 18°05'·7E), a ten-minute

* where at times there is hardly room to pass

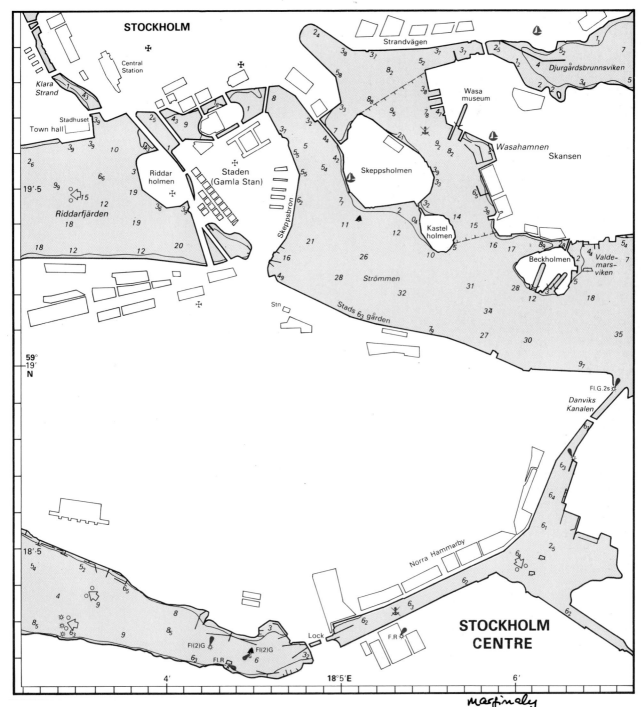

marginally

walk from the city centre, is probably the most convenient and most expensive of the available harbours. In 1991 an overnight mooring fee of around £12 was charged for a yacht 12 metres long, and included electricity. The showers require coins.

Mooring in Wasahamnen is at pontoons with narrow fingers along both sides of the boat. Most of the fingers are only 3·5 to 4m wide, and there is not a great deal of space for turning. Good fendering along both sides is desirable.

Because of its location, Wasahamnen tends to be crowded, so it is best to arrive early. On arrival, take any vacant berth and report as soon as convenient to the harbour office for instructions.

Two quieter and ✓ cheaper harbours, less convenient for the city centre, lie on either side of Valdemarsudde, on Djurgården. The Royal Swedish Sailing Association (KSSS) harbour is at 59°19'·6N 18°07'·4E, and the Navishamnen is at 59°19'·3N 18°06'·9E. The KSSS harbour is close to the house, *Manilla,* and garden of the artist Prince Eugéne, and has frequent water buses to the city. Navishamnen, less prepossessing at first sight, is very hospitable. Biskopksudden no longer accepts visiting yachts.

Formalities

It is surprisingly difficult to obtain customs clearance if entering the Stockholm archipelago

* The outside berths at both can be very uncomfortable because of the wash

143

Wasahamnen, the main yacht harbour near the centre of
Stockholm.

The picturesque old part of Stockholm.

from another country, as the outlying customs posts are not easy to locate. If intending to cruise before reaching Stockholm, the best plan is to call customs on VHF Ch 16 when in the region of Nynäshamn, Sandhamn or Kapellskär, and ask for instructions. If it is not intended to stop, and Stockholm is the first port of call in Sweden, advice should be sought locally after arrival on how and where to contact customs.

General facilities

Bread, groceries and green groceries are available from a small supermarket within the marina.

Stockholm has all the facilities of a modern city, and the shopping is of the highest standard. Top quality goods of all types can be bought – at a price.

The main tourist information office is in the shopping centre of the city.

The bridge over the Skurusund, near Stockholm.

The narrow Baggensstäk channel near Stockholm.

Yachting services

There are several fuelling berths within the precincts of Stockholm harbour.

At Wasahamnen there are water, electricity, toilets, showers, a sauna, a laundry, a sailmaker and even a television room. In a back street, about ~~ten minutes~~' ½ hr walk away, there is a good chandler's shop with general chandlery and very good stocks of charts and books, as well as a shop which specialises in flags and ensigns of all nations. Get directions at Wasahamnen.

Repairs can be arranged by consultation with the various harbourmasters.

*

Communications

Telephone, facsimile and telex facilities are widely available.

Travel

Air, rail, coach and ferry services between Stockholm and other parts of Europe are excellent.

Arkösund

58°29'N 16°56'E

Distances

Stockholm 80M, Västervik 45M, Visby 65M.

Charts and guides

Admiralty charts *2361, 3217, 3218* and *3219*
Swedish charts *72, 621* and *724*
Baltic Pilot Volume II (NP 19)

Lights

1. **Norra Fällbåden** 58°26'·5N 17°06'·4E Fl(3)WRG. 16m11·7M Black concrete tower, white top, yellow band, grey base, 17m. Wind generator. 108·5°-G-114·5°-W-116°-R-122°-G-180°-R-245°-G-253°-W-315°-R-333·5°

General

Arkösund visitors' harbour is the first of two yacht harbours on the west side of Arkösund. It is a small, attractive harbour in a rural setting, with only a few houses and hotels amongst the trees surrounding the harbour.

Approach

From the open sea, pass close north of North Fällbåden lighthouse to enter the Arkö approach channel, marked at intervals with spar buoys on both sides, on a course of 292°. The channel is also indicated by the Arkö leading marks, but these are not easily visible. However, the buoyage is clear in daylight, and once the Arkö light is reached the

* The S C Club (SXK) shop at Karlevägen 67, a ½ hr walk, has a very good stock of yachting publications & charts at advantageous prices.
camping gas cylinders may be exchanged at Wasahammen & Navis-hammn.

145

ARKÖSUND APPROACHES

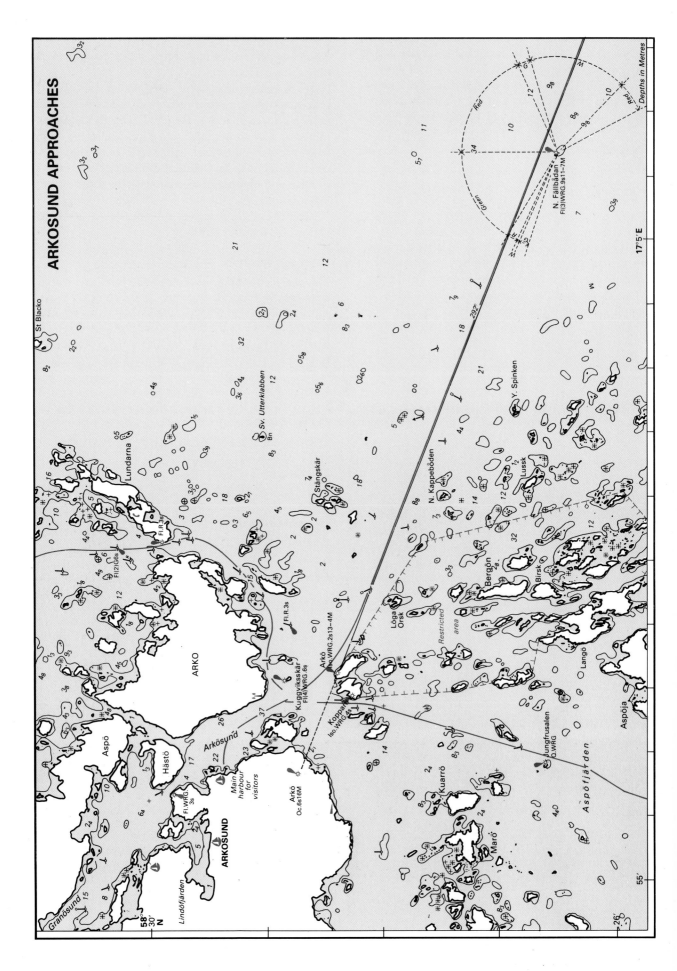

St Blacko

Lundarna

Sv. Utterklabben
Bn

Stängskär

Aspö

Hästö

ARKO

Arkösund

ARKÖSUND

Granösund

Lindöfjärden

FI.WRG
3s

Main
harbour
for
visitors

Arkö
Oc.6s16M

FI.R.3s

FI.R.3s

Arkö
Iso.WRG.2s13–4M

Kuggviksskär
FI(4)WRG.6s

Koppa
Iso.WRG.4s

FI(2)G6s

Loga
Orsk

Restricted
area

N. Kappebåden

Y. Spinken

Lussk

Bergön

Birsk

Langö

Aspöja

Kuarrö

Marö

Jungfrusalen
Q.WRG

Aspöfjärden

N. Fällbådan
FI(3)WRG.9s11–7M

Red

Green

Red

297°

Depths in Metres

17°5'E

55'

58°
30'
N

146

entrance becomes obvious. Entry is not recommended at night or in conditions of poor visibility.

Anchorage

There are no restrictions on anchoring in this area.

Berthing

This is a small, popular harbour with only a limited number of berths, so it is advisable to time one's arrival to be reasonably early. Mooring is bows-to with stern to buoy. There are no reserved berths, so take any vacant berth and report as soon as convenient to the harbour shop at the fuelling berth.

In 1991 an overnight mooring fee of approximately £4 was charged for a yacht 12 metres in length.

In 1993 a new yacht harbour was constructed which should relieve congestion.

Formalities

There are no customs or immigration officials at Arkösund.

General facilities

Water is available at the fuelling berth. There is electricity within reach of each berth.

The yacht harbour at Arkösund.

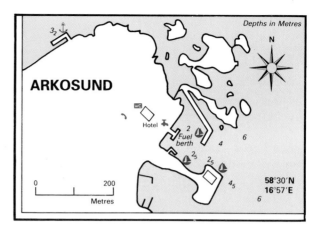

The showers and toilets are in a wooden building at the side of the harbour.

There is a small grocery shop in a wooden building on the quay, and a stall selling smoked fish.

The nearby village has a restaurant and several small hotels, but no tourist information office or banks.

Yachting services

Charts and a limited range of chandlery can be bought at the shop at the fuelling berth.

Repair facilities at Arkösund are limited to those available for local fishing boats.

Weather forecasts in English are broadcast on VHF Ch 27 of the Stockholm net at 0933 and 2133 UT.

Communications

There is a nearby telephone kiosk from which international calls can be made.

The area is served by Stockholm Radio through a satellite transmitter at Norrköping, on VHF Ch 27. Public correspondence services are available.

Travel

There is a bus service from Arkösund to Norrköping.

Västervik

57°45'N 16°39'E

Distances

Arkösund 45M, Visby 55M, Kalmar 65M.

Charts and guides

Admiralty charts 2361 and 3435
Swedish charts *72* and *623*. *6231* is useful but not
  necessary.
Baltic Pilot Volume II (NP 19)

Lights

1. **Västerbaden** 57°44'·8N 16°44'·6E Oc.WRG.10s14m 14-10M Red tower, black base, floodlit, 15m 112°-G-113·5°-R-258·5°-G-268°-W-269·5°- R-309°-G-321°-R-011°-G-040° Racon all round 12M
2. **Kungsgrund** 57°41'·2N 16°54'·5E LFl(2)WRG.27m 16-12M White lantern, black tower, red band 005°-R-048°-G-088·5°-R-122°-G-193°-W-005° Racon all round 17M
3. **Spårö Ldg Lts** 323° *Rear* 57°42'·8N 16°43'·9E Iso.6s 36m14M White tower, 8m
4. **Idö Stångskär** *Front* 3·1M from rear 57°40'·3N 16°48'E Q.WRG.13m8-5M White lantern, red base 145°-G-150°-W-152°-R-302°-G-321°-W-324°-R-338°

General

Västervik is a small industrial town with a modern harbour for small ships. It is a pleasant, unpretentious town, not without charm. It has good shopping facilities, and the Blå Kustens (Blue Coast) marina is perhaps one of the most modern and well equipped yacht harbours on the eastern coast of Sweden. It is an excellent centre from which to explore the famous Blå Kustens archipelago to the south.

Approach

From seaward there are two main approaches: from the east, passing 4 miles north of Kungsgrund light[2] heading towards Vasterbaden light[1]; and from the

southeast, heading towards Idö Stångskär light[4] on a bearing of 323° and passing close northeast of it.

The well charted and well marked inshore channels from north and south join these two approach routes shortly before entry to Lusärnafjärden, which must be crossed to reach the port of Västervik.

Anchorage

There are no restrictions on anchoring in this area.

Berthing

Immediately on entry to Lusärnafjärden there is a quiet yacht harbour, Solbergsudde, tucked away behind a group of small islands to the south. Alternatively, after rounding the north of the island of Lusärna to enter the inner harbour, the commercial port is clearly to be seen. There is a small marina immediately northwest of the commercial quays, but although it is close to the town, it is suitable only for shallow-draught yachts. Half a mile north is the well equipped Blå Kustens yacht harbour. Mooring is bows-to with stern to buoy. Many of the berths are reserved, so it is important for visitors to check at the harbour office immediately on arrival. In 1991 an overnight mooring fee of £14 was charged for a yacht 12 metres long, but this included free use of the showers, sauna, laundry and swimming pool.

General facilities

Blå Kustens: showers, sauna, toilets, laundry and swimming pool, together with a restaurant, a supermarket, a chandlery and a wide range of other shops, all form part of the administration block at the side of the marina.

Should it not be possible to satisfy one's requirements from these shops, the town centre is approximately one mile away.

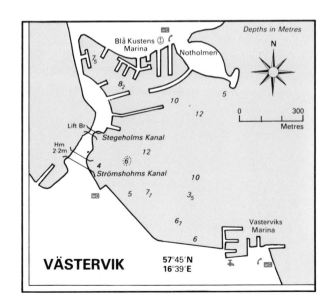

Log raft at the entrance to Västervik.

Blå Kustens marina, Västervik.

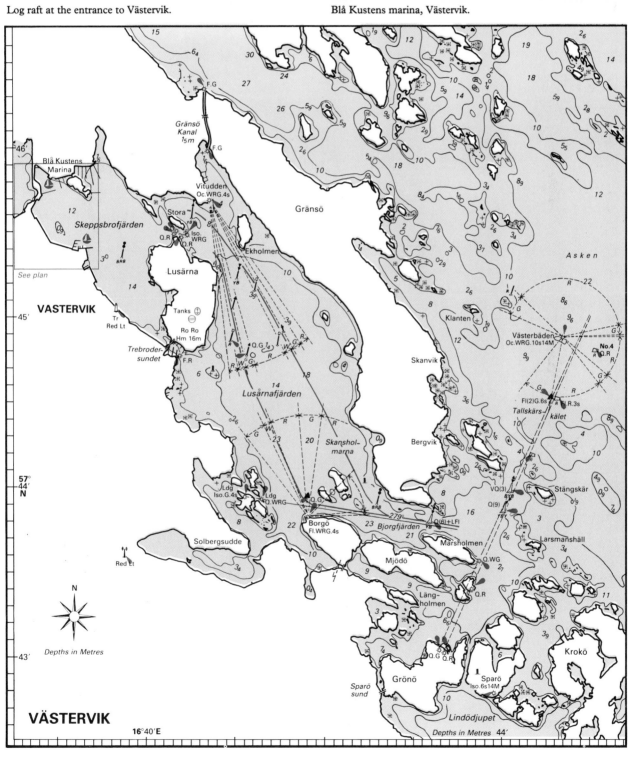

VÄSTERVIK

16°40'E

149

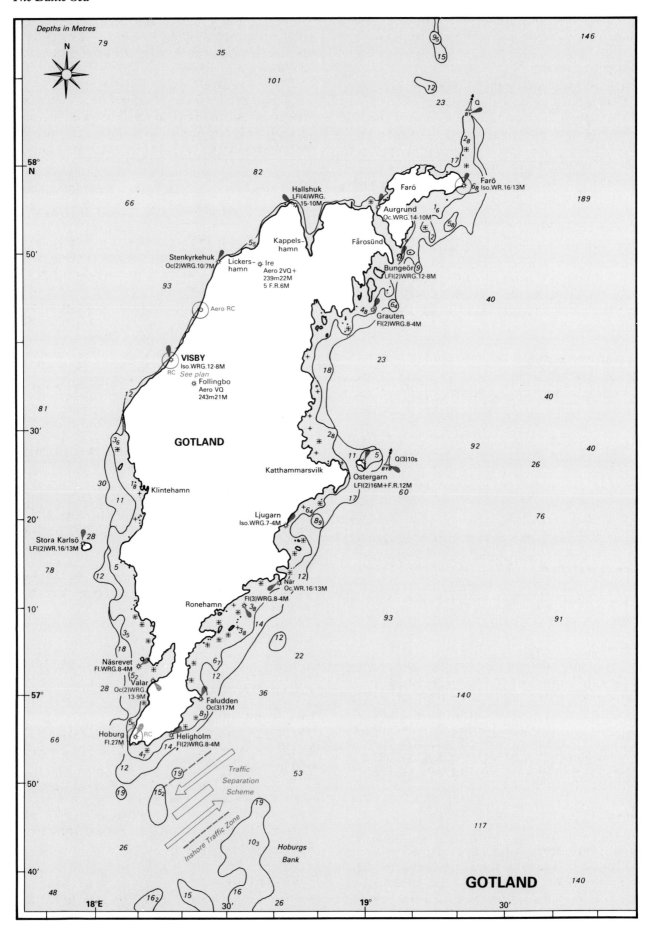

Depths in Metres

N

79

35

101

146

95

15

12

23

Q
BY

58°
N

82

2 8

17

66

Hallshuk
LFl(4)WRG.
15-10M

Farö

6 8   Farö
Iso.WR.16/13M

189

50'

Kappels-
hamn

Aurgrund
Oc.WRG.14-10M

1 6

Stenkyrkehuk
Oc(2)WRG.10/7M

Lickers-
hamn

Ire
Aero 2VQ+
239m22M
5 F.R.6M

Fårosünd

5 8

2

40

93

Bungeör (9)
LFl(2)WRG.12-8M

Aero RC

6 4

4 8   Grauten
Fl(2)WRG.8-4M

VISBY
Iso.WRG.12-8M

RC   *See plan*

Follingbo
Aero VQ
243m21M

23

18

40

81

30'

GOTLAND

2 8

3 6

11   5   Q(3)10s
BYB

92

26

40

30

1 8   Klintehamn

Katthammarsvilk

Ostergarn
LFl(2)16M+F.R.12M

60

11

20'

Stora Karlsö   28
LFl(2)WR.16/13M

Ljugarn
Iso.WRG.7-4M

6 4

8 9

17

76

78

5

12

När
Oc.WR.16/13M

12

10'

Ronehamn

Fl(3)WRG.8-4M

3 8

14

93

91

3 5

3 8

18

12

22

Näsrevet
Fl.WRG.8-4M

6 7

5 2   Valar
28   Oc(2)WRG.
13-9M

12

36

140

57°

Faludden
Oc(3)17M

8 7

5 5

Hoburg
Fl.27M

RC   Heligholm
Fl(2)WRG.8-4M

4 7   14

66

12

19

Traffic
Separation
Scheme

53

50'

15 2

19

19

117

26

10 3   Hoburgs
Bank

40'

48

16 2   15   16   26   **GOTLAND**   140

18°E   **30'**   **19°**   **30'**

Banks, restaurants and hotels can be found in the town. There is also a tourist information office.

Yachting services

There are water and electricity on the pontoons, and a fuelling berth within the marina.

Chandlery can be bought on the marina site, and arrangements can be made for most types of repair.

English-language weather forecasts are broadcast at the normal times, morning and evening, on Stockholm Radio. The marina office also publishes daily forecasts for the local area.

Communications

International calls can be made from telephone kiosks within the marina. Facsimile and telex services are available through the marina office.

Stockholm Radio, through its satellite transmitter at Västervik, provides facilities for link calls on VHF Ch 23 and 85.

Travel

There are coach services from Västervik to the major centres, and there is a regular ferry sailing to Visby.

Visby

57°39'N 18°17'E

Distances

Vastervik 55M, Arkösund 65M, Kalmar 95M.

Charts and guides

Admiralty charts *2361, 2251* and *2288*
Swedish charts *72, 73* and *731*
Baltic Pilot Volume II (NP 19)

Lights

1. **Ire** 57°49'N 18°37'E Aero 2 VQ(vert)239m22M and 5F.R.6M Radio tower. This light is 3M inland.
2. **Visby** 57°38'·1N 18°16'·6E Iso.WRG.4s11m12-8M Round white concrete structure, floodlit, 8m 007°-R-044°-G-055°-W-087°-R-209°-G-239°-W-245°-R-296 RC 290·5kHz *VY* (···−/−·−−) 30M
3. **Stora Karlsö** 57°17'·5N 17°57'·8E LFl(2)WR.12s56m 16-13M White tower on dwelling, 18m 340°-W-193°-R-212°-W-233°-R-340°

General

Through its position in the Baltic, Visby became one of the most important trading centres of Europe in the 10th and 11th centuries, and later a principal depot of the Hanseatic League. Its wealth and its strategic position led to conflict, and the island of Gotland changed hands many times between the Swedes, the Danes and lastly the Russians (most

recently in 1808). Visby's 13th-century towers and walls are a striking sight from the sea, and they and the ten early medieval churches are good evidence of her former importance.

Visby now has a population of 20,000 and is the only town of any size on Gotland. It is a pleasant mixture of old and new, and attracts many tourists. Its harbour is very popular with yachtsmen, and can be very crowded and noisy during the warm summer nights.

Approach

Entry to Visby should not be attempted in bad weather.

The approach from the west is straightforward, keeping a west cardinal buoy to starboard in order to avoid the shoals to the south of the fairway leading into the harbour mouth.

There are four or five tall radio masts in various parts of the island of Gotland, equipped with extremely bright white strobe lights, and these should not be confused with Ire light[1]. The masts are difficult to identify on the chart, and at night tend to give the impression that the island is closer than it is in reality.

Anchorage

The coast near Visby is very exposed, and anchoring outside the harbour is not recommended.

Berthing

The yacht marina occupies the north end of the harbour. Mooring is with bows to a pontoon and stern to a buoy. The harbour office is in a wooden building beside the pontoons.

In 1990 an overnight mooring fee of £8 was charged for a 12 metre yacht. Showers operate on a coin-in-the-slot principle.

Formalities

If Visby is the first port of call in Sweden and if it is desired to obtain customs clearance, there is a customs office near the harbour.

General facilities

Water and electricity are provided on the pontoons. There are toilets and showers, crowded at times, near the marina office.

There are plenty of sources of food supplies in the town, within a few hundred metres of the harbour.

The tourist information office is beside the harbour, and there are banks, restaurants and hotels within a few minutes' walk.

Yachting services

Fuel can be purchased from a fuelling point on the quayside. There is a general chandlery near the marina.

The busy yacht harbour at Visby.

Visby is not a good place for repairs, although some help may be obtainable from various firms which exist for the benefit of the fishing boats and commercial shipping.

Weather forecasts in English are broadcast at 0933 and 1933 UT on VHF by Stockholm Radio.

Communications

There are numerous telephone kiosks in the vicinity of the yacht harbour.

VHF public correspondence is transmitted though the three remotely controlled transmitting stations of Stockholm Radio on Gotland. One is at Visby, operating on Ch 25, one at Fårö in the north of the island, operating on Ch 28, and one at the Hoburgen in the south, on Ch 24.

Travel

There are frequent air and ferry connections with the mainland, and there are buses to all parts of Gotland.

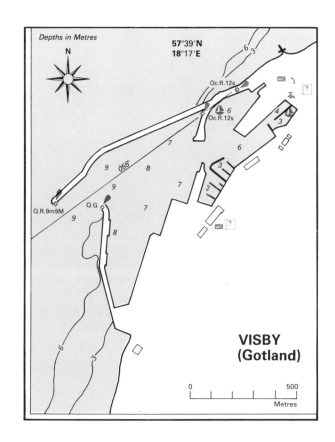

152

Kalmar

56°40'N 16°21'E

Distances

Simrishamn 100M, Visby 95M, Vastervik 65M.

Charts and guides

Admiralty charts *2251* and *3435*
Swedish charts *81, 712, 713* and *819*
Baltic Pilot Volume II (NP 19)

Lights

1. **Dämman** 57°03'·4N 16°41'·7E Iso.WRG.4s20m16-12M Orange tower, black band, grey base, floodlit, 21m 010°-G-021°-W-024'·5-R-120°-G-169°-W-209°-R-010°
2. **Slottsbraden** 56°55'·7N 16°36'·3E Fl(2)WRG.6s20m 14-10M Black tower, green band and lantern, grey conical base, floodlit, 21m 018°-W-022°-R-048°-G-098°-R-184°-G-202°-W-208°-R-359°-G-018°
3. **Utgrunden** 56°22'·5N 16°15'·7E LFl.WRG.8s26m11-7M Horn 30s Black tower, white band and lantern, grey conical base, 28m. 019°-R-096°-G-153°-R-166°-G-185°-W-192°-R-265°-G-292°-R-316·5°-G-349°-W-019° Racon all round
4. **Ölands Södra Udde** 56°11'·8N 16°24'E Fl(2)30s41m 26M and F.WRG.19m19-14M Round white stone tower, black bands, floodlit, 42m 153·5°-G-159°-W-167·5°-R-to shore

5. **Ölands Södra Grund** 56°04'·2N 16°40'·8E Iso.8s 33m21M Horn Mo(R)30s Black tower, red bands, grey base, floodlit, 35m. RC 313·5kHz *ÖG* (−−−·/−−·) 70M
6. **Utklippan south rock** 55°57'·2N 15°42'·2E Fl.15s 31m23M and Iso.WRG.4s30m16-12M Horn(2)30s Red framework tower on old fort, 30m. 134°-G-140°-R-189°-G-223°-W-240°-R-299°-W-134°

General

Kalmar is one of Sweden's oldest towns, and the scene of the Union of Kalmar, 1397. It was originally a Viking stronghold, and became one of the major ports of the Hanseatic League.

The present town, with a population of around 50,000, has many historic buildings dating back to the 17th century, a fine baroque cathedral and a picturesque castle, parts of which are over 800 years old, standing in a dominating position overlooking Kalmarsund. The castle museum has an exciting exhibition of articles from the sunken galleon *Kronan*.

Kalmar has a very good shopping centre, within easy walking distance of the harbour.

Approach

The sound between the mainland and Öland is for the most part about 5 miles wide, and it can funnel the wind to provide some very brisk sailing.

Ölands Bridge at Kalmar, the longest bridge in Europe.

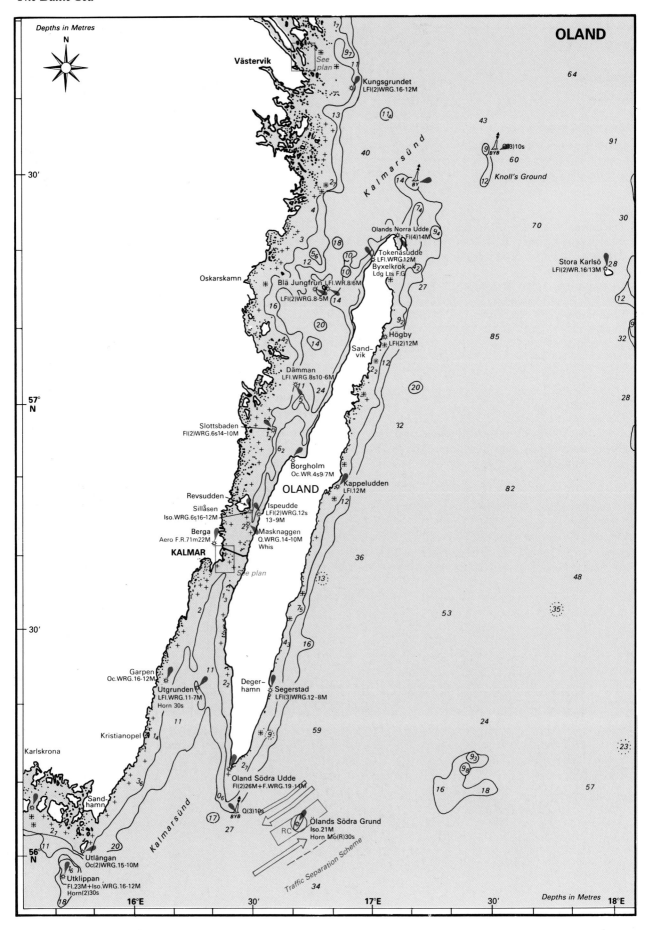

OLAND

Depths in Metres
N

30'

Västervik

See plan

Kungsgrundet
LFl(2)WRG.16-12M

64

91

30'

Knoll's Ground

30

70

Olands Norra Udde
LFl(4)14M

Tokenäsudde
LFl.WRG.12M
Byxelkrok
Ldg Lts F.G

Stora Karlsö
LFl(2)WR.16/13M

12

Oskarskamn

Blå Jungfrun LFl.WR.8/6M
LFl(2)WRG.8-5M

Högby
LFl(2)12M

Sand-
vik

85

32

57°
N

Dämman
LFl.WRG.8s10-6M

28

Slottsbaden
Fl(2)WRG.6s14-10M

32

Borgholm
Oc.WR.4s9/7M

OLAND

Kappeludden
LFl.12M

82

Revsudden

Sillåsen
Iso.WRG.6s16-12M

Ispeudde
LFl(2)WRG.12s
13-9M

Berga
Aero F.R.71m22M

Masknaggen
Q.WRG.14-10M
Whis

KALMAR

See plan

36

48

30'

53

35

Garpen
Oc.WRG.16-12M

Degerhamn

Segerstad
LFl(3)WRG.12-8M

24

Utgrunden
LFl.WRG.11-7M
Horn 30s

Kristianopel

59

23

Karlskrona

Oland Södra Udde
Fl(2)26M+F.WRG.19-14M

Sand-
hamn

57

Kalmarsünd

Q(3)10s

Ölands Södra Grund
Iso.21M
Horn Mo(R)30s

RC

56
N

Utlängan
Oc(2)WRG.15-10M

Utklippan
Fl.23M+Iso.WRG.16-12M
Horn(2)30s

Traffic Separation Scheme

34

16°E   30'   17°E   30'   Depths in Metres   18°E

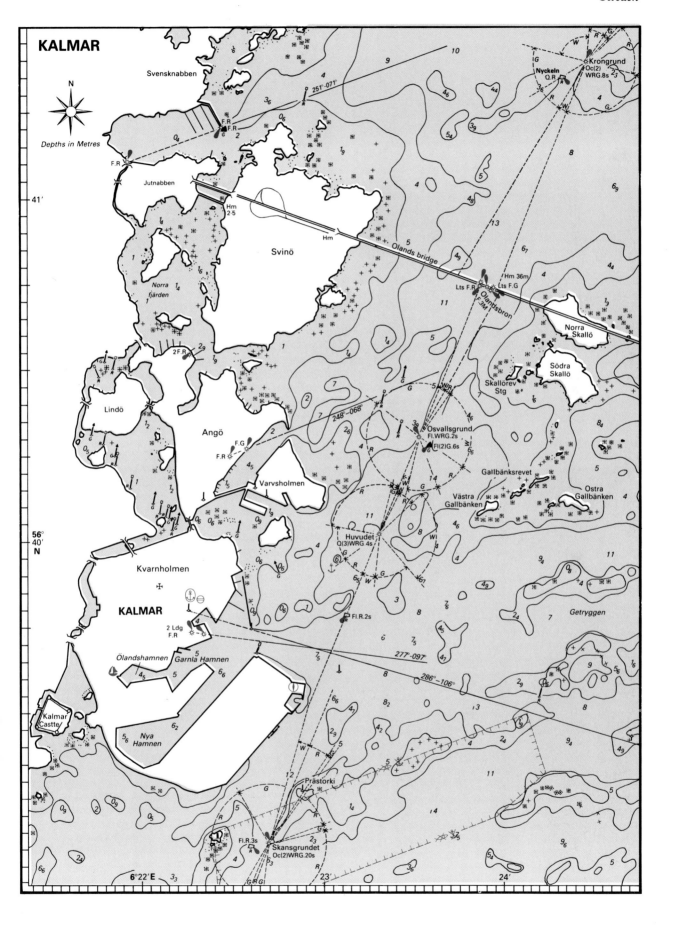

Kalmar castle and the entrance to the yacht harbour.

The Ölands Bridge at Kalmar.

From the north, pass either side of the conical island of Blå Jungfrun, a nature reserve, and sail down the centre of Kalmarsund, eventually following the broad but winding channel between Slottsbraden, Silläsen, Ispeudde and Masknaggen lighthouses into the Kalmarsunds Djupränna, leaving Krongrund lighthouse to port at the entrance. The harbour entrance is to starboard shortly after passing under the spectacular 3·5 mile long bridge (clearance 36m) which connects the island of Öland to the mainland.

From the south, steer up the centre of Kalmarsund, passing either side of Utgrunden lighthouse, and enter Kalmarsunds Djupränna, the dredged channel 2·5 miles long which leads N–S immediately opposite Kalmar. Its north and south limits are marked by Krongrund and Skansgrund lighthouses respectively, and the entrance to Kalmar harbour leads off it to the west. There is a traffic separation scheme around Ölands Södra Grund.

Anchorage

It is not permitted to anchor in the immediate vicinity of Kalmar harbour.

Berthing

The commercial quays to the south of the town should be ignored. Yachts will find it far more satisfactory to use the older harbour, whose entrance is off the west side of the Kalmarsunds Djupränna, south of the bridge.

From the harbour entrance, there is a choice between the customs quay opposite the entrance and the yacht harbour, which is in the inner harbour, just past the new shopping centre which has been created in a complex of old quayside warehouses.

Mooring at the customs quay is free, but there are no facilities. The inner harbour, which has been made into a yacht harbour, is perhaps more comfortable, but there was a charge in 1990 of about £7 a night. Mooring is with bows to the dockside and stern to a buoy, as in most Scandinavian harbours.

Formalities

If entering Sweden at Kalmar and requiring customs clearance, contact the customs by telephone through the harbour office. Tying up in the customs harbour near the main harbour entrance does not seem to attract the attention of the customs officers.

General facilities

Water and electricity are both available on the quayside. There are toilets and showers by the harbour office. All food supplies are within easy walking distance.

The tourist office is situated within 200 metres of the harbour, and there are many banks, restaurants and hotels.

Yachting services

Fuel can be purchased at the quayside. There is a well stocked chandlery close to the harbour, and *Camping Gaz* could be purchased. There are facilities for most types of repair.

Weather forecasts can be heard on Stockholm Radio at 0933 and 2133 UT, VHF Ch 26.

Communications

There are numerous telephone kiosks within easy reach of the harbour.

Stockholm Radio has a satellite transmitter at Emmaboda, not far from Kalmar, and provides a public correspondence service on VHF Ch 26.

Travel

The railway station is about 200 metres from the harbour, and there are good services to all major towns. There are also coach services to many parts of Sweden.

Simrishamn

55°33'N 14°22'E

Distances

Gislövs Läge 50M, Kalmar 100M.

Charts and guides

Admiralty chart *2360*
Swedish charts *82, 83* and *839*
Baltic Pilot Volume II (NP 19)

Lights

1. **Simrishamn** 55°33'·5N 14°22'E Iso.WRG.6s16m13-9M Horn 60s White tower, 15m. Shore-G-160°-W-223°-G-238°-W-279°-R-285°-W-355°-R-shore
2. **Sandhammaren** 55°23'N 14°11'·8E Fl.5s31m22M Red metal tower, framework base

General

Simrishamn is a small town of around 8,000 inhabitants, with a commercial harbour and, leading off it, a well equipped yacht harbour. It is a very convenient stopping place on the way to or from the northern Baltic.

Approach

The windmill above the town and Simrishamn lighthouse are good landmarks, and there are leading marks on a line of 250° leading into the wide harbour entrance. There are no significant hazards.

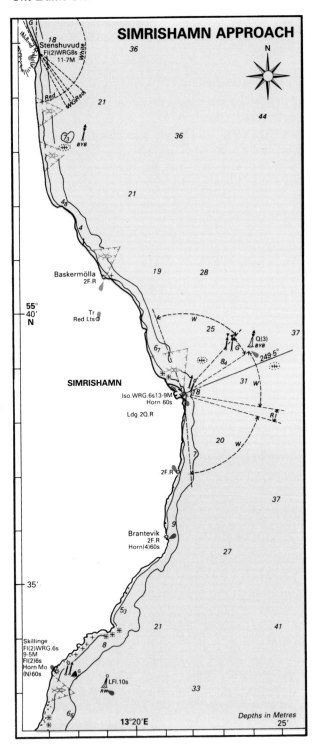

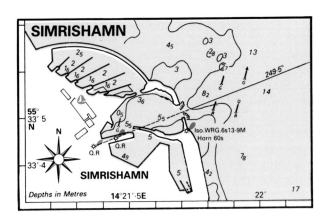

The charge for an overnight stay for a yacht 12 metres long was approximately £5 in 1991, with showers extra.

Formalities

Should customs clearance be required, it is best to ask the harbour office to telephone for officers to come to the marina.

General facilities

Water and electricity are both available on the pontoons, and there are toilets, showers and washing machines ashore.

Food supplies can be obtained in the town, less than one kilometre away from the harbour.

A tourist office, banks, restaurants and hotels are all within easy reach of the harbour.

Yachting services

Fuel will be delivered by arrangement through the harbourmaster.

There is a yachting shop which sells charts and clothing, together with some items of chandlery.

Motor and electronics repairs can be arranged, and there is a sailmaker who can be contacted through the harbour office.

English-language weather forecasts can be heard at 0933 and 2133 UT on Stockholm Radio.

Communications

There are telephone kiosks near the harbour.

Stockholm Radio, through a remotely controlled transmitter at Kivik, operates on VHF Ch 28 for public correspondence services and weather forecasts.

Travel

There is a bus station approximately 300 metres from the harbour.

Anchorage

The coast near Simrishamn is very exposed and steep-to. Anchoring outside recognised harbours is not recommended.

Berthing

The yacht marina is immediately to starboard after entering the main harbour. Mooring is to pontoons with stern buoys or narrow fingers.

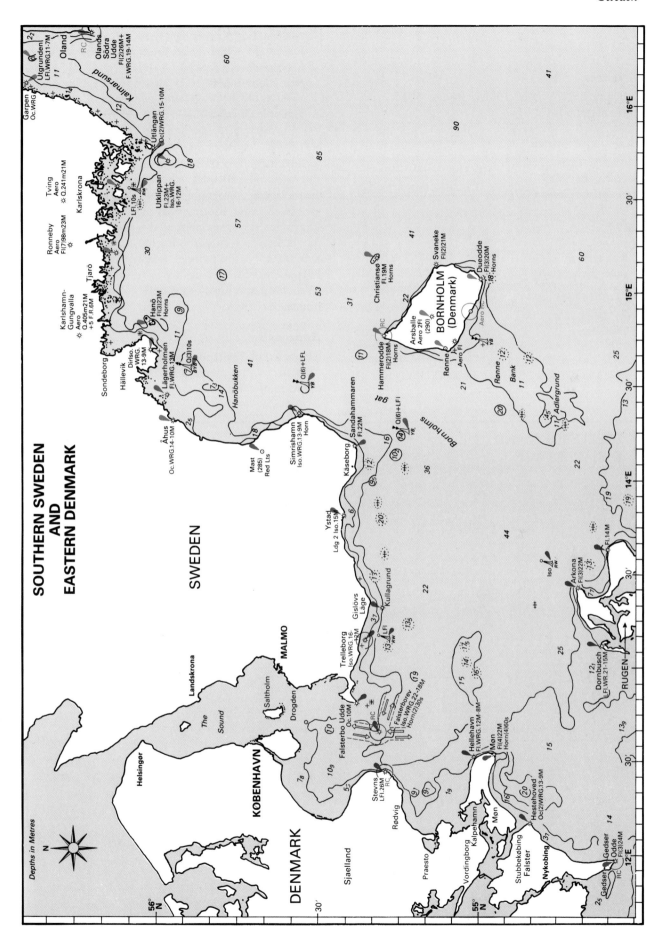

SOUTHERN SWEDEN
AND
EASTERN DENMARK

Depths in Metres

N

SWEDEN

DENMARK

MALMO

KOBENHAVN

Landskrona

Helsingor

The
Sound

Saltholm

Drogden

Sjaelland

Falster

Mon

Gislövs Läge

55°21'·3N 13°14'·5E

Distances

København 35M, Kiel 135M, Rønne 55M, Simrishamn 50M.

Charts and guides

Admiralty chart *2360, 2115*
Swedish chart *839*
Baltic Pilot Volume I (NP 18)

Lights

Approach

1. **Kullagrund** 55°17'·9N 13°19'·5E Iso.WRG.4s18m16-12M Red tower with black band, white lantern, floodlit, 20m 181°-R-244°-G-271°-W-105°-R-120°-G-181°
   Racon all round 14M
2. **Trelleborg** 55°21'·4N 13°09'·1E Iso.WRG.8s12m16-12M Grey conical base, black tower with white band, white lantern, floodlit, 15m 279°-G-311·5°-W-060°-R-082°-G-110°-W-279° Racon all round 13M

Entrance

3. **Gislövs Ldg Lts** 022·5° *Front* 55°21'·3N 13°13'·9E F.R.4m7M White ▲, red bands on framework tower.
   Inner pier heads floodlit
   Rear 201m from front 55°21'·4N 13°14'E F.R.11m7M White ▼, red bands on framework tower
4. ~~**West pier head** 55°21'·3N 13°13'·9E Horn Mo(A)60s~~

General

Gislövs Läge is a pleasant yacht harbour 5M east of the town of Trelleborg, which has a major ferry port and a large commercial harbour, but no facilities for yachts. Several fishing boats are based at Gislövs Läge, but the main part of the harbour is reserved for yachts, and is administered as one of the civil amenities of Trelleborg. Ashore, there is a small village, partly serving as a residential area for Trelleborg and partly as a quiet location for holiday homes.

Approach

The town of Trelleborg is very obvious from the sea, marked by the continual comings and goings of passenger ferries and other large vessels.

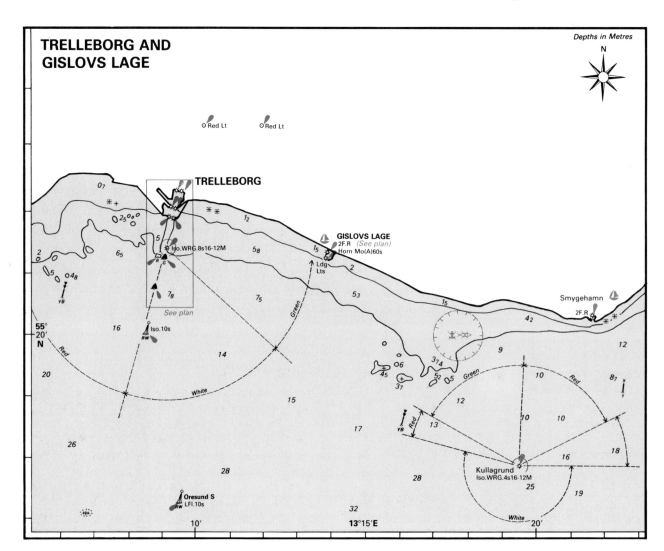

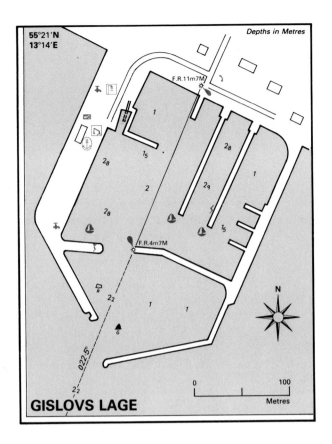

GISLOVS LAGE

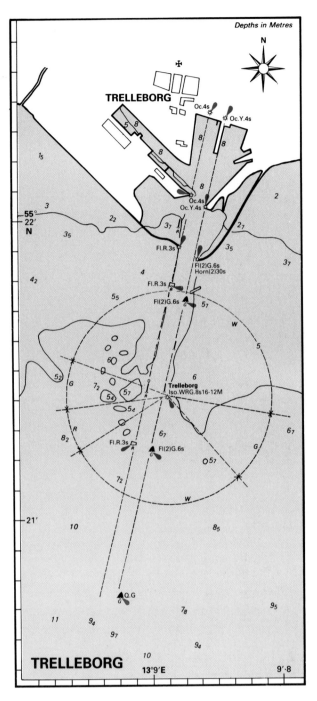

TRELLEBORG

Once within three miles of the coast, in normal visibility the entrance of Gislövs Läge can be seen without difficulty, by day or night approximately 5M east of Trelleborg. Approach is at 022·5°, with leading lights in line. Unlit channel markers indicate the last half mile of the approach, and the pier heads can be seen clearly from a distance of one mile.

There is a small outer harbour with several small red and green buoys just inside the entrance indicating the way into the inner harbour, which has a uniform depth of approximately 2 metres.

Anchorage

The coast on each side of the harbour entrance is gently shelving, and there are no restrictions on anchoring, except in marked fairways. If all berths are full, it is permitted to anchor temporarily in the harbour.

Berthing

There is a new pontoon in the centre of the harbour, specially reserved for visitors. Mooring is with bows to the pontoon and stern lines to posts.

Harbour dues are collected from the yacht. In 1991 an overnight mooring fee of approximately £4 was charged for a yacht 12 metres long.

Formalities

Customs authorities can be contacted through the yacht club if needed. If a yacht has goods to declare it must go to the customs quay in Trelleborg.

General facilities

Water and electricity are within reach of every boat. The toilets, showers and washing machines are near the yacht club at the side of the harbour.

Food supplies can be purchased at a small super-market about 10 minutes' walk from the harbour. Bread is available at the kiosk in the harbour.

The nearest tourist information office is 5 miles away in Trelleborg, which can be reached easily by bus. There are also banks, restaurants and hotels in Trelleborg.

Reflections at Gislövs Läge.

Yachting services

Fuel is available on the quayside.

VHF weather forecasts can be obtained twice daily on Stockholm Radio.

Communications

The telephone kiosk near the visitors' pontoon is card operated, but there is a coin box near the supermarket.

The area is served by the Smygehuk radio transmitter, controlled remotely as part of Stockholm Radio, and operating on VHF Ch 24 for public correspondence. Göteborg radio can be received on Ch 21.

Travel

There are frequent ferries from Trelleborg to Travemünde and Bornholm, rail services to Malmö and Stockholm, and buses to most parts of southern Sweden.

Other ports in the Skargard + on the East Coast

The east coast of Sweden is an extremely attractive cruising area, characterised by many thousands of small islands, many of them with interesting harbours or anchorages. Rather than attempt to provide comprehensive coverage of every harbour and anchorage, the notes below describe a selection of smaller harbours likely to be attractive or convenient to visiting yachtsmen.

Gräddö 59°46'N 19°02'E
A small, picturesque harbour. Interesting stop on the way to Åland if time is not pressing.

Granhamn 59°44'N 19°07'·9E
A good place to wait for favourable conditions for a crossing to Mariehamn. The mooring rings were used by clippers; English graffiti dates from 1759.

Furusund 59°39'·7N 18°55'·3E
Small yacht harbour overlooked by windmill. Shops and a restaurant. A convenient overnight stop en route between Stockholm and Mariehamn.

Rödlöga 59°35'·8N 19°10'·5E
Beautiful natural harbour. Moor bows to rocks.

The yacht harbour at Furusund.

Möja 59°24'·7N 18°54'E
Small fishing village.

Vaxholm 59°24'N 18°21'E
Ancient castle overlooking the water. Good small yacht harbour, but very popular and subject to considerable wash. Fuel available.

Sandhamn 59°17'N 18°55'E
The Cowes of Sweden, with frequent ferries to and from Stockholm. Picturesque. Each year around 500 yachts start from Sandhamn to compete in the famous round-Gotland race.

Saltsjöbaden 59°17'N 18°18'E
A spa and summer holiday resort only half an hour by rail from Stockholm. Good yacht harbour, shops, hotels and restaurants.

Runmarö 59°16'·5N 18°43'·9E
Royal Swedish Sailing Club quay, but nothing else. Well maintained. 6 boats or so only.

Södertälje 59°12'N 17°38'E
Commercial port on the Södertälje Kanal, the 'back entrance' to Stockholm. Tie up to wooden quay southwest of sea locks. Can be shallow (1·8m). *Calor Gas* and *Camping Gaz* available at Oljehamnen, to the south of the town.

Dalarö 59°08'N 18°25'E
Small marina on east side, ferry and fishing harbour on south side. Marina has water, electricity and toilets but no showers. Picturesque, higgledy-piggledy wooden houses.

Utö 58°58'N 18°19'·5E
Favourite destination for yachtsmen from Stockholm. Interesting historical site of 300m-deep iron mine, now filled with water. Miners used to take food for a week because of the difficulty of climbing into and out of the mine. Special liqueur now unobtainable from mining days: strong version for men and weak version for women.

Nynäshamn 58°54'N 17°57'E
Not particularly attractive, but a good marina and market. Ferries to Gotland and Poland.

Trosa 58°54'N 17°33'E
Known as 'the end of the world'. Very picturesque indeed. Situated on a small river. Yacht harbour ~~in centre of town~~. Very popular.

1m S~~E~~ of town centre ★

Oxelösund 58°40'N 17°06'E
A steel town,~~ but~~ ★★ attractive. It has a large and pleasant ~~yacht harbour~~ with good facilities.

★★ with 2 marinas + good facilities. Long walk to town shops

Fårösund 57°52'N 19°04'E
Small town at the northernmost tip of Gotland. Preferred to Visby by many people.

★ fasthamn to E of river mouth is shallow; deep draft boats moor in river on starboard bank where there is W & E

163

The Baltic Sea

Kappelshamn 57°51'N 18°47'E
A pleasant small commercial and fishing port on the island of Gotland.

Lickershamn 57°50'N 18°31'E
Attractive fishing harbour on the island of Gotland.

Oskarshamn 57°16'N 16°27'E
A pleasant small town. Famous for a woodcarver who carved caricatures of fishermen and animals.

Sandvik 57°04'N 16°52'E
Holiday village on the island of Öland, with small yacht harbour.

Borgholm 56°53'N 16°39'E
Attractive and popular harbour. Town popular for jet-set parties. The king of Sweden has a castle nearby.

Byxelkrok 56°19'·7N 17°00'·5E
A nice combined fishing and yacht harbour with good fish and bread.

Utklippan 55°57'N 15°42'E
A collection of tiny islands joined by concrete quays to form a minuscule harbour. Complete shelter.

Enter in calm weather only from east or west by rock-fringed but well buoyed channels. Lighthouse keepers collect dues. No services, but very wild and attractive.

Karlskrona 56°10'N 15°36'E
Major naval base, but also attractive yachting port. Detailed chart necessary for entry.

Tjärö
Beautiful but very popular island with pontoon and various anchorages.

Hanö 56°00'·8N 14°50'·9E
Attractive island with small fishing harbour and village. English cemetery dating from 1810. Popular with local yachtsmen.

Sölvesborg 56°03'N 14°35'E
Small, sheltered yacht harbour in a small town at the head of a long inlet. Trains to Malmö and Stockholm.

The bridge over the Falsterbo Canal.

Kivik 55°41'N 14°14'E
Small fishing harbour with several resident yachts.
Bronze Age grave.

Kåseberga 55°23N 14°04'E
Tiny fishing harbour with fish smokery and
Stonehenge-like stones.

Ystad 55°26'N 13°50'E
Approach shared with ferries, but separate entrance
to small well kept marina with all facilities. Town
centre close by. A convenient and interesting staging
post on the way to or from more northerly places.

Falsterbo 55°25'N 12°50'E
Coming from København this is a likely entry point
for Sweden. There is a swing bridge over the canal
and a waiting area just inside the north end of the
canal. Customs clearance can be obtained.

see corrections for Lake Mälaren

7. Denmark

This guide is concerned only with that part of the kingdom of Denmark which lies along one of the main routes to the Baltic. Of the remnants of her overseas interests, which have included amalgamations with England, Sweden and Norway, Iceland became an independent republic in 1944; Greenland and the Faroe Islands are integral parts of the kingdom, with full internal self-government.

Sailing is very popular amongst Danes, and there are numerous attractive and well equipped harbours throughout the kingdom. The only problem is that, such is their attractiveness, they are often full, not only of Danes but of Germans and Swedes as well; however, Scandinavian schools return to work in early August, and the congestion thereafter lessens.

A brief history

From the 11th to the 17th century the Danes were concerned to establish trading and territorial rights throughout the Baltic, a process in which contact often resulted in conflict. Denmark early established trading posts in the east of the Baltic en route to Russia (for instance, Tallinn in 1219) but she did not hold them for long. After dispute, an act of union was signed at Kalmar in 1397, nominally uniting the three Scandinavian countries, and Eric of Pomerania was crowned as king. However, the three tended to act as separate entities, and in due course the eastern part of Sweden established a separate existence.

When Denmark has not been involved with Norway and Sweden in their common objective of stemming German intrusion, her history has been largely that of her attempts to consolidate her own institutions and territories, and to ensure a revenue from the operations of her own traders and from her control of the Sound. This has at various times brought her into conflict, not only with Sweden and Germany, but also with the Dutch, who replaced the Hanseatic League as the carriers of the Baltic trade, and were squeezed by dues at the Sound (see København). Despite the difficulties which the Danes had with the Germans, by the end of the 17th century Denmark had a decidedly German stamp. German was the language of administration, of command in the army, and of the court, which became absolutist. Much was spent on the maintenance of the court, on building decorative but unnecessary castles, and on the upkeep of the army and navy. At the same time the navy and the academic world, including the church, were strongly nationalistic. A great interest in the country's own language, literature and history developed, as did interest in science and agriculture.

After a remarkable increase in Baltic trade in 1730, ship owners and merchants gained a new confidence. The combination of interest and confidence led to the establishment being questioned on such matters as its control of trade and its policy towards agriculture, which was badly in need of reform. At the end of the century a series of reforms was started. Old monopolies were abolished, agriculture was further improved, the Danish peasant was released from his 'serfdom' and landowners were prevented from swallowing up small holdings – the effect of the last is noticeable in the landscape. Denmark, with good internal policies, did well through her insistence upon her right as a neutral to carry anyone's goods in her ships. This insistence was one factor which brought her into conflict with the British, who, concerned with their fight with the French, pretended a right to search ships at sea. Although the British claim was enforced after the Battle of Copenhagen in 1801, differences were not settled, and Nelson's bombardment of København in 1807, together with the seizure of the Danish fleet, drove the Danish monarchy to side with the French, against the wish of the majority in both Denmark and Norway. The result was the ruin of trade, war with Russia and Sweden, the loss of Norway to Sweden and national bankruptcy.

It was difficult enough to recover economically, and internal reform was further slowed by the problem of Schleswig and Holstein, to which both Denmark and Germany had a claim through the two intermingled populations. Germany resorted to force, and in 1864 Denmark ceded both territories. Feeling that her aspirations were neglected by the rest of Europe, Denmark concentrated her efforts on internal matters, agriculture, economics and science. Politically there continued to be sharply different points of view, with the richer urban population sharing a position with the landowners and many of the civil and military leaders, and the producers, steadily coming up in the world, allied to liberal opinion in commerce and the professions. A constitution was not settled until 1915, but there was steady improvement in the performance of agriculture and industry.

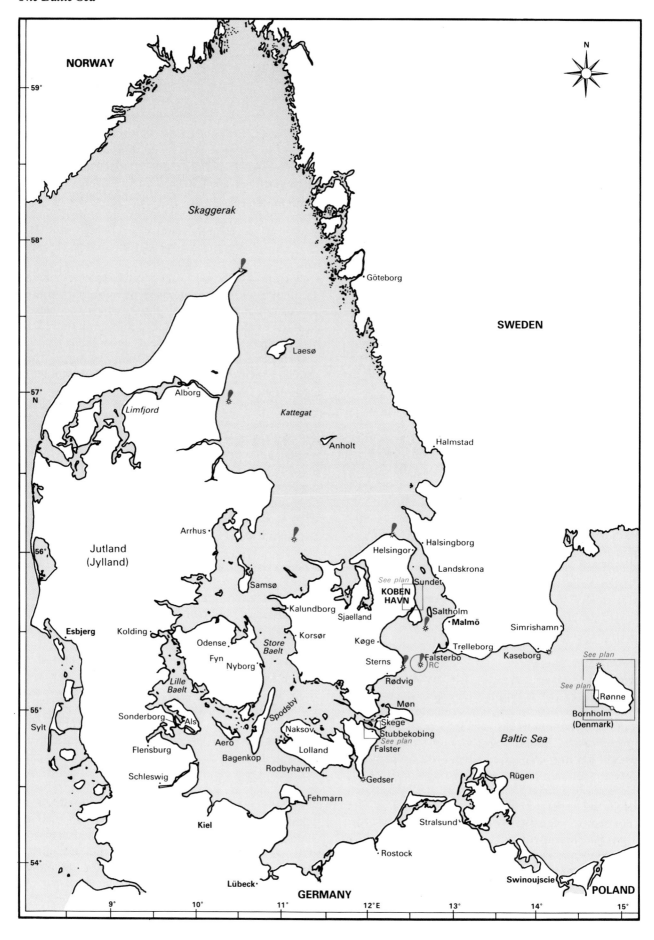

NORWAY

59°

Skaggerak

58°

Göteborg

SWEDEN

Laesø

57°
N

Alborg

Limfjord

Kattegat

Anholt

Halmstad

Arrhus

Jutland
(Jylland)

56°

Helsingor

Halsingborg

Landskrona

See plan Sundet

Samsø

KOBEN
HAVN

Saltholm

Kalundborg

Malmö

Esbjerg

Kolding

Sjaelland

Korsør

Simrishamn

Odense

*Store
Baelt*

Køge

Trelleborg

Falsterbo
RC

See plan

Fyn

Nyborg

Sterns

Kaseborg

See plan

*Lille
Baelt*

55°

Sylt

Sonderborg

Als

Spodsby

Rødvig

Møn

Skege

Ronne

Bornholm
(Denmark)

Flensburg

Aero

Bagenkop

Naksov

Lolland

Stubbekobing

See plan
Falster

Baltic Sea

Schleswig

Rodbyhavn

Gedser

Rügen

Fehmarn

Kiel

Stralsund

54°

Rostock

Swinoujscie

POLAND

Lübeck

GERMANY

9°   10°   11°   12°E   13°   14°   15°

Denmark remained neutral in the First World War; she sold her West Indian possessions to the USA in 1917, gave Iceland her independence under the crown in 1918, and, after a plebiscite, recovered northern Schleswig in 1920. Between the wars her agricultural and industrial efficiency was further improved despite a generally difficult trading situation. In the Second World War, Denmark submitted under protest to a German invasion in 1940, and the situation deteriorated into a state of war in 1943. By the time the Germans left in 1945 they had pillaged the country. Since then, and with some pain, Denmark has re-established her position as a leading agricultural producer, besides developing a significant manufacturing industry. The present constitution of Denmark is founded on the charter of 5 June 1953, which places the legislative power with the crown and a single chamber, the Folketing, and the executive power with the crown through its ministers, the judiciary being separate.

The people

Some 90% of the population of over five million is estimated to belong to the Lutheran Church, which was established in 1536 and is the national church, under the direction of the state. Education has been compulsory since 1814, and there are three universities and two university centres, besides various other institutions of higher education. A comprehensive social security system covers health, pensions, industrial accidents, unemployment and certain other hazards.

The Danes are friendly, tolerant and relaxed. They enjoy their pleasures and are happy for other people to enjoy theirs. Within sailing circles, however, they are under pressure from the recent great increase in visiting yachts.

The economy

Denmark has one major natural resource, the land, and a small but significant capacity for oil production. But the Danish work force is well educated, and has played a substantial role in developing Denmark's industries. Although she is best known for agricultural and fishery products, the value of her exports of those commodities is less than half the value of products manufactured from imported raw materials – metal working generally, machinery, transport, electrical, pharmaceuticals, textiles. Her largest markets are Germany, the UK, Sweden, Norway and the USA.

Money

The unit of currency is the Danish crown.

Exchange is straightforward, and traveller's cheques, Eurocheques and major credit cards are widely used.

Shopping

Housekeeping costs are similar to those in Germany, perhaps 10–20% up on those in the UK. Alcoholic drinks, however, are more expensive but easily available – Denmark here contrasts with Sweden and Finland. Shops usually close on Saturday afternoons.

Yacht services and chandlery

Chandlery is widely available.

Overnight mooring fees tend to be in the range of £5–£10, and diesel costs around the same price as it does in England.

Coast radio stations will give a weather forecast in English on request. Be ready to give the forecast area required.

Communications

All coin and card telephones can be used for international calls. Dial 009 for the international exchange. Facsimile and telex services are widely available. Mail takes 2–3 days to or from England.

Coast radio stations handle public correspondence, but Kiel Radio and Göteborg Radio may also be used.

Travel

Denmark can be reached very easily from most parts of western Europe by air, rail, coach and ship.

Time

Denmark is one hour ahead of UT in winter and two hours ahead from the last Sunday in March until the Saturday before the last Sunday in September.

Formalities

There are few restrictions on yachting in Denmark. Unless carrying dutiable goods, yachts from EC or Scandinavian countries are not required to report to customs. If clearance is required, however, it may be quite difficult to find customs officers (København telephone numbers are listed later).

Yachts from EC countries may stay in Denmark for up to three months. A longer stay can be arranged after arrival, but it is best to make arrangements through a Danish consulate before starting a cruise.

The Danish flag is red with a white Scandinavian cross. It is nearly square; some British flag makers have been cutting them in a pronounced rectangle.

UK representation

British Embassy Kastelvej 36/38/40 DK-2100 København ☎ (45) 31 26 46 00 *Fax* (45) 31 38 10 12 *Telex* 19908.

Rønne (Bornholm) Consulate Fiskerivej 1 DK-3700 Rønne ☎ (45) 56 95 21 11 *Fax* (45) 56 95 25 67 *Telex* 48137.

Danish Embassy in London 55 Sloane Street SW1X 9SR ☎ 071-235 1255.

Navigation

Admiralty charts are useful for the main channels around Denmark, but Danish charts are necessary for exploring the inner channels and visiting the attractive smaller harbours and anchorages. They are obtainable at all yachting centres in Denmark. Mean level is used for chart datum and the wind effect may result in a depth differing by as much as one metre.

Baltic Pilot Volume I (NP 18) covers the Danish islands in great detail but is not the most convenient publication for everyday pilotage.

Cruising guide to Germany and Denmark by Brian Navin (Imray).

Hafenführer Dänemark (DK Edition, Maritim), in German, is extremely useful.

Cruising areas

The most attractive areas for cruising in Denmark are generally considered to be the waters between the two major islands of Fyn and Sjaelland and the islands immediately to the south of them. Under *Other ports,* several smaller harbours have been listed as representing some of the more interesting places to visit without straying too far from the Baltic shores of Denmark. Christiansø, northeast of Bornholm, is also worth visiting if time allows.

København

55°41'N 12°36'E

Distances

Stubbekøbing 55M, Gislövs Läge (Sweden) 35M.

Charts and guides

Admiralty charts *2595, 790* and *3194*
Danish small-craft charts *Series 1*
NV charts *Series 2, Lübecker Bucht bis Bornholm und Kopenhagen*
Baltic Pilot Volume I (NP 18)
Cruising guide to Germany and Denmark Brian Navin, Imray
Hafenführer Dänemark DK Edition Maritim

Lights

1. **Trekroner** 55°42'·2N 12°37'E Oc.WRG.10s20m20-16M White round tower, 12m 175°-R-195°-G-207°-R-214°-G-219·8°-W-222·9°-R-255°-G-316·5°-W-320°-R-336°

General

A friendly city with a strong feeling of history. There is much for the tourist, better described in one of the numerous shore-based guide books than here. The centre of the city can be walked.

After the treaty of Kalmar, Denmark controlled both sides of the Sound, and in 1429 Eric, recognising its potential profitability, imposed a toll on all shipping passing through it. To administer and enforce this toll, he appropriated København (then a Hanseatic town) to the crown and built a second fortification at Helsingör, opposite Hälsingborg. The toll continued to be levied after Denmark lost control of the Swedish shore, and lasted until 1856, when, after increasing numbers of complaints from several countries, the United States simply refused to pay. The duties were abolished by treaty a year later.

Approach

The approaches to København are well marked and well lit. Given any one of the more detailed charts, there is little difficulty in entering this large and busy port. By day and in poor visibility, however, care should be taken in the vicinity of the offlying island of Saltholm, which is surrounded by shoal water and is very low-lying: so much so that it is very easy to misjudge distances.

Anchorage

There are no restrictions on anchoring in the København area except in the channels.

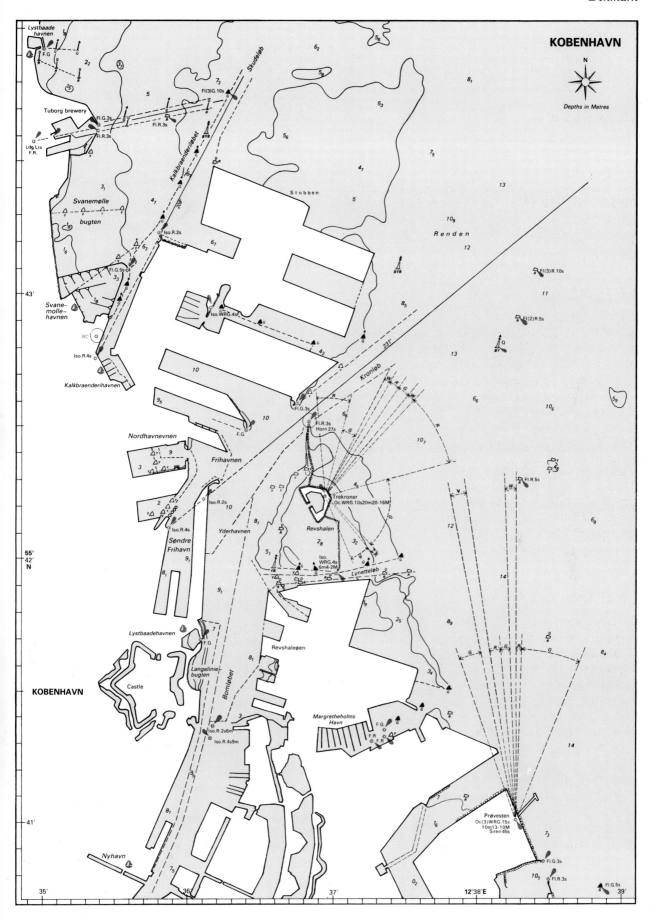

KOBENHAVN

N

Depths in Metres

The small yacht harbour at Hellerup, København.

Nyhavn, København.

Berthing

There are four yacht harbours close to the centre of København: Nyhavn, Langelinie, Svanemølle and Hellerup.

Nyhavn is the picturesque old harbour, close to the city centre, which frequently figures in publicity photographs. Yachts are permitted to tie up near the many historic vessels permanently moored here, but although this is a lively and exciting place to lie for a short while, it can be extremely noisy and uncomfortable for a longer stay. Mooring is alongside the rather high quayside or, more likely, outside other vessels already moored there. There is considerable wash from commercial vessels passing outside. There are no facilities, although there is the convenience of being adjacent to the main shopping centre.

Langelinie is a large and well equipped marina about a kilometre from the city centre. It is always busy, but is useful for its proximity to the city. It lies amongst the parks and gardens near the Little Mermaid, which sits on a rock at the water's edge near Langelinie promenade. Mooring is bows to quay with stern line to a buoy. To be sure of finding a vacant berth it is advisable to arrive at Langelinie early in the day.

Svanemølle, close south of the prominent Tuborg brewery, is 4km from the main shopping centre, but the excellent public transport system makes it easy to travel there, leaving one's boat in relative quiet and safety. The approach is in a southwesterly direction, leaving green buoys to starboard. This harbour tends to be less crowded than Langelinie.

Hellerup is a small yacht harbour 6km from the city centre and 500m north of the Tuborg factory. It is administered by the Hellerup Yacht Club, and comprises a small square basin flanked by trees and overlooked by the yacht club. There is an obvious buoyed channel leading to the south-facing harbour entrance. Mooring is bows-to with stern lines to posts. Visitors are automatically members of the yacht club for the duration of their stay; its facilities include water and electricity on the quayside, toilets, showers, a sauna and an excellent restaurant with umbrella-shaded tables on the balcony overlooking the sea. There is no fuelling berth. In 1991, overnight mooring cost about £9 for a yacht 12 metres in length. A very good meal was around £6 a head, including beer. Hellerup shopping centre is about 300m away, with a wide range of shops, banks, restaurants etc.

Formalities

If København is the first port in Denmark and clearance is needed (i.e. there are dutiable goods on board), it is advisable to contact customs by VHF. If ashore, the two relevant offices are District 2 (the inner city) ☎ (45) 01 54 22 88, and District 6 (north) ☎ (45) 02 80 77 11. The head office is on ☎ (45) 01 15 73 00.

General facilities

Except for Nyhavn, the yacht harbours provide a full range of facilities, and provisions can be bought from any number of shops in their vicinity. There are many banks, restaurants and hotels. The main tourist information office is in H C Andersens Boulevard.

Yachting services

There are several chandlers in København, and most repairs can be arranged. Fuel can be purchased with ease, but *Camping Gaz* is available only from certain petrol stations which are not easy to find.

Danish, Swedish, German and British charts and pilot books may be bought from Iver Weilbach & Co a/s, Toldbodgade 35, København DK 1253.

Communications

The VHF service for the København area is provided by Lyngby Radio, with its transmitter on the island of Saltholm, Ch 03 26 and 66.

Telephone kiosks throughout København can be used for international calls.

Travel

København is well served by air, rail, road and sea communications with all parts of Denmark and the rest of Europe.

Stubbekøbing
54°54'N 12°03'E

Distance
København 55M, Kiel 85M, Gislövs Läge 50M.

Charts and guides
Admiralty chart *2138*
Danish small-craft charts *Series 1*
NV charts *Series 2, Lübecker Bucht bis Bornholm und Kopenhagen*
Baltic Pilot Volume I (NP 18)
Cruising guide to Germany and Denmark Brian Navin, Imray.
Hafenführer Dänemark DK Edition Maritim

Lights
1. **Hestehoved** 54°50'·1N 12°10'E Oc(2)WRG.6s14m 13-9M White house, 4m 216·5°-R-264°- G-290°-W-342°-R-007°-G-024°

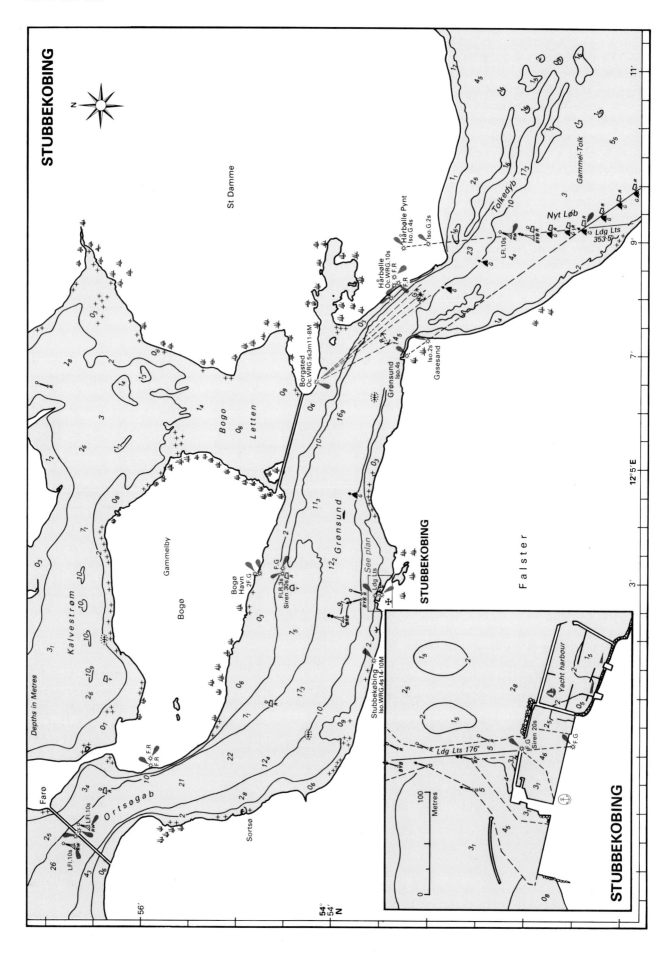

STUBBEKØBING

STUBBEKØBING

STUBBEKØBING

N

Depths in Metres

St Damme

Kalvestrøm

Gammelby

Bogø

Bogø Letten

Borgsted
Oc.WRG.5s3m11·8M

Bogø
Havn

Bogø

FI.R.3s F.G
Siren 30s

2F.G

Grønsund

Grønsund

See plan

Ldg Lts

Stubbekøbing
Iso.WRG.4s14·10M

Hårbølle Pynt
Iso.G.4s Iso.G.2s

Hårbølle
Oc.WRG.10s
F.R
F.R

Gasesand

Iso.2s

Iso.4s

Tolkedyb

Nyt Løb

Gammel-Tolk

Ldg Lts
353·5°

Farø

Faro

LFI.10s

LFI.10s

Ortsøgab

Sortsø

F.R
F.R

Falster

Yacht harbour

Ldg Lts 176°

F.G
Siren 20s

F.G

100
Metres

0

12°5′E

11′

9′

7′

3′

56′

54°
54′
N

174

General

Stubbekøbing is a very useful stop on the way from Kiel to southern Sweden. It is a pleasant small town and commercial port, with a comfortable yacht harbour and friendly yacht club.

Approach

The yacht harbour is at the eastern end of the commercial port.

Approaching from the west, make as if to enter the commercial port, then go along close outside the harbour wall to the east-facing entrance to the yacht harbour.

From the east, leave the main buoyed channel opposite the yacht harbour entrance and turn through 90° to enter the yacht harbour. Do not cut the corner.

Berthing

Mooring is bows to quay with stern lines to posts, plus a few alongside berths. The spacing of some of the posts, however, is only around 3m.

The harbour is divided into two basins, and, although the first basin has a depth of 2m, the second one is considerably less than this between the post situated in the centre of the basin and the boats moored on the south shore.

In 1991 the overnight mooring fee was about £7 for a boat 12 metres in length.

General facilities

Electricity and water are provided on the quays, and there are good showers and toilets nearby.

There is a kiosk selling a limited number of groceries and drinks beside the commercial harbour, and there is a modest shopping centre in the town some 500m further away.

There are banks, hotels and restaurants in the town.

Yachting services

There is a fuelling point in the commercial harbour.

Urgent repairs can be arranged through the yacht club.

Communications

Lyngby Radio's remotely controlled VHF transmitter on the island of Møn is within range: Ch 02 and 64. There are telephone kiosks near the harbour.

The nearest railway station is Nykøbing, some 20km away.

Other ports

Rønne (Bornholm) 55°06'N 14°42'E (See plan)
Major port with straightforward entry. A very useful stopping place en route for the central Baltic. The yacht harbour near the church in the northeast corner of the harbour has a depth of 1·8m, but larger yachts can moor in other parts of the harbour.

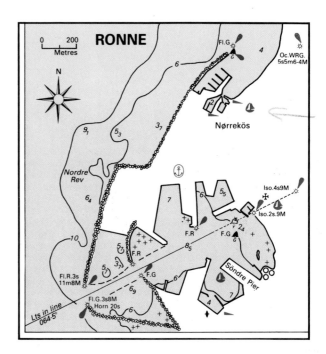

Christiansø 55°19'·4N 15°11'·1E
Gorgeous small island northeast from Bornholm. Moor in the sound between Christiansø and Frederiksö; entry from south.

Rødvig 55°15'N 12°22'·6E
A pleasant small harbour, and a useful stop on the way to København from the south. The yacht harbour to the right of the entrance is often congested; the fishing harbour to the left is relatively clear, and has greater character, but no facilities. The harbour entrance should be approached in a NNE direction to avoid the many fishing stakes just offshore, and entry should not be attempted at night. Fuel, water, electricity and showers in yacht harbour. Shop nearby. *Camping Gaz* available at fuel berth.

Praesto 55°07'·5N 12°02'·8E
Danish chart 190 advisable. Attractive village/town with yacht harbour comprising wooden jetties. Depth varies 1·5–2m but bottom soft. Fuel from garage.

Rødvig

Yacht moorings at Praesto.

København.

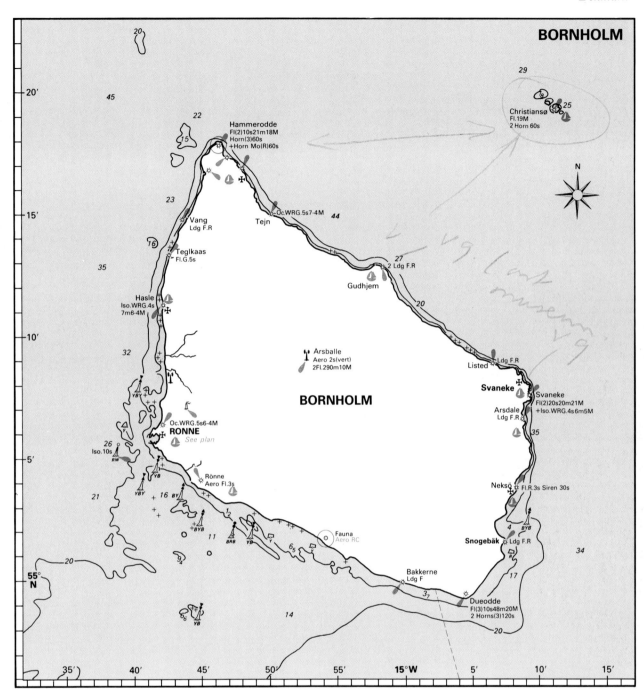

BORNHOLM

BORNHOLM

Rødbyhavn 54°39'·1N 11°20'·8E
Busy ferry port. Useful stop on way from Kiel to Sweden. Berth in basin at north end of harbour. Beware ferries on entry. A few shops but no facilities.

Vordingborg 55°00'·2N 11°55'E
Danish chart *161* advisable. Approach by wide partially buoyed channel with depths varying 1·5–1·8m. First two jetties only 1·5m, but 2m at furthest jetty. Winds between east and southeast reputed to lower water level by up to 1m. Castle, museum, good shopping.

Gedser 54°35'N 11°56'E
Ferry port, but useful stopping place. It has a fishing harbour with 4m in the east corner.

Neksø Bornholm 55°04'N 15°07'E
A large deep-sea fishing port. Centre for all Baltic states' offshore fishing boats who trade through this port. Small yacht harbour off main harbour, to right of commercial harbour on entry, 2.5m. Good shopping, and fuel. Toilets and showers.

The bridge and yacht harbour at Kalvehave.

Appendix

I. Bibliography

GUIDE BOOKS
The Fodor Series: separate volumes on Germany, Poland and Scandinavia. Fodor's Travel Publications Inc., New York & London.
The Green Michelins.

PILOTS AND CHARTS
The publications listed below can be obtained in the UK through Imray, Laurie, Norie & Wilson Ltd, Wych House, The Broadway, St Ives, Huntingdon, Cambridgeshire PE17 4BT England ☎ 0480 62114 *Fax* 0480 496109.

They are available from abroad as follows:

Germany
Nautischer Dienst, Kapt Stegmann & Co
Schleuse, Maklerstrasse 8
Postfach 8070
2308 Kiel-Holtenau 17
☎ (49) 31 33 17 72
Fax (49) 31 33 17 61

Bade & Hornig GmbH
Herrengraben 31
Postfach 11 20 45
2000 Hamburg 11
☎ (49) 40 37 48 11 0
Fax (49) 40 36 64 00

Eckhardt & Messtorff GmbH
Rödingsmarkt 16
2000 Hamburg 11
☎ (49) 40 37 13 34
Fax (49) 40 37 30 28

Finland
O.Y. Maritim AB
PO Box 46
SF 00211 Helsinki
☎ (358) 0-67 3331
Fax (358) 0-692 7917

Sweden
Nautic Center AB
Skeppsbroplatsen 1,
S411 18 Göteborg
☎ (46) 31 112421
Fax (46) 31 115357

Nautiska Forlaget A/B
Norrtullsgaten 4,
S113 29 Stockholm
☎ (46) 8 736 6005
Fax (46) 8 736 6001

Denmark
Iver Weilbach & Co A/S
Toldbodgade 35,
København DK1253
☎ (45) 33 13 5927
Fax (45) 33 93 5927

General
Admiralty *Baltic Pilot Volumes I, II, III (NP 18, 19, 20)*.
Admiralty *List of Lights Volume C Baltic Sea (NP 76)*.
Admiralty *List of Radio Signals Volume 1 Part 1 Coast Radio Stations (NP 281(1))*.
Reeds Almanac – Baltic Edition Thomas Reed Publications Ltd.

Germany – pilots
Cruising guide to Germany and Denmark Brian Navin, Imray, Laurie, Norie & Wilson Ltd.
Küstenhandbuch Mecklenburg-Vorpommern (Travemünde bis Ueckermünde mit Rügen und den Boddengewässern) M. Brandenburg, DK Edition Maritim. In German.
Der Grosse NV Hafen Lotse Volumes 1 and 4 Nautische Veröffentlichung (complements *Serie 1 and 4* of their charts). In German.

For the German canals:
Sportschiffahrtskarten Binnen by Nautische Veröffentlichung. *Band 1 Berlin & Märkische Gewässer. Band 2 Berlin & Mecklenburger Gewässer. Band 3 Die nördliche Oder und die Peene. Band 4 Die Elbe und ihre Kanäle Hamburg-Magdeburg-Hanover.*

Poland – pilots

Hafenführer Polen Bodo Müller (Stettiner Haff, Pommersche Bucht, Danziger Bucht, Frisches Haff) DK Edition Maritim. In German.

Der Grosse NV Hafen Lotse Volume 4 Nautische Veröffentlichung (complements *Serie 4* of their charts). In German.

Finland – pilots

Stora Hamnboken (Suuri Satamkirja)

Vol I Åbo Skägård (Turun saaristo)

Vol II Åland Skärgård (Akvenanmaa)

Vol III Finska Viken (Suomenlahti) (The Gulf of Finland)

Although in Swedish and Finnish, the text is short and subsidiary to the large-scale plans.

Sweden – pilots

Seglarhamnar på Ost Kusten (Sailing Harbours of the East Coast).

Batleder på Ost Kusten (Small Boat Fairways of the East Coast).

Svenska Kryssarklubbens Forsaljningsaktiebolag (Swedish Cruising Club), Stockholm.

Küstenhandbuch Schweden Volumes 2 and 3 DK Edition Maritim. In German. Based on the Swedish official pilots.

Denmark – pilots

Cruising guide to Germany and Denmark Brian Navin, Imray Laurie Norie & Wilson Ltd.

Hafenführer Dänemark DK Edition Maritim.

Der Grosse NV Hafen Lotse Volumes 1 and 2 Nautische Veröffentlichung (complements *Serie 1 and 2* of their charts). In German.

BRITISH ADMIRALTY CHARTS

Chart	Title	Scale
33	Approaches to Kieler Hafen	60,000
53	Ports on the east coast of Sweden	
	Luleå	20,000
	Piteå and approaches: Approaches to Luleå	50,000
57	Ports on the east coast of Sweden	
	Skelleftehamn: Ornsköldsvik: Husum	20,000
	Holmsund Umea Hamn	25,000
	Approaches to Skelleftehamn	50,000
	Approaches to Ornsköldsvik	50,000
	Approaches to Husum: Approaches to Holmsund	50,000
58	Ports on the east coast of Sweden	
	Sundsvall	20,000
	Approaches to Sundsvall	55,000
70	Ports on the east coast of Sweden	
	Hudiksvall	20,000
	Söderhamnsfjärden, Ljusnefjärden	25,000
	Approaches to Hudiksvall; Approaches to Ljusnefjärden and Söderhamnsfjärden	50,000
173	Porkkalanselkä to Söderskär	75,000

Chart	Title	Scale
185	Approaches to Świnoujście	60,000
	Świnoujście	24,400
	Szczecin	25,000
259	Baltic sea	1,270,000
523	Ports in southwest Finland	
	Turku and Hanko	20,000
613	Mariager fjord, Randers fjord and Grenå	50,000
	Mariager: Hobro	5,000
	Randers: Grenå	10,000
	Approaches to Grenå	60,000
696	Kieler hafen	60,000
790	Approaches to København	40,000
1088	Approaches to Loviisa and Valkom	55,000
1089	Approaches to Kotka and Hamina	55,000
1090	Ports in the Gulf of Finland	
	Kotka	20,000
	Hamina	20,000
	Vysotsk	20,000
	Vyborg and approaches	35,000
2115	The Sound	150,000
2116	Little Belt and Kieler bucht	150,000
2118	Great Belt	150,000
2120	Samso Bælt, including Århus bugt and Isefjord	150,000
	Holbæk	6,000
	Hundested	7,500
	Horsens	10,000
	Århus	15,000
2138	Gronsund and the Storstrom	75,000
2150	Arkona to Ustka	200,000
	Kolobrzeg	10,000
2182a	North sea – southern sheet	750,000
2215	Gulf of Rīga	200,000
	Pärnu	36,000
2222	Gotska Sandön to Hiiumaa	200,000
2223	Gotland to Saaremaa	200,000
2224	Helsinki	20,000
2225	Approaches to Novotallinskiy	27,500
2227	Tallinn and approaches	27,500
	Vana Sadam	5,000
2241	Entrance to the Gulf of Finland	200,000
2248	Gulf of Finland – western part	200,000
2251	Öland to Gotland with Kalmarsund	200,000
2252	Gulf of Bothnia	750,000
2256	Rīga and approaches	25,000
2264	Gulf of Finland – eastern part	200,000
2276	Approaches to Klaipėda	35,000
	Klaipėda	12,500
2277	Ventspils and approaches	25,000
2288	Rozewie to Ventspils	350,000
2294	Ports on the east coast of Sweden Härnösand: Svanön and Sandö:	
	Kramfors	25,000
	Angermanälven – Härnön to Svanön	50,000
2296	Södra Kvarken to Hornslandet	225,000
2297	Saaristomeri and Ålands Hav	225,000
2298	Isokari to Gåshällan	225,000
2299	Hudiksvall to Husum	225,000
2300	Skagsudde to Stora Fjäderägg and Södra Björkö to Pietarsaari	225,000
2301	Holmsund to Skellefteå and Pietarsaari to Tauvo	225,000

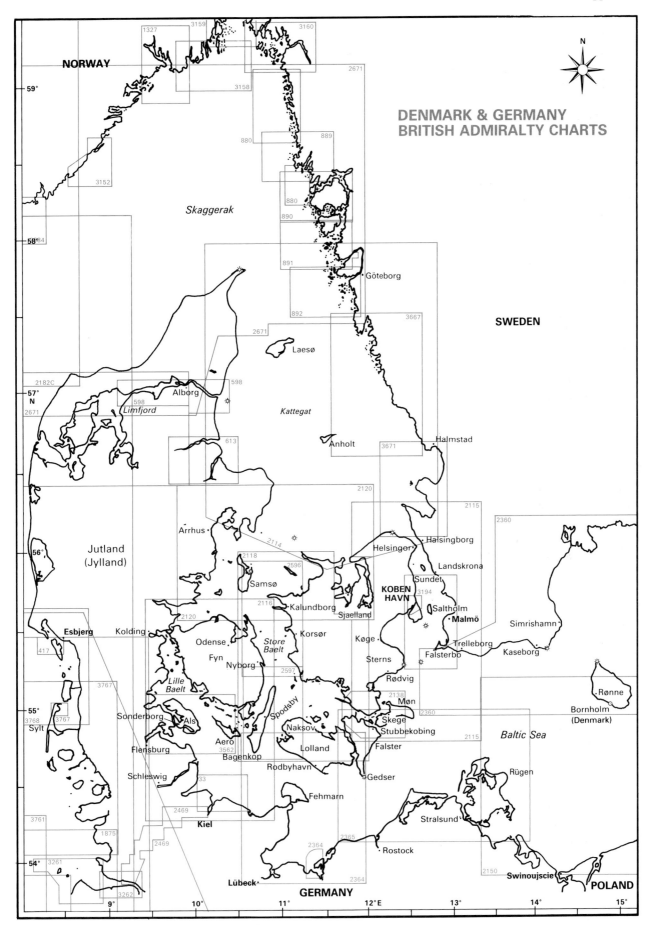

**DENMARK & GERMANY
BRITISH ADMIRALTY CHARTS**

NORWAY

59°

Skaggerak

58°

57°
N

Limfjord

Alborg

Laesø

Kattegat

SWEDEN

Göteborg

Anholt

Halmstad

56°

Jutland
(Jylland)

Arrhus

Helsingør

Halsingborg

Landskrona

Sundet

Samsø

KOBEN
HAVN

Saltholm

Malmö

Kalundborg

Sjaelland

Simrishamn

Esbjerg

Kolding

Odense

Store
Baelt

Korsør

Køge

Sterns

Trelleborg

Falsterbo

Kaseborg

Fyn

Nyborg

Rødvig

Rønne

55°

Lille
Baelt

Spodsby

Møn

Bornholm
(Denmark)

Sylt

Sønderborg

Als

Naksov

Skege

Stubbekobing

Baltic Sea

Aero

Lolland

Falster

Flensburg

Bagenkop

Rügen

Schleswig

Rodbyhavn

Gedser

Stralsund

Fehmarn

Rostock

54°

Kiel

Lübeck

GERMANY

Swinoujscie

POLAND

9°   10°   11°   12°E   13°   14°   15°

Chart numbers: 1327, 3159, 3160, 2671, 3158, 889, 880, 880, 890, 891, 3152, 984, 892, 2671, 3667, 2182C, 598, 598, 2671, 613, 3671, 2120, 2115, 2360, 2114, 2118, 2596, 2116, 3194, 2120, 417, 2597, 2138, 2360, 3767, 2115, 3768, 3767, 3562, 33, 3761, 2469, 1875, 2469, 2364, 2365, 3261, 2364, 2150, 3262

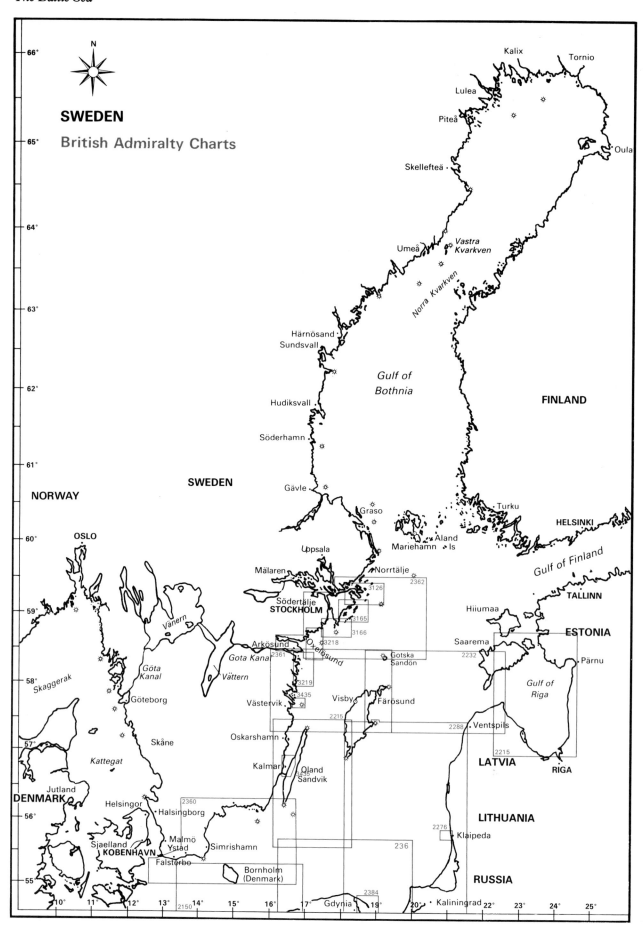

SWEDEN
British Admiralty Charts

N

NORWAY

OSLO

Skaggerak

Vänern

Göta Kanal

Vättern

Göteborg

Kattegat

Skåne

Jutland

DENMARK

Helsingor

Halsingborg

Sjaelland
KOBENHAVN

Malmö
Ystad

Falsterbo

Simrishamn

Bornholm
(Denmark)

SWEDEN

Härnösand
Sundsvall

Hudiksvall

Söderhamn

Gävle

Graso

Uppsala

Mälaren

Södertälje
STOCKHOLM

Arkösund

Gota Kanal

Oxelösund

Västervik

Oskarshamn

Kalmar

Oland
Sandvik

Gulf of Bothnia

Kalix

Lulea

Piteå

Skellefteå

Umeå

Vastra
Kvarkven

Norra Kvarkven

Turku

FINLAND

HELSINKI

Aland
Mariehamn · Is

Norrtälje

Gulf of Finland

Hiiumaa

Saarema

Gotska
Sandön

Visby

Färosund

TALLINN

ESTONIA

Pärnu

Gulf of
Riga

Ventspils

LATVIA

RIGA

Tornio

Oula

Klaipeda

LITHUANIA

Kaliningrad

Gdynia

RUSSIA

2362

3126

3165

3166

3218

2361

3219

3435

2215

2232

2288

2215

3435

2360

2276

236

2384

2150

Chart	Title	Scale
2302	Furuögrund and Tauvo to Tornio	225,000
2303	Ports on the west coast of Finland	
	Kemi and approaches: Kristiinankaupunki	
	and Kaskinen: Vaasa and approaches	50,000
2331	Hankoniemi to Porkkalanselkä	75,000
2335	Simpnäsklubb and Gisslan to Argosgrund,	
	including Södra Kvarken	100,000
	Osthammar	20,000
2336	Argosgrund to Iggö	100,000
	Gävle hamn and approaches:	
	Skutskär-Harnäs	25,000
2340	Norra Kvarken	125,000
2356	Söderskär to Tiiskeri	75,000
2360	Falsterbo to Öland	200,000
	Rønne	10,000
	Trelleborg. Ystad	20,000
2361	Öland to Gotska Sandön	200,000
	Visby	10,000
	Fårösund	75,000
2362	Approaches to Stockholm	200,000
2369	Darlowo to Mys Taran including Gulf of	
	Gdańsk	200,000
2370	Warnemünde and Rostock	20,000
	Warnemünde	10,000
2371	Plans on the coast of Sweden	
	Sölvesborg: Karlshamn: Stilleryd	15,000
	Ahus and approaches: approaches to	
	Sölvesborg: approaches to Karlshamn	50,000
2377	Gdańsk and Gdynia	15,000
2384	Approaches to Gdańsk and Gdynia	75,000
2395	Approaches to Gdańsk Leningrad	50,000
	Leningrad: Kronstadt	25,000
2469	Nord-Ostsee-kanal	50,000
	Brunsbüttel: Holtenau	12,500
	Rendsburg	20,000
2594	The Sound – northern part	60,000
	Helsingør	8,046
	Höganäs: Helsingborg: Sydhamnan and	
	Kopparverkshamnan	15,000
	Landskrona	20,000
2595	The Sound – southern part	60,000
2596	Great Belt – northern portion	70,000
	Korsør	12,000
	Nyborg	15,000
	Kalundborg	25,000
2597	Great Belt – southern portion	70,000
	Agersø sund	50,000
2816	Baltic sea – southern sheet	750,000
2817	Baltic sea – northern sheet and Gulf of	
	Finland	750,000
3062	Ports on the west coast of Finland	
	Oulu	20,000
	Approaches to Oulu	60,000
	Kokkola and approaches	75,000
3114	Stockholms hamn	20,000
3126	Approaches to Stockholm – Sandhamn	
	entrance	50,000
3127	Approaches to Stockholm – Söderarm	
	entrance, Marö to Tisterögrundet	50,000
3163	Approaches to Stockholm – Arholma	
	and Söderarm to Marö	50,000
	Norrtälje	15,000

Chart	Title	Scale
3165	Approaches to Stockholm – Landsort	
	entrance	
	Nynäshamn to Fjärdhällan	50,000
	Dalarö	25,000
3166	Approaches to Stockholm – Landsort to	
	Himmerfjärden and Nynäshamn	50,000
	Nynäshamn	25,000
3169	Oregrunds Skärgård	50,000
	Continuation of Ortalaviken and Väddö	
	Kanal (on the same scale)	
	Hargshamn: Hallstavik	10,000
	Oregrund and approaches	25,000
3194	Københavns havn, Malmö and Limhamn	
	Københavns havn	12,500
	Malmö	20,000
	Limhamn	20,000
3196	Approaches to Stockholm – Himmerfjärden	
	entrance	50,000
	Södertälje	20,000
3217	Approaches to Söderköping and	
	Norrköping	50,000
	Norrköping: Fläskoärna: Stegeborg	25,000
3218	Norra Fällbådan to Nyköping	50,000
	Nyköping	10,000
	Oxelsund	25,000
	Hävringe	25,000
3219	Stora Askö to Norra Fållbådon	50,000
3415	Approaches to Mäntyluoto and Tahkoluoto	
	Approaches to Rauma	50,000
	Tahkoluoto: Mäntyluoto and Reposaari	20,000
	Rauma	25,000
3435	Plans on the southeast coast of Sweden	
	Oskarshamn	15,000
	Karlskrona:	20,000
	Kalmar and the Narrows: Vastervik	25,000
	Kalmar sund – inner part: Approaches to	
	Oskarshamn: Approaches to Vastervik	50,000
	Ronneby and approaches: Approaches	
	to Karlskrona	50,000
3465	Little Belt – northern part	70,000
	Assens	6,000
	Vejle	8,000
	Haderslev: Fredericia	10,000
	Kolding	12,000
	Snaevringen	30,000
3501	Usikaupunki (Nystad) and approaches	75,000
3562	Little Belt southern part	70,000
	Abenra: Enstedvaerket: Sønderborg	15,000
	Flensburg	20,000
	The Narrows off Holnis	50,000
3671	Tylö to Viken	100,520
	Halmstad harbour	25,000
3891	Åland islands	75,000
3894	Saaristomeri – southwestern part including	
	–Degerö, Vardö, Kumlinge and Kökar	75,000
3896	Saaristomeri – northern part, Vardö to	
	Kaurissalo and Mossala	75,000
3897	Saaristomeri – southern part, Bogskär and	
	Utö to Korppoo	75,000
3898	Saaristomeri – southeastern part,	
	Grisselborg to Hankoniemi	75,000
3899	Saaristomeri – northeastern part,	
	approaches to Turku	75,000

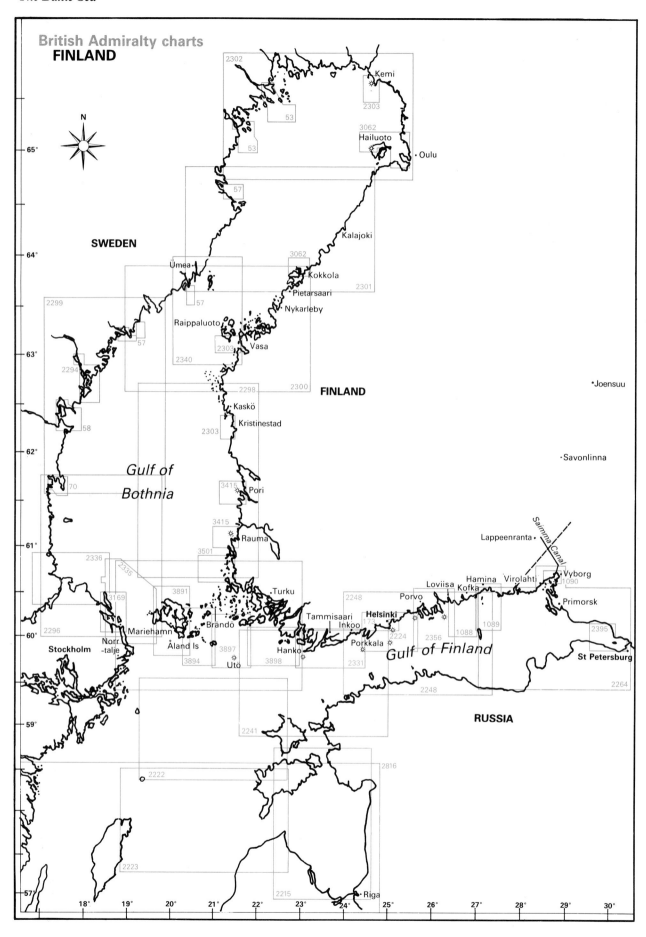

GERMAN CHARTS

Bundesamt für Seeschiffahrt und Hydrographie,
Bernhard-Nocht-Strasse 78 Postfach 30 12 80 D-2000
Hamburg 36.

Chart	Title	Scale
30D	Kieler Bucht	100,000
31D	Gewässer um Fehmarn, Heiligenhafen bis Dahmeshöved	50,000
32D	Falshöft bis Holtenau	50,000
33	Ansteuerung der Kieler Förde	12,500
34	Häfen von Kiel	12,500
35	Neustädter Bucht	25,000
36D	Travemünde bis Gedser Odde	100,000
42	Nord-Ostsee-Kanal	50,000
43D	Gabelsflach bis Heiligenhafen	50,000
44D	Elbmündung	50,000
46	Die Elbe von der Oste bis Brunsbüttel und Krautsand	30,000
47	Die Elbe von Krautsand bis Schulau	30,000
51	Die Trave von Travemünde bis Große Holzwiek und Dassower See	12,500
52	Die Trave von Große Holzwiek bis Lübeck	12,500
87D	Borkum bis Neuwerk and Helgoland	150,000
103D	Helgoland bis Rømø	25,000
141	Rigaischer Meerbusen (Riškij zaliv)	200,000
142D	Lyserort (Oviši) bis Ristna	200,000
143D	Memel (Klaipéda) bis Lyserort (Oviši)	200,000
144D	Rixhöft (Rozewie) bis Memel (Klaipéda)	200,000
145D	Kolberg (Kołobrzeg) bis Rixhöft (Rozewie)	200,000
148D	Baltisch Port (Paldiski) von Hogland (Gogland)	200,000
152D	Hogland (Gogland) bis St Petersburg	200,000
154D	Einfahrt in den Finnischen Meerbusen, Klipsaarenukk bis Hanko	200,000
157	Ansteuerung von Reval (Tallinn)	25,000
158	Ansteuerung von Novotallinnskij	25,000
1411	Hafen von Riga (Riga)	25,000
1421	Irbenstraße (Irbenskij proliv)	100,000
1431	Ansteuerung von Windau (Ventspils)	25,000
1441	Ansteuerung und Hafen von Memel (Klaipéda)	25,000
1443	Danziger Bucht (Zatoka Gdańska), westlicher Teil	50,000
1444	Hafen von Danzig (Gdańsk)	15,000
1511	Greifswalder Bodden, Ostansteuerung von Stralsund	50,000
1512	Peenestrom, nördlicher Teil	25,000
1513	Peenestrom, südlicher Teil, und Kleines Haff	50,000
1514	Ansteuerung von Swinemünde (Świnoujście) und Große Haff (Wielki Zalew)	50,000
1515	Die Oder von Ziegenort (Trzebiez) bis Stettin (Szczecin)	25,000
1516D	Prorer Wiek	25,000
1522	Hafen von Memel (Klaipéda)	7,500
1578	Greifswalder Bodden, nördlicher Teil	25,000
1579	Der Strelasund von Palmer Ort bis Stralsund	25,000
1621	Nördliche Rügensche Bodden	30,000
1622	Nordansteuerung von Stralsund	25,000
1623	Boddengewässer Barhöft bis Ribnitz-Damgarten	50,000

Chart	Title	Scale
1641D	Ansteuerung von Wismar	25,000
1671D	Ansteuerung von Rostock	50,000
1672D	Hafen von Rostock	12,500

Small-craft charts (in sets)

3003	Karten der Ostsee von Flensburg bis Kiel	
3004	Karten der Ostsee von Kiel bis Lübeck	
3005	Karten der Ostsee von Travemünde bis Stralsund	
3006	Karten der Ostsee von Stralsund bis Stettiner Haff	

Nautische Veröffentlichung

Four sets of yachtsmen's charts in plastic wallets.

Serie 1 Rund um Fünen – Kieler Bucht

Chart	Title	Scale
S1	Kieler Bucht	140,000
S2	Kieler Förde	40,000
S3	Kieler Bucht Süd-West	80,000
S4	Flensburger Förde	80,000
S5	Kleiner Belt Süd	80,000
S6	Kleiner Belt Mitte	80,000
S6a	Alssund u. Augustenborg	25,000
S7	Kleiner Belt Nord	80,000
S7a	Stromkarte Kleiner Belt	
S8	Nord Fünen	80,000
S9	Großer Belt Nord	80,000
S10	Großer Belt Mitte	80,000
S10a	Stromkarte Großer Belt	
S11	Großer Belt Süd	80,000
S11a	Nakskov Fjord	33,000
S12	Süd Fünen	80,000
S12a	Svendborgsund	15,000

Serie 2 Lübecker Bucht bis Bornholm und Kopenhagen

Chart	Title	Scale
S13	Fehmarn	80,000
S14	Lübecker Bucht	80,000
S14a	Die Travemündung	17,000
S15	Mecklenburger Bucht	150,000
S16	Mön Südost	160,000
S16a	Wismar Bucht	33,000
S17a	Häfen von Rostock	25,000
S17	Smaalandsfahrwasser West	80,000
S18	Smaalandsfahrwasser Ost	80,000
S19	Grönsund	60,000
S19A	Guldborg Sund	60,000
S20	Fakse Bucht	60,000
S20a	Salzhaff	33,000
S21	Sund Mitte	80,000
S21a	Die Untertrave	15,000
S22	Hanö Bucht	260,000
S22a	Kopenhagen/Nakskov Fjord	40,000
S23	Sund Süd	140,000
S24	Klintholm bis Bornholm	220,000
S25	Bornholm	140,000

Serie 3 Gewässer um Samsö, Sund und Kattegat

Chart	Title	Scale
S26	Sund Nord	80,000
S26a	Oberflächenströmung im Sund	
S27	Isefjord	80,000
S28	Samsö Belt	100,000
S29	Aarhus Bucht	100,000
S30	Kattegat Süd	180,000
S31	Kattegat Mitte	180,000

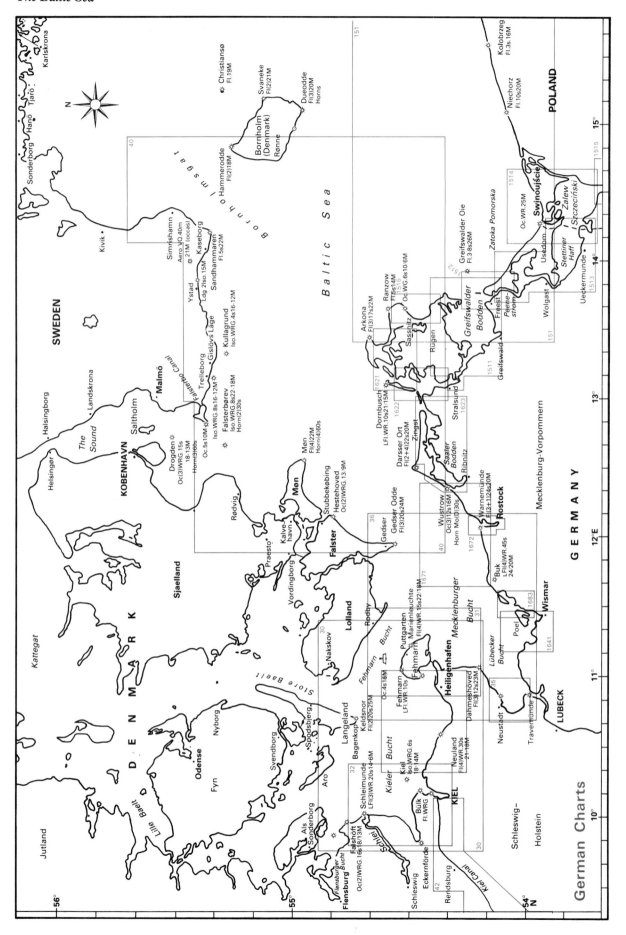

Sonderborg · Hanö · Tjärö ·
Karlskrona

N

Kivik ·

☆ Christiansø
Fl.19M

Svaneke
Fl(2)21M

Dueodde
Fl(3)20M
Horns

Kolobrzeg
Fl.3s.16M

POLAND

Niechorz
Fl.10s20M

Bornholmsgat

Baltic Sea

Simrishamn ·
Aero VQ.40m

☆ 21M (occas)

Kaseborg

Sandhammaren
Fl.5s22M

Ystad

Ldg.2Iso.15M

SWEDEN

Kullagrund
Iso.WRG.4s16-12M

Greifswalder Oie
Fl.3.8s26M

Oc.WR.25M

Świnoujście

Zalew
Szczeciński

Stettiner
Haff

Usedom

Zatoka Pomorska

Wolgast

Ueckermünde

Arkona
☆ Fl(3)17s22M

Ranzow
Fl.5s14M

Oc.WG.6s10/6M

Greifswalder

Bodden

Freest

Peene

Strom

Halsingborg ·

Landskrona ·

Malmö

Falsterbo Canal

Trelleborg

Gislövs Läge

Falsterbrev
Iso.WRG.8s22-18M
Horn(2)30s

Iso.WRG.8s16-12M ☆

Oc.5s10M ☆

Saltholm

Sassnitz

Rügen

Greifswald

Stralsund

Mecklenburg-Vorpommern

The Sound

Helsingör ·

Dragden
Oc(3)WRG.15s
Horn)9)60s

KØBENHAVN

Møn
Fl(4)22M
Horn(4)60s

Dornbusch
Fl(3)17s22M

Darsser Ort
Fl(2+4)22s20M

Saaler Bodden

Zingst

Saaler Bodden

Ribnitz

Rödvig ·

Præstø ·

Kalve-
havn

Stubbekøbing

Hesthoved
Oc(2)WRG.13.9M

Møn

Gedser Odde
Fl(3)20s24M

Wustrow
Oc(3)12s16M

Warnemünde
Fl(3±1)24s20M

Rostock

Horn Mo(D)30s

Kattegat

Sjaelland

Vordingborg ·

Falster

Gedser ·

Buk
LFl(4)WR.45s
24.20M

GERMANY

Store Baelt

Lolland

Nakskov ·

Rödby

Fehmarn Bucht

Puttgarten
Fehmarn Marienleuchte
Fl(4)WR.15s22/18M

Fehmarn
Fl(4)WR.30s

Wismar

Poel

Spodsbjerg ·

Langeland

Keldsnor
Fl(2)20s25M

Bagenkop

Fehmarn
Oc.4s16M

Fehmarn
LFl.WR.10s

Heiligenhafen

Dähmeshoved
Fl(3)12s23M

Lübecker

Bucht

Nyborg

Svendborg ·

Odense

Fyn

Kiel
Iso.WRG.6s
18·14M

Neuland
Fl(4)WR.30s
21·18M

Neustadt ·

Travemünde

LÜBECK

Lille Baelt

D E N M A R K

Aro

Kieler Bucht

Schleimünde
LFl(3)WR.20s14·6M

Bulk
Fl.WRG

KIEL

Schleswig-
Holstein

Sönderborg

Als

Falshöft
Fl.WRG.16s18/13M

Schlei

Eckernförde ·

Flensburg
Flensburger Bucht
Oc(2)WRG.16s

Schleswig ·

Rendsburg ·

Kiel Canal

Jutland

German Charts

56°

55°

54°
N

15°

14°

13°

12°E

11°

10°

N

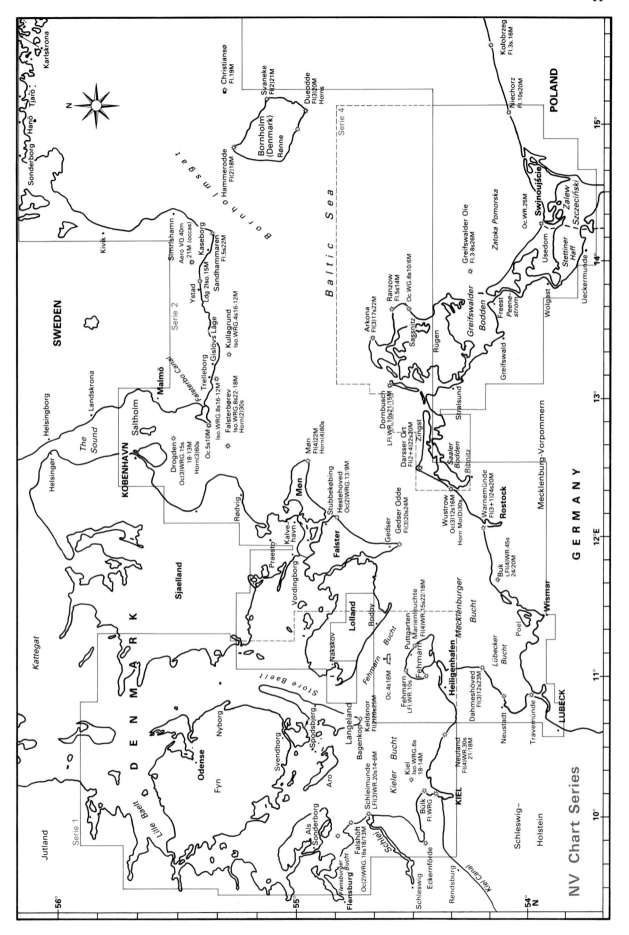

NV Chart Series

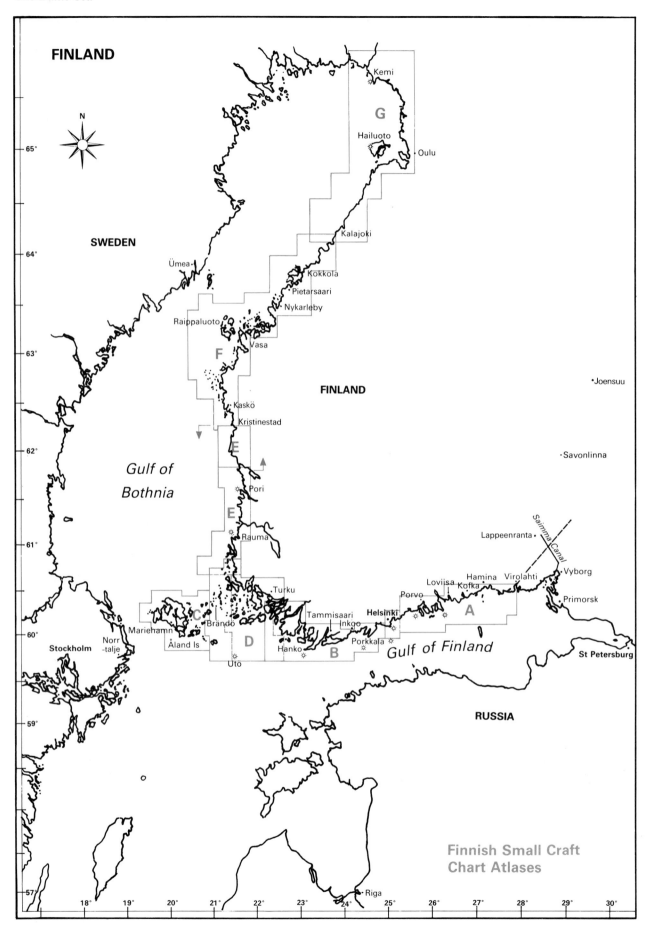

FINLAND

N

SWEDEN

FINLAND

Gulf of
Bothnia

Gulf of Finland

SWEDEN

Stockholm

RUSSIA

Finnish Small Craft
Chart Atlases

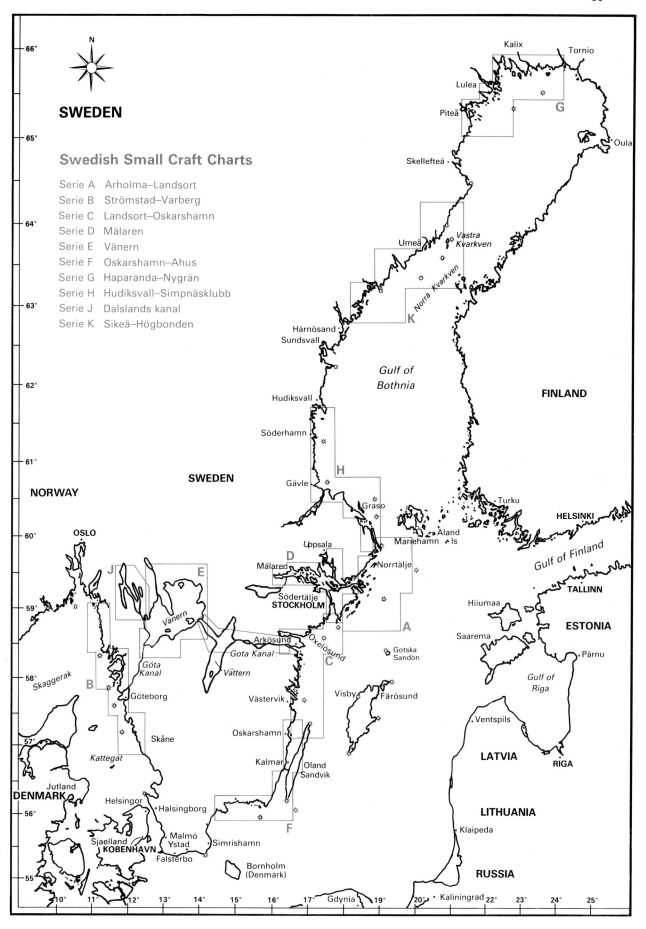

SWEDEN

Swedish Small Craft Charts

Serie A   Arholma–Landsort
Serie B   Strömstad–Varberg
Serie C   Landsort–Oskarshamn
Serie D   Mälaren
Serie E   Vänern
Serie F   Oskarshamn–Ahus
Serie G   Haparanda–Nygrän
Serie H   Hudiksvall–Simpnäsklubb
Serie J   Dalslands kanal
Serie K   Sikeä–Högbonden

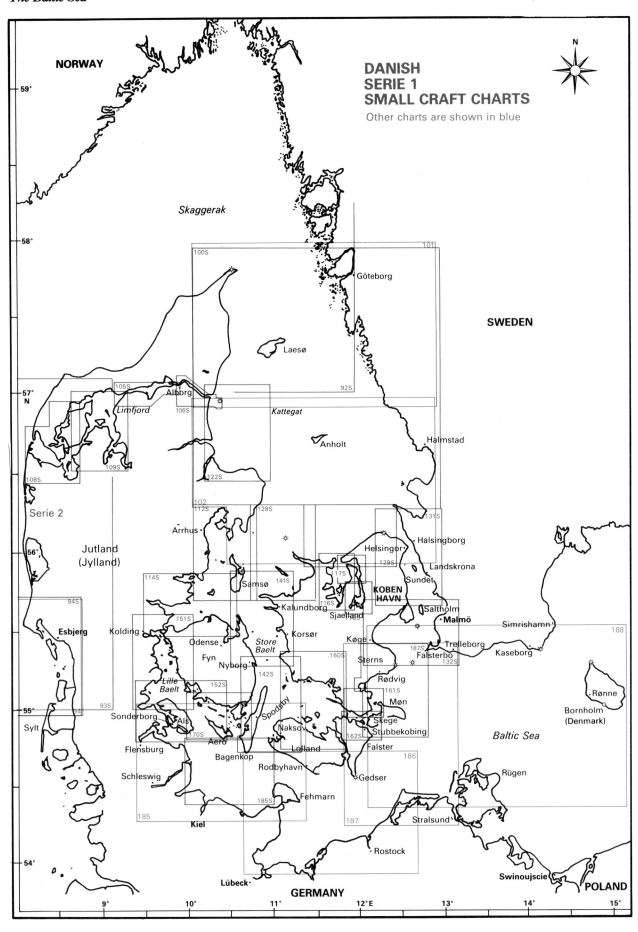

NORWAY

59°

Skaggerak

**DANISH
SERIE 1
SMALL CRAFT CHARTS**
Other charts are shown in blue

N

58°

100S

101

Göteborg

SWEDEN

Laesø

105S

57°
N

Alborg

92S

Limfjord

106S

Kattegat

Halmstad

109S

108S

Anholt

122S

Serie 2

102

112S

128S

131S

Arrhus

Halsingborg

56°

Helsingor

114S

141S

117S

129S

Samsø

Landskrona

94S

116S

Sundet

**KOBEN
HAVN**

Esbjerg

151S

Kalundborg

Sjaelland

Saltholm

**Jutland
(Jylland)**

Kolding

Korsør

Malmö

Simrishamn

Odense

*Store
Baelt*

Køge

188

Fyn

160S

Sterns

187S

Trelleborg

Nyborg

142S

Falsterbo

132S

Kaseborg

*Lille
Baelt*

152S

Rødvig

161S

93S

Sonderborg

Als

Spodsoy

Møn

Rønne

55°

170S

Naksov

Skege

Sylt

Aerö

162S

Stubbekobing

Baltic Sea

**Bornholm
(Denmark)**

Flensburg

Bagenkop

Lolland

Falster

186

Rügen

Schleswig

Rodbyhavn

Gedser

185S

Fehmarn

Stralsund

185

187

Kiel

Rostock

54°

Lübeck

Swinoujscie

POLAND

GERMANY

9°   10°   11°   12° E   13°   14°   15°

Chart	Title	Scale
S32	Kattegat Nord	180,000
S33	Mariager-Randers-Fjord	40,000
S34	Ansteuerungen und Hafenpläne	
S35	Ansteuerungen und Hafenpläne	

Serie 4 Rund um Rügen Boddengewässer-Stettin

Chart	Title	Scale
S36	Die Bodden südl. Zingst	60,000
S37	Strelasund Nord	60,000
S38	Hiddensee bis Jasmund	60,000
S39	Strelasund Süd	60,000
S40	Greifswalder Bodden West	60,000
S41	Greifswalder Bodden Ost	60,000
S42	Peenestrom Süd	60,000
S43	Stettiner Haff	80,000
S44	Die Oder bis Stettin	30,000
S45	Hiddensee bis Swinemünde	240,000

Der Nord – Ostsee Kanal – 2 charts at 1:55,000

FINNISH CHARTS

Merenkulkuhallitus – Merikarttaosasto, Vuorimiehenkatu 1, Helsinki.

Småbåtssjökort series. A series of spiral bound volumes of 1:50,000 charts with many larger scale plans; *Volumes A, B, C and D* are relevant. See diagram. They are cheaper than the standard charts, but are not corrected after publication.

Chart	Title	Scale
A	Itäinen Suomenlahti Ostra Finska viken	50,000
B	Läntinen Suomenlahti Västra Finska viken	50,000
C	Åland Ahvenanmaa	50,000
D	Turunmaan saaristo, Abolands skärgård	50,000
E	Selkämeri Bottenhavet	50,000
F	Merenkurkku Kvarken	50,000
G	Perämeri Bottenviken	50,000
L	Saimaan vesistö, eteläosa	50,000
M	Savonlinna – Kuopio	40,000
N	Tampere – Virrat	30,000
O	Tampere – Hämeenlinna	30,000
P	Valkeakoski – Längelmävesi – Hauho	30,000
R	Pielisjoki	20,000
T	Oulujärven kartasto	40,000
	Saimaan kanavan kartasto Viipuri – Lappeenranta	10,000

Merikarttojen (Sjökorts). Sheet charts, mainly 1:50,000.

These publications can be bought in most large towns in Finland.

SWEDISH CHARTS

Sjöfartsverkert, Sjökarteavdelningen, S-601 78, Norrköping.

Beteckningar och förkortningar i sjörkort (symbols and abbreviations used on Swedish charts) interprets conventional signs in Swedish and English. Available free of charge.

Båtsportkort Serie A, C and F. See diagram. The small charts in these books are taken from the normal charts. They are cheaper than the originals, but are not corrected after publication. They can be bought in shops in most large towns in Sweden, but supply may run short in mid-summer.

DANISH CHARTS

Kost-og Matrikelstyrelsen, Søkortkontoret, Rente-mestervej 8, Dk-2400 København NV.

Yachting charts (*Søsportskort*) *Serie 1.* See index diagram.

II. Conversion tables

1 inch = 2.54 centimetres (roughly 4in = 10cm)
1 centimetre = 0.394 inches
1 foot = 0.305 metres (roughly 3ft = 1m)
1 metre = 3.281 feet
1 pound = 0.454 kilograms (roughly 10lbs = 4.5kg)
1 kilogram = 2.205 pounds
1 mile = 1.609 kilometres (roughly 10 miles = 16 km)
1 kilometre = 0.621 miles
1 nautical mile = 1.1515 miles
1 mile = 0.8684 nautical miles
1 acre = 0.405 hectares (roughly 10 acres = 4 hectares)
1 hectare = 2.471 acres
1 gallon = 4.546 litres (roughly 1 gallon = 4.5 litres)
1 litre = 0.220 gallons

Temperature scale

$t°F$ to $t°C$ is $5/9$ $(t°F -32) = t°C$
$t°C$ to $t°F$ is $9/5$ $(t°C +32) = t°F$

So:

70°F = 21·1°C	20°C = 68°F
80°F = 26·7°C	30°C = 86°F
90°F = 32·2°C	40°C = 104°F

metres–feet

m	ft/m	ft
0·3	1	3·3
0·6	2	6·6
0·9	3	9·8
1·2	4	13·1
1·5	5	16·4
1·8	6	19·7
2·1	7	23·0
2·4	8	26·2
2·7	9	29·5
3·0	10	32·8
6·1	20	65·6
9·1	30	98·4
12·2	40	131·2
15·2	50	164·0
30·5	100	328·1

centimetres–inches

cm	in/cm	in
2·5	1	0·4
5·1	2	0·8
7·6	3	1·2
10·2	4	1·6
12·7	5	2·0
15·2	6	2·4
17·8	7	2·8
20·3	8	3·1
22·9	9	3·5
25·4	10	3·9
50·8	20	7·9
76·2	30	11·8
101·6	40	15·7
127·0	50	19·7
254·0	100	39·4

metres–fathoms–feet

m	fathoms	ft
0·9	0·5	3
1·8	1	6
3·7	2	12
5·5	3	18
7·3	4	24
9·1	5	30
11·0	6	36
12·8	7	42
14·6	8	48
16·5	9	54
18·3	10	60
36·6	20	120
54·9	30	180
73·2	40	240
91·4	50	300

kilometres–statute miles

km	M/km	M
1·6	1	0·6
3·2	2	1·2
4·8	3	1·9
6·4	4	2·5
8·0	5	3·1
9·7	6	3·7
11·3	7	4·3
12·9	8	5·0
14·5	9	5·6
16·1	10	6·2
32·2	20	12·4
48·3	30	18·6
64·4	40	24·9
80·5	50	31·1
120·7	75	46·6
160·9	100	62·1
402·3	250	155·3
804·7	500	310·7
1609·3	1000	621·4

kilograms–pounds

kg	lb/kg	lb
0·5	1	2·2
0·9	2	4·4
1·4	3	6·6
1·8	4	8·8
2·3	5	11·0
2·7	6	13·2
3·2	7	15·4
3·6	8	17·6
4·1	9	19·8
4·5	10	22·0
9·1	20	44·1
13·6	30	66·1
18·1	40	88·2
22·7	50	110·2
34·0	75	165·3
45·4	100	220·5
113·4	250	551·2
226·8	500	1102·3
453·6	1000	2204·6

litres–gallons

l	gal/l	gal
4·5	1	0·2
9·1	2	0·4
13·6	3	0·7
18·2	4	0·9
22·7	5	1·1
27·3	6	1·3
31·8	7	1·5
36·4	8	1·8
40·9	9	2·0
45·5	10	2·2
90·9	20	4·4
136·4	30	6·6
181·8	40	8·8
227·3	50	11·0
341·0	75	16·5
454·6	100	22·0
1136·5	250	55·0
2273·0	500	110·0
4546·1	1000	220·0

III. Abbreviations used on Russian charts

Glossary

IALA System A	МАМС
List of lights	список маяков
light	свет огонь

Structures

lighthouse	маяк (Мк)
light vessel	пл. Мк
radiobeacon (RC)	РМк
beacon	зн
column	колонна
framework tower	ажурная
	установка
	ферма
house	дом
building	здание
	домик
hut	будка
mast	мачта
post	столб
tower	башня (бня)
concrete	бетон(ный)
iron	желез(ный)
metal	металл(ический)
stone	камен(ный)
wooden	дерев(янный)
band	горизонтальная полоса
stripe	вертикальная полоса
destroyed	разруш(енный)
occasional	случ(айный)

Lights

temporary	врем(енный)
extinguished	погаш(енный)
F	П
Oc	Зтм
Iso	Изо
Fl	Пр
Q.	Ч. Пр
IQ	прер. Ч. Пр
Al	пер
Oc(. .)	Гр. Зтм
Fl(. .)	Гр. Пр
F.Fl	П. Пр
F.Fl(. .)	П. Гр. Пр
LFl	Дл. Пр
sec	С
leading light	Ств.

Examples

Fl.7s8M	Пр 7С 8М
Iso.7M	Изо 7М
Fl(3)15s12/10M	Пр(3) 15С 12/10М
Q.5M	Ч. Пр 5М
leading light, Q	Ств Ч. Пр
leading light, Iso	Ств Изо

Supplementary information

whistle	(Рев)
horn	(Н)
gong	(гонг)
bell	(К)
explosive	(В)
cannon	(п)
reed	(Г)
siren	(С)

Colours

black	чр.
violet	фл.
blue	сн.
green	зл.
orange	ор.
red	кр.
white	бл.
yellow	жл.
brown	кч.
grey	ср.
pale blue	гл.

or abbreviated, as in:

black/red/black	ч к ч
black/yellow/black	ч ж ч
yellow/black/yellow	ж ч ж
red/white	к б

Bottom

bottom	грунт
broken, cracked	б
pebbles, shingle	гк
clay	гл
gravel, sand with small stones	гр
mud, silt, sludge	И
clay, mud, silt	гл. И
lime	Изв
stone	К
small stones	мК
large stone, boulders	кК
shallow	м
soft	мг
coarse	к
hard, firm	т
sand	П
fine sand	мП
coarse sand	кП
plate, slab	Пл
shells	Р
cliff, rock face	С
medium, average	с
weed	вд
firm, fine sand and mud	тмПИ

magnetic variation	Магн. скл.
(former) spoil dumping ground	(бывшая) свалка грунта

Index